A Calendar of Catholic Devotion

Julien Chilcott-Monk is a writer, composer and choir director, who lives with his wife in Winchester and occasionally in their retreat in Brittany. He is the author of *Walking the Way of the Cross, A Basic Dictionary of Bible People* and co-author, with Bishop Geoffrey Rowell, of *Flesh, Bone, Wood, The Nails and The Cross* and *Come, Lord Jesus!*

A Calendar of
Catholic Devotion

Julien Chilcott-Monk

Introduced by
The Duchess of Norfolk

CANTERBURY
PRESS
Norwich

First published in 2008 by the Canterbury Press Norwich
(a publishing imprint of Hymns Ancient & Modern Limited,
a registered charity)
13–17 Long Lane, London EC1A 9PN

www.scm-canterburypress.co.uk

British Library Cataloguing in Publication data

A catalogue record for this book is available
from the British Library

ISBN 978-1-85311-859-3

Typeset by Regent Typesetting, London
Printed in the UK by CPI William Clowes
Beccles NR34 7TL

Contents

Acknowledgements

Scriptural quotations are taken from the Catholic Edition copyright 1965 and 1966 of the Revised Standard Version of the Holy Bible copyright 1946, 1952 and 1957 by the Division of Christian Education of the National Council of the Churches of the USA, and are used by permission. All Rights Reserved.

I acknowledge my enormous debt to the splendid 12-volume set of Burns & Oates' *New Full Edition of Butler's Lives of the Saints* as a reliable source of the dates and details of the lives of the saints featured in this book.

To His Holiness Pope Benedict XVI

Foreword

I am glad to commend Julien Chilcott-Monk's *A Calendar of Catholic Devotion*. A generation of Catholics has grown up without sufficient information about or devotion to the saints of the calendar, and this book makes up for those deficiencies. Saints are the real heroes of the Catholic Church, and Catholics will be very grateful indeed to Julien Chilcott-Monk for his excellent guide to the saints. It will help many people not only to know more about the saints but also to pray to them for their intercession.

+Cormac Cardinal Murphy-O'Connor
Archbishop of Westminster
(Saint Francis of Lucera)

Introduction

It is striking what an amazing variety in the lives of holy men and women is featured within these covers – from the humble poor, to those who used their wealth for the good of others; from those who relinquished earthly reward and position for the hermitage or cloister, to those who used their elevated position or remarkable skills and talents to do good; and from those who simply confessed the Faith, to those who lived every day in fear of being discovered a priest, a Catholic, or even simply a Christian. The list is almost endless.

What is noteworthy (and of some comfort too) is that they all possessed, to a greater or lesser degree, deficiencies and weaknesses, just as we possess them. However, a saint is simply someone who fulfils his or her God-given vocations while overcoming or controlling those handicaps with the help of Christ. Most of the saints we celebrate fell short of the ideal at some stage in their lives.

I am so pleased to make this introduction to the book and give to each month of the year a prelude commending to you two or three saints who are of particular interest and significance to me, or for whom I have a special devotion. But all the saints featured in this book will daily inform and guide our meditations, intercessions and general prayer, and become signposts on our journey through life.

Georgina Norfolk
(Saint Ermengild)

Preface and How to Use this Book

I am grateful for the Cardinal Archbishop's kind words and for the Duchess of Norfolk's enthusiasm. It is clear that if we ignore the examples of the saints, we do so to the detriment of our daily prayer and intercession and, in consequence, our spiritual life. The saints are our signposts and lighthouses and give us direction and warning throughout our journey. By their overcoming error, weakness and countless difficulties we are instructed and gain strength; by their insights our thinking is illuminated; by their examples we are encouraged: we are thereby ably and daily assisted in our general vocation to become 'other Christs'.

The purpose of this book is to give us a daily glimpse of the saints, to encourage our interest in them and study of them. At the same time we have the discipline of a sensible routine for daily prayer and meditation. If we pray each morning, the saint's story, and therefore his or her strength and teaching, will remain in our minds throughout the day. The saint will give direction to our daily intercession and, indeed, will *assist* with our intercession because we daily ask for this. The suggested topics for the intercession are not exclusive or exhaustive: intercession will flow from our reaction to the day's texts.

If we are extraordinarily busy people, the daily entry on its own, together with the Paternoster, will suffice. If we can spend a little more than a few moments, a suggested format is included below. The expanded Paternoster, also included, may be used to embody more formally the thoughts we wish to express. In addition, a number of other prayers are provided, in both Latin and English. (The use of Latin is encouraged by His Holiness and connects us with the faithful living throughout the world; and with the custom and practice of all the saints of all ages and nationalities.) The style of English employed has been chosen to sit most comfortably with the versions of the Paternoster and Ave Maria with which we are most familiar.

There have been recent revisions of and modifications to the Universal and Local Calendars, and to the Roman Martyrology but the dates in this book largely accord with those sources. The saints featured within have been chosen to provide us with such variety of material that our intercession throughout the year ought to embrace most of those who need our prayers. For the most part only one saint is chosen to represent each day although others are mentioned, on occasions, beneath the title of the day, especially when the chosen saint of the day is less well known. Many of the saints chosen are, sadly, little known. Let us get to know them and be encouraged to know all the other citizens of heaven whose lives have been recorded and whose examples have been valued. Here and there a saint associated with the subject of the day is mentioned and date given but not featured otherwise in the book.

When the daily quotation is a verse or two from the Book of Psalms, I have given, in brackets, the number of the psalm found in the Septuagint and Catholic versions of the Holy Bible. Where the names of the books vary, the name generally found in Catholic versions is used, for example, Sirach for Ecclesiasticus.

From time to time the daily devotion will fall upon a Day of Obligation in the Temporal Cycle, in which case the text provided may form part of our private preparation for Mass.

Julien Chilcott-Monk
(Saint Henry Morse)

A Calendar of Catholic Devotion

January

I love the saints of whom we catch but glimpses – saints such as the martyrs Agnes (January 21) and Sebastian (20), about whom so little is now known to us, and, in contrast, the wonderful John Bosco (31) who, I think I am right, was either the first saint to give a press conference or the first to talk to newspaper reporters!

January 1   Mary the Mother of God

It is the Octave of Christmas, of the Nativity of Our Lord. Both the celebration of Mary, Mother of God (*Theotokos*), and the celebration of the Holy Family, which occurs today if January 1 falls on a Sunday, make a splendid beginning to the year. From the title *Theotokos* flow all the other titles that are Our Lady's, who was chosen to enable Almighty God to present the Logos, the Word that was with God from the very beginning, in the person of Jesus. Into Jesus God pours himself, and Mary is the selfless and willing servant.

In the beginning God created the heavens and the earth. (Genesis 1.1)
In the beginning was the Word and the Word was with God, and the Word was God. He was in the beginning with God. (John 1.1,2a)
'For he who is mighty has done great things for me, and holy is his name.' (Luke 1.49)

It is impossible for us to picture with any accuracy the vastness of the swirling gases before the birth of our solar system, and to grasp fully the idea of Almighty God, the Creator, realizing his intentions as they unfold. And what of other systems, other universes; what of knowable space, and what lies beyond? There are those who live their lives making these enquiries and employing their God-given intellects and gifts.

3

Before the explosive preludes to the swirls of matter, the Word was already with God, as he had always been, and that Word became flesh at a precise moment in time and in space, thousands of millions of years later. God's pinpoint precision is awe-inspiring; from the vastness he picks and makes a creature the mother of the Word, his Son; the Son who is equal to him as God, but inferior to him as man. How did Mary carry such a burden?

In our prayers: thanks for the life, example and intercession of Our Lady, Mother of God; for all scientists, researchers and those who seek after knowledge of Creation.

Pray for us, Holy Mother of God, that we may be made worthy of the promises of Christ.
Holy Mary, pray for us, and for all churches and institutions dedicated in your name.

୧୫୪୬୨

January 2 Basil the Great *(Bishop and Doctor of the Church)*
(Also today, Gregory Nazianzen [*Bishop and Doctor of the Church*].)

It is difficult to exaggerate Basil's contribution to the Church. He was born of wealthy parents in Caesarea. Dismissing a promising career, he toured the monasteries of Egypt and Palestine, became a monk and, later, a hermit. However, he was persuaded into Holy Orders and succeeded the Bishop of Caesarea in 370. Basil used his family wealth to improve the conditions of the poor and for the reform of prostitutes and robbers. He persuaded his clergy into a dedicated priestly life, and was able to bring monasticism within the embrace of the Church so that both benefited.

Basil is known for his contribution to the understanding of Trinitarian theology. He died in 379.

And even though you go unnoticed by . . . [mankind], you will not go unnoticed by our God. The prizes which he has put before us for good works are great. (From a letter by Basil)
What does it profit, my brethren, if a man says he has faith but has not

4

works? Can his faith save him? If a brother or sister is ill-clad and in lack of daily food, and one of you says to them 'Go in peace, be warmed and filled' without giving them the things needed for the body, what does it profit? So faith by itself, if it has no works, is dead. (James 1.14–17)

Basil was indeed one of the 'great' men. His work remains a guide and a pool of inspiration to this day. Not everyone is called to such extensive and varied works, and it is certainly not an essential feature of greatness to be noticed and lauded by our fellows, as Basil himself points out. Basil's fine theological mind prompts us, and his generosity to the poor and to those fallen into sin nudges us to perform works in a similar theme.

In our prayers: thanks for the life, example and intercession of Saint Basil the Great; for the victims of poverty and sin, and for the organizations dedicated to their relief.

Saint Basil, pray for us, for the poor, and for all places dedicated in your name.

January 3   Saint Genevieve of Paris

After the death of her parents, Genevieve lived with her godmother in Paris. Her reputation as a charitable worker grew quickly as she cared for and fed the hungry and destitute people of Paris and other cities. Gradually she became honoured throughout Paris not only for her work with the less fortunate, but also for her sanctity. She was an energetic and tireless worker, and galvanized the citizens of Paris to build a church in honour of Saint Denis (October 9), a patron of France. Genevieve died in about 500, probably in her seventies.

Unless the Lord builds the house, those who build it labour in vain. Unless the Lord watches over the city, the watchman stays awake in vain. (Psalm 127[126].1)
Do good O Lord to those who are good, and to those who are upright in their hearts! (Psalm 125[124].4)

Those who are like Genevieve have the gift of organizing people and projects. They can be overbearing, formidable; they can use charm and gentle persuasion. It is important that we do everything with the face of Christ clearly visible within our own. We are all called to be 'other Christs'. We are here to serve in one way or another using the strengths we have been given. Genevieve's organizational efforts were performed with sanctity: she was a gentle persuader of people. If we have these skills, Genevieve gives us a fine example. Are we menacing and frightening? Do we contribute in any way to the maintenance of the church building with which we have an association?

In our prayers: for the life, example and intercession of Saint Genevieve of Paris; for the victims of hunger in our cities and those who feed them.

Saint Genevieve, pray for us, and for Paris.

༺❀༻

January 4   Saint Elizabeth Ann Seton *(Foundress)*

Elizabeth was born in the United States of America in 1774. She married, and produced five children. Elizabeth then set about a long-held desire to work for the relief of widows and their young children. She spent some time in Italy and embraced the Catholic Faith on her return to America. She opened successful schools for girls and for boys, orphanages and other charitable institutions. Elizabeth and her fellow workers formed a community, which became known as the Daughters of Charity of Saint Joseph. She died in 1821 and was canonized in 1975.

And he sat down and called the twelve; and he said to them 'If any one would be first, he must be last of all and servant of all.' And he took a child, and put him in the midst of them; and taking him in his arms, he said to them 'Whoever receives one such child in my name receives me; and whoever receives me, receives not me but him who sent me.' (Mark 9.35–37)

Elizabeth's vocation to raise a family was fulfilled, but she did not then rest on her laurels; she responded to another call. She spent time to consider carefully her understanding of the Faith and its teachings. It is so easy to be complacent, to make no endeavour to learn more, to study. (We can be sure that the 'why?' uppermost in our minds has long ago been answered. Pray to God for wisdom and understanding.) Armed now with a more secure grasp of the Faith, Elizabeth began to fulfil her second vocation. It is doubtful that the law would these days permit an individual to fulfil a vocation in this way. However, there are other ways to assist with the education of orphans, of children in difficulties, of children with parents separated, and so on.

In our prayers: thanks for the life, example and intercession of Saint Elizabeth Ann Seton; for all orphans and those who care for them.

Soul of Jesus, sanctify me. Humility of Jesus, humble me. Cross of Jesus, support me. Embrace of Jesus, receive me with thy saints in glory evermore. Let me adore thee in thy life-giving Sacrament as my God; listen to thee as my Master; obey thee as my King; imitate thee as my Model; follow thee as my Shepherd; love thee as my Father; seek thee as my Physician, who will heal all the maladies of my soul. Sustain me, O heavenly Manna, through the desert of this world, until I behold thee unveiled in thy glory. Amen. (From the Anima Christi of Elizabeth Ann Seton)
Saint Elizabeth, pray for us, for the United States of America and its President, and for all establishments specializing in the education of the impoverished and neglected.

January 5 Saint John Nepomucene Neumann *(Bishop)*

A Bohemian by birth, John was educated at the Charles Ferdinand University in Prague. Responding to a missionary call, he left for the United States in 1836 and was ordained in the New York diocese. Caring for both German immigrants and American Indians, and building churches and schools for them, John was drawn to the Redemptionists and was received into the Congregation of the Most Holy Redeemer. He was responsible for establishing many more schools in the United States and was also noted for his holiness and enthusiasm. His elevation to the See of Philadelphia allowed him to continue this work of building and founding. John died suddenly in 1860 and was canonized in 1977.

By the waters of Babylon, there we sat down and wept . . . How shall we sing the Lord's song in a foreign land? (Psalm 137[136].1,4)
Praise the Lord, all nations! Extol him, all peoples! For great is his steadfast love towards us . . . (Psalm 117[116].1,2a)

Drawn to the United States of America from outside, John began work as an alien serving both aliens and also indigenous natives, who were themselves alienated. His call from Bohemia may remind us, perhaps, of an ancient prophet called out of the obscurity of one place to minister and preach in another. A fresh eye can sometimes see what we cannot see or refuse to see upon our own doorstep. Perhaps John's work underlines this for us and helps us not only to see what is before us but also to help in whatever way we can by supporting appropriate charities, by intercession, by volunteering.

In our prayers: thanks for the life, example and intercession of Saint John Nepomucene Neumann; for those who feel alien in a strange land.

Saint John, pray for us, for American Indians, German families living in the United States, and for the Redemptorists.

January 6 Epiphany of Our Lord; Saint Raphaela Mary *(Foundress)*

(Today is the traditional date for the Solemnity of the Epiphany of Our Lord: it is now generally kept on the Sunday falling between January 2 and 8.)
　　Raphaela was joint foundress with her sister of the Sisters of Reparation of the Sacred Heart. Many homes were established in Spain and in other countries. The name was changed to Handmaids of the Sacred Heart of Jesus, whose mission was the education of children and the provision of facilities and assistance for retreats. Raphaela was elected superior general in 1877, but by 1893 her sister had replaced her. For over 30 years Raphaela fulfilled a simple and modest role within the community. She died in 1925 and was canonized in 1977.

And an argument arose among them as to which of them was the greatest . . . and [Jesus] said to them '. . . he who is least among you all is the one who is great'. (Luke 9.46–48)
And going into the house they saw the child with Mary his mother, and they fell down and worshipped him. Then, opening their treasures, they offered him gifts, gold, frankincense and myrrh. (Matthew 2.11)

We can easily convince ourselves that we are 'great'. Some of us enjoy being in charge, having responsibility. These things may be performed well in humility, but it is not always so easy to be gracious and humble when given the most menial task, the task so obviously beneath us. How better to fulfil this aim than to assist and encourage those who continue the work and duties of Raphaela's Handmaids? In this way we can do our part in making Christ manifest in our lives and in the lives of others.

In our prayers: thanks for the life, example and intercession of Saint Raphaela Mary; for the victims of discrimination and humiliation; for those who find it difficult to take the lowest place.

Saint Raphaela, pray for us, and for all those who provide facilities for retreats and quiet days.

January 7   Saint Raymond of Peñafort

Raymond, an aristocrat and lecturer in law at Bologna University, joined the Dominican Order in the 1220s. He was renowned as a preacher and confessor, and he became master general of the Order. He worked carefully on the rewording of the Order's constitution and then resigned as superior. Raymond's remaining 30-odd years were spent diligently taking the gospel to the Jews and the Moors, many thousands of whom accepted baptism. Raymond died in 1275 and was canonized in 1601.

The Lord appointed seventy others, and sent them on ahead of him, two by two, into every town and place where he himself was about to come. And he said to them, 'The harvest is plentiful, but the labourers are few; pray therefore the Lord of the harvest to send out labourers into the harvest.' (Luke 10.1,2)

Raymond had the appropriate background for the work of setting down on paper a constitution. Once achieved, Raymond immediately resigned from the position that had given him the authority to do the job, in order to perform the greater challenge – his vocation to those who did not know Christ. Raymond nudges us and reminds us of our general vocation to make Christ known to others by the very way we live our lives. We are not all called to Raymond's more direct form of evangelization, but the witness of our lives can do much to propagate the Faith, slowly and surely and secretly. However, our lives may do the opposite. Does mine?

In our prayers: thanks for the life, example and intercession of Saint Raymond of Peñafort; for all missionaries and those responsible for sending them.

Saint Raymond, pray for us, and pray for the Dominican Order and for all missionary societies.

January 8   Saint Laurence Giustiniani *(Bishop)*

Laurence was an ascetic, having turned his back on family wealth and joined the Congregation of Canons Regular of Saint Augustine. He became a priest in 1406. He was known for setting humility high in the scale of virtues. In 1433 he became Bishop of Castello, and Archbishop of Venice in 1451. His years in both appointments were noted for his personal care of souls and for the provision of food and clothing for tramps and the destitute. Laurence died in 1455 and was canonized in 1690.

Let me hear what God will speak, for he will speak peace to his people, to his saints, to those who turn to him in their hearts. Surely his salvation is at hand for those who fear him that glory may dwell in our land. Steadfast love and faithfulness will meet; righteousness and peace will kiss each other. Faithfulness will spring up from the ground, and righteousness will look down from the sky. (Psalm 85.8–11)

And here is a man, an ascetic, who does not shun the tramp. It is so easy to avoid, to walk away from those in need and to ignore the genuine charities dedicated to the destitute. Even in his exalted position as Archbishop of Venice, the soiled and the unwholesome and unlovely were not beneath his attention. Are we able to turn fully to Christ and ignore the downtrodden? No, because we shall be turning away from the face of Christ himself.

In our prayers: thanks for the life, example and intercession of Saint Laurence Guistiniani; those who minister to the needs of the unlovely; for victims of depression, fear and poverty.

Saint Laurence, pray for us, and for all Orders and Foundations dedicated to the relief of the disadvantaged.

January 9 Saint Adrian of Canterbury *(Abbot)*

Adrian, an African and abbot in Naples, accompanied Theodore when the latter was appointed to the See of Canterbury. Theodore asked Adrian to become abbot of what would eventually become Saint Augustine's. This became a most important academy for scholars from far and wide. For 40 years until his death in about 710, Adrian worked here devotedly for the instruction of the young.

Therefore I prayed, and understanding was given me; I called upon God, and the spirit of wisdom came to me. May God grant that I speak with judgement; for we and our words are in his hand, as are all understanding and skill in crafts; for it is he who gave me unerring knowledge of what exists, to know the structure of the world and the activity of the elements. (Wisdom of Solomon 7.7,15a,16,17)

Instruction and education of the young is a constant feature of the lives of the saints. In this case, Adrian travels to a foreign land and remains there until he dies, quietly and efficiently fulfilling his vocation to guide and nurture the young in the Faith and in other matters of learning. Who can doubt the heavenly Father's cry of 'Well done, good and faithful servant!' on Adrian's entry to the heavenly realms? Do we lack application and dedication? Are we content to leave a task unfinished?

In our prayers: thanks for the life, example and intercession of Saint Adrian of Canterbury; for all teachers and lecturers; for those who find faith difficult.

Saint Adrian, pray for us, and for all abbots and head teachers.

January 10   Saint Gregory of Nyssa *(Bishop)*

Gregory, the younger brother of Saint Basil (January 2), became bishop in 372. He was no administrator and had little flair for ecclesiastical politics. However, after the death of Basil, he found his nîche. He did all he could to promote orthodoxy in his writings and addresses. Gregory was a significant figure in the Council of Constantinople in 381. For his towering intellect, emphasis on the study of Scripture and a defence of orthodoxy, Gregory was highly regarded. He died towards the end of the fourth century.

And he said to them 'O foolish men, and slow of heart to believe all that the prophets have spoken! Was it not necessary that the Christ should suffer these things and enter into his glory?' And beginning with Moses and all the prophets, he interpreted to them in all the scriptures the things concerning himself. (Luke 24.25–27)

The Fathers of this period of the Church's history often lived in danger and were never far from controversy. Many popular heresies arose, and the great intellects in the early Church had to wrestle and reason their way to gain and maintain an orthodox understanding of theology. Born of this work and meticulous purification of the understanding of the Faith is the catechism we now hold dear. These great minds of the early centuries have given us clarity and purity of thought to arm us against error and to strengthen us in the promotion of the Faith. We ourselves are not all called to dispute in matters of the intellect, but do we help others understand the Faith? Do *I* understand the Faith? Do *I* read and endeavour to understand Scripture?

In our prayers: thanks for the life, example and intercession of Saint Gregory of Nyssa; for the enemies of orthodoxy.

Saint Gregory, pray for us, and for all seminaries and places of learning.

January 11   Saint Paulinus of Aquileia *(Bishop)*

Paulinus, a farmer's son, was blessed with a bright intellect. He became professor of grammar and then Bishop of Aquileia. He also had the role of adviser in Charlemagne's court in Aachen. Paulinus was instrumental in the court's encouraging orthodoxy in the Faith; insisting on proper instruction for converts, and good quality sermons for the edification of the laity; and providing secular leaders with guidance as to their obligations towards their citizens and subjects. Paulinus died in 802.

For the Lord has chosen Zion; he has desired it for his habitation: 'This is my resting place for ever; here I will dwell, for I have desired it. I will abundantly bless her provisions; I will satisfy her poor with bread. Her priests I will clothe with salvation, and her saints will shout for joy. (Psalm 132[131].13–16)

Again, we have a saint who points us clearly along the way of orthodoxy. Paulinus's encouragements were not extraordinary – he merely urged faithfulness in religion, clarity in the instruction of the Faith, and responsibility towards others. Paulinus's example shows us that we must continue to learn and seek after wisdom in the Faith; we must be sure that we inform others correctly and without our own particular slant. Do we study Scripture too little or not at all? Do we miss opportunities to pass on to others what they are anxious to know? Do we really consider everyone to be our neighbour? How do we express what we think?

In our prayers: thanks for the life, example and intercession of Saint Paulinus of Aquileia; for those who instruct others in the Faith.

Saint Paulinus, pray for us, and for all teachers of the Faith.

❧❦☙

January 12 Saint Antony Mary Pucci
(Also today, Saint Benedict Biscop [*Abbot*].)

Of Tuscan peasant stock, Antony entered the priory of the Annunciation, Florence, in 1837. After a grounding in classics and theology, he was ordained in 1843 and immediately appointed to a parish in Viareggio, becoming its parish priest in 1847. Antony served in this capacity for 45 years until his death in 1892. He was the perfect parish priest, possessing all the appropriate skills and a genuine love of the sick and poor of the parish. Antony was canonized in 1962.

I will look with favour on the faithful in the land, that they may dwell with me; he who walks in the way that is blameless shall minister to me. (Psalm 101[100].6)
So I exhort the elders among you . . . tend the flock of God that is your charge . . . [by] being examples to the flock. (1 Peter 5.1–3)

Antony's vocation was clear. Not for him the elevation to the episcopacy, not for him the solemn assemblies. His vocation was down to earth, demanding patient dedication without the yearning for anything other than the ability and steadfastness to minister to his appointed flock. Are we ever dissatisfied with our lot, or do we always carry out our God-given vocation willingly, cheerfully and without demur? Do we lavish time and energy upon our Christian duties? If we are not parish priests, do we offer our parish priest our talents and skills? Do we share Antony's love of the sick and poor? How do we show it?

In our prayers: thanks for the life, example and intercession of Saint Antony Mary Pucci; for all parish priests and those who assist them.

Saint Antony, pray for us, and for all parish priests.

❦

January 13 Saint Hilary of Poitiers *(Bishop and Doctor of the Church)*

Hilary was converted and baptized in 350. By popular demand he became Bishop of Poitiers and for a number of turbulent years seemed to be the lone voice of orthodoxy. He spent some time in exile but he was always striving to encourage and argue orthodoxy in the many synods during the period after Constantine's death. Hilary has left us a large collection of writings. He died in 367. Pope Pius IX declared him Doctor of the Church in 1851.

And in case the soul should err and linger in some delusion of heathen philosophy, it receives this further lesson of perfect loyalty to the holy Faith, taught by the Apostle in words inspired. (Hilary of Poitiers, Book 1: On the Holy Trinity)
See to it that no one makes a prey of you by philosophy and empty deceit, according to human tradition . . . and not according to Christ. For in him the whole fullness of the deity dwells bodily, and you have come to

fullness of life in him, who is the head of all rule and authority. (Colossians 2.8–10)

With Hilary we return to the theme of purity of Faith. Hilary was made to suffer for orthodoxy from time to time during his life. Great men were striving to grasp ideas and put them into words, to clarify and to assist. Not for everyone are these intellectual struggles, but for everyone is the fruit of Hilary's work. For everyone is the great benefit of the quiet contemplation of our Lord and Saviour in the Most Holy Sacrament. In Christ 'the whole fullness of the Deity dwells bodily'. Do we thank God for this gift or do we take it for granted?

In our prayers: thanks for the life, example and intercession of Saint Hilary of Poitiers; for all theologians and philosophers; for those who find aspects of the Faith difficult.

Saint Hilary, pray for us, and for all those who do not accept the teaching of the Church.

જ✵ℐ

January 14 Saint Sava of Serbia *(Abbot and Bishop)*

Sava was a son of Prince Stephen I of Serbia. At 17 he left the household for Greece and established himself as a monk on Mount Athos. His father joined him in 1198, having given up the throne to his eldest son, Stephen II. Father and son now established a monastery of Serbian monks, a monastery that exists to this day. Sava became abbot. Later, Sava was consecrated bishop in Nicaea and returned to Serbia and reorganized the Church, building churches and monasteries throughout Serbia. Sava died in 1237, a gentle trainer of monks in Mount Athos, a tireless reformer of the whole ecclesiastical structure of Serbia.

O Lord, who shall sojourn in thy tent? Who shall dwell on thy holy hill? – He who walks blamelessly, and does what is right; and speaks the truth from his heart. (Psalm 15[14].1,2)
Preserve me O God, for in thee I take refuge. I say to the Lord, 'Thou art my Lord; I have no good apart from thee.' (Psalm 16[15].1,2)

We do not find it incomprehensible that as Sava was of ascetic temperament he should seek solitude in order to reach a decision as to his future. God had called him to contemplation; not for him was a life at court. The tasks set for him were formidable and in great contrast to one another. However, the training received in his first calling prepared him for the important work of the second. Sava's life was one of complete dedication and submission to God's will. Do we ever remain silent long enough to consider carefully what God demands of us? Do we listen? Most of us are not called upon to reform the Church, but we are all called upon to reform ourselves. Often we avoid looking too intently at ourselves as we know the experience likely to be uncomfortable.

In our prayers: thanks for the life, example and intercession of Saint Sava of Serbia; for men and women who live the contemplative life; for Serbia.

Saint Sava, pray for us, and for all church administrators.

January 15 Ita of Killeedy *(Foundress and Abbess)*

Ita founded a religious house in County Limerick in the sixth century. There she established a boys' school. Ita was elected abbess. Among others who would eventually achieve sainthood, Brendan (May 16) came within her sphere of influence. Ita required nothing more than a humble life and was content with her kitchen garden, her small school and religious community. Her life was lived in faith, gratitude and in charity. She was buried in the house she founded, in about 570.

We know that in everything God works for good with those who love him, who are called according to his purpose. (Romans 8.28)
And he fell on his face at Jesus' feet, giving him thanks. Now he was a Samaritan. Then said Jesus, 'Were not ten cleansed? Where are the nine? Was no one found to return and give praise to God except this foreigner?' (Luke 17.16–18)

The lingering memory after Ita's death was that her life had been lived in faith, gratitude and charity. What a splendidly sufficient legacy; what a clear signpost for the faithful! A life in faith and good works is often what attracts the observer; the gratitude of the individual is often less obvious to the observer. Giving thanks is so often the happy duty we tend to overlook. Our petitions and intercessions may be full and exhaustive, but our thanks is often sparing or non-existent. Do we thank others appropriately? If so, why are we so niggardly in giving thanks to God? Ita thanked him for her simple life, her kitchen garden, the boys who attended the school, the opportunities she was given for performing charitable acts. Do we always see when we are given the opportunity to perform a charitable act? Often we realize it when it is too late.

In our prayers: thanks for the life, example and intercession of Saint Ita of Killeedy; for those simple workers of the Faith who work in contentment and gratitude.

Saint Ita, pray for us, and for those who do not appreciate the simple things of life.

January 16   Saint Romanus the Bulgarian

Romanus left his home and entered a monastery, and then travelled to become a disciple of Gregory of Sinai. He assisted in the construction of a monastery on the borders of Bulgaria and the Byzantine Empire. There he was responsible for the sick and elderly monks, and was known for his kind and gentle demeanour. Romanus then took to Mount Athos and became a well-loved spiritual director to monks from many different countries and backgrounds. He ended his days near Belgrade and died around 1374.

I will sing of thy steadfast love, O Lord, for ever; with my mouth I will proclaim thy faithfulness to all generations. For thy steadfast love was established for ever, thy faithfulness is firm as the heavens. (Psalm 89[88].1,2)
They were bewildered, because each one heard them speaking in his own language. And all were amazed and perplexed, saying to one another, 'What does it mean?' (Acts 2.6b,12)

Romanus, rather like Sava (January 14), left home to lead the contemplative life. However, Romanus was never called to a life outside these circumstances. He worked hard to develop the monastic life for others and in so doing discovered his special vocation to the sick and elderly monks. What gifts of generosity and patience he possessed and exercised! We know that the sick and the elderly can sometimes be difficult to care for, requiring from the nurse or companion both those gifts in abundance. But to show generosity and patience in these circumstances there must first be self-denial. Time must be given freely – we need time to serve and time in which to be patient.

In our prayers: thanks for the life, example and intercession of Saint Romanus the Bulgarian; for all organizations dedicated to the care of the sick and elderly; for Bulgaria.

Saint Romanus, pray for us, and for those who care for the sick and elderly.

༺ຊ❀ຊ༅

January 17   Antony of Egypt *(Abbot)*

Antony was of a wealthy Christian family. When his parents died, he sold his inheritance and gave it to the poor. He then began life as a hermit, eventually moving himself to an abandoned hill-fort in the desert. Early in the fourth century, he began to take disciples and founded a monastery – in fact, a rather loose collection of cells. He founded a second on the east bank of the River Nile. With his disciples he received a large number of visitors anxious to hear the word of this desert father. He was known for his gentleness of spirit and wise counsel. Of devils and demons he would sagely comment that they could only be given form by our invitation. Antony died in 356, or thereabouts.

'Fear not, little flock, for it is your Father's good pleasure to give you the kingdom. Sell your possessions, give alms; provide yourselves with purses that do not grow old, with a treasure in the heavens that does not fail, where no thief approaches and no moth destroys. For where your treasure is, there will your heart be also.' (Luke 12.32–34)

The desire to 'get away from it all' often seems to prevail in these short biographies of the saints – certainly during this early period. Antony felt he had no need for his riches and simply did as our Lord had bidden him. The poor benefited. Are we all called to live as solitaries or in a monastic community, in poverty and asceticism? No, we all have different callings, but we must all possess the *spirit* of self-denial, and exercise it appropriately. In other words, we must use what we have for the benefit of others, and we may do this in many different ways in accordance with our vocation. The demon of avarice, and its associated failings, is certainly given form when we entertain him.

In our prayers: thanks for the life, example and intercession of Saint Antony of Egypt; for all ascetics; for priestly confessors.

Saint Antony, pray for us, and for those who give form to demons.

❦

January 18   Saint Margaret of Hungary

Margaret, born in 1242, was the daughter of the Hungarian king, Bela IV, and had been dedicated to the nuns at Vesprem as a thank-offering for military success against the Tartars. The king built a convent for Margaret and there she was professed. She set herself the lowliest duties in the convent and took her fasting to extreme lengths. Her short life of prayer and humility came to an end in 1270. She was canonized in 1943.

And he said to them, 'If any man would come after me, let him deny himself and take up his cross daily and follow me. For whoever would save his life will lose it; and whoever loses his life for my sake, he will save it.' (Luke 9.23,24)

Is this rather a waste of a princess's life, anyone's life, to fast to the detriment of the body? After all, can any good be done on earth by a weakened body? Perhaps we should concentrate, in the alternative, on the example set by the life of this saint, on Margaret's response to God's vocation for her. She was called to the cloister and there made herself the least among her sisters. She humbled herself from princess to scullery maid for the sake of Christ. Furthermore, she denied herself the pleasure of food and drink, taking only sufficient sustenance to enable her to continue her life of prayer – and a life of prayer in a monastery or a convent is a life of prayer for others. This short life of extreme self-denial and intercession actually follows Christ's words to the letter! If we are not called to the ascetic life, what can we learn from Margaret? Perhaps, her absolute confidence in Christ is the answer, because into his hands she placed herself.

In our prayers: thanks for the life, example and intercession of Saint Margaret of Hungary; for those who constantly intercede for others; for abbots and abbesses of contemplative Orders.

Saint Margaret, pray for us, and for those who have not the strength to deny themselves.

January 19   Saint Wulfstan *(Bishop)*

Wulfstan received his education from the Benedictines at Evesham and Peterborough. After ordination, he entered the Benedictine priory at Worcester Cathedral, rising to prior in about 1050. Twelve years later, Wulfstan was bishop of the diocese. He laboured tirelessly for both diocese and priory. He rebuilt the cathedral; he was renowned as a preacher and social reformer; he halted the trade in slaves from Bristol docks. Above all, he was a humble and generous man. He died in 1095 while washing the feet of 12 destitute men.

When he had washed their feet, and taken his garments and resumed his place, he said to them, 'Do you know what I have done to you? You call me Teacher and Lord; and you are right, for so I am. If I, then, your Lord and Teacher, have washed your feet, you also ought to wash one another's feet.' (John 13.12–14)

What a man was Wulfstan! He was a fine bishop – he literally built up the Church in his diocese, and was scrupulous about what happened in the churches in his diocese and in the cathedral. However, in these days of much self-satisfaction over our sensitivity, and outrage at the insensitivity of past ages, it is startling to discover that 1,000 years ago Wulfstan possessed the character and determination to act in defence of the downtrodden. Why do we believe that only *we* know how to follow in the footsteps of Christ? When did we last wash the feet (or give shoes to) *one* destitute man or woman?

In our prayers: thanks for the life, example and intercession of Saint Wulfstan; for those who are slaves; for bishops and senior clergy; for those in authority.

Saint Wulfstan, pray for us, and for all bishops.

January 20 Saint Sebastian *(Martyr)*
(Also today, Saint Fabian [*Pope and Martyr*].)

Little is known about Sebastian. He is pictured in some mosaics and frescoes as a mature, bearded man – not the smooth-skinned youth of the Renaissance. It is probable that he was born in Milan and martyred in Rome during Diocletian's slaughter of Christians. If a soldier at the time, there is no doubt his martyrdom would have been doubly horrific. A basilica was built in his honour on the Appian Way, in the fourth century. He died at the beginning of that century.

Therefore be imitators of God as beloved children. And walk in love, as Christ loved us and gave himself up for us – a fragrant offering and sacrifice to God. (Ephesians 5.1,2)

If we assume Sebastian to have been an army officer of some seniority and maturity, on the evidence of the frescoes, it is probable that he embraced Christ in middle life. The pressures on him in the Roman army would have been considerable. If discovered, the Christian in the Roman army would find himself tortured and killed with more enthusiasm than that lavished on the ordinary citizen. It was difficult to keep your faith secret – you would refuse the obligatory worship of the Roman gods; your demeanour would give you away eventually. Some, of course, boldly admitted their faith. Is our Christianity and Catholic Faith likely to be discovered from our demeanour?

In our prayers: thanks for the life, example and intercession of Saint Sebastian; for victims of oppression and religious hate; for magistrates, judges and lawmakers; for athletes and those engaged in sports.

Saint Sebastian, pray for us, and for all soldiers and those under command.

January 21 Saint Agnes *(Martyr)*

Like Sebastian (January 20), Agnes was a victim of Diocletian's bloody purge. She was beheaded – tradition has it that she was then but a 13-year-old – in Circus Agonalis. The church of Saint Agnes now stands there. Her story, like Sebastian's, became encrusted with fabulous tales; but her simple ardent faith and her holy defiance always shine through. Agnes died early in the fourth century.

For the Lord knows the way of the righteous, but the way of the wicked will perish. (Psalm 1.6)

It is interesting to read the stories that embroider Agnes's martyrdom. They simply serve to underline her sanctity. That she was so young but resolute in her faith, clearly caught the imagination of her contemporaries because her courage was hailed at her martyrdom not on the strength of the later stories. Would that our faith and courage were as strong and resolute in difficult times. Do we assist in nurturing the faith of the young?

In our prayers: thanks for the life, example and intercession of Saint Agnes; for all those who are young in the Faith; for those who are responsible for young people.

Saint Agnes, pray for us, and for all churches dedicated in your name, and for all young people growing up in the Faith.

୧୧✤୨୨

January 22   Saint Vincent Pallotti *(Founder)*
(Also today, Saint Vincent of Zaragoza [*Martyr*].)

Born in Rome in 1795, Vincent was ordained in 1818. God was at the core of all the work he undertook. He was zealous in his desire to ensure the laity were properly valued for their particular skills, and employed in good works. He was alarmed that the lines of demarcation between religious and secular clergy were sharply defined and so between clergy and laity. He formed the Congregation of the Catholic Apostolate, and the Sisters of the Catholic Apostolate. These foundations developed into international missionary societies. Vincent died in 1850 and was canonized in 1963.

It is neither the intellect nor the will, but God; it is not worldly goods or riches, but God. It is neither honours nor distinction, but God; it is not dignities or advancement, but God. God is always the centre of everything. (Paraphrase of Vincent Pallotti's diary entry)

Nothing is more straightforward than Vincent's God-centred philosophy. If only we had the resolve to say and to mean 'Whatever task we perform, we perform it for God, because it is his will; because it builds up the body of Christ.' How often we fall short of this ideal. But the helping hand of God's good grace raises us up to try again. Whatever we do, wherever we go, we are on a mission for Christ.

In our prayers: thanks for the life, example and intercession of Saint Vincent Pallotti; for the administrators of missionary societies.

Saint Vincent, pray for us, and for those who support the work of missionaries.

January 23   Saint Ildephonsus of Toledo *(Abbot and Bishop)*

Ildephonsus was a monk in Agalia near Toledo. He became abbot and subsequently was elected Archbishop of Toledo at a relatively peaceful time for the Church in Spain. He established a convent of nuns in the region. Ildephonsus developed a great devotion to Our Lady and encouraged this devotion in others. He was passionate also that the laity should be properly educated in the Faith and that their understanding of the Faith ought to be at a high level. He died in 667.

For whatever was written in former days was written for our instruction, that by steadfastness and encouragement of the scriptures we might have hope. (Romans 15.4)

Whether we are priest or lay, priest religious or lay religious, we need to be educated in the Faith, to study the Scriptures, the Fathers and Doctors of the Church. In our contemplation God will speak. So fired by his devotion to Our Lady, Ildephonsus sought to share his enthusiasm with others. Her title of Mother of God and the example of her steadfastness are the points of departure for fruitful meditation. And we benefit from the contemplation of all the Mysteries of her Rosary. Do we spend sufficient time considering all these matters?

In our prayers: thanks for the life, example and intercession of Saint Ildephonsus; for all teachers and instructors of the laity; for those who encourage devotion to Our Lady.

Saint Ildephonsus, pray for us, and for all catechists.

❧✣❧

January 24   Francis de Sales *(Bishop and Doctor of the Church)*

After studying theology in Paris and law in Padua, Francis was ordained in 1593. He was given a mission to a remote part of Geneva, where he successfully restored the Catholic Faith and re-established it in a few years. In 1602, he was consecrated Bishop of Geneva and set about re-educating his clergy and re-organizing the 400 or so parishes. He preached, taught and wrote thousands of letters of instruction and guidance.

Patience, humility and hard work were Francis's hallmarks. He died in 1632, was canonized in 1665, and declared Doctor of the Church in 1877.

It is not only wrong but heretical to suggest that a life in the army, the factory, the court or the home is incompatible with devotion. God commands Christians, the living branches of the vine, to bear fruit by practising devotion according to their state in life. (From Introduction to the Devout Life, *Francis de Sales)*

Francis was a great correspondent and he achieved much of his work by letter; he was able to remain in contact with priests and laity in the remote parts of Geneva. In this way he performed his duties as shepherd most perfectly. His writing and his visits to the private oratory were of equal importance; both were part of his devotional life. For most of us, our devotional life may be largely practised in the general operation of our duties and as we work, although quiet contemplation also is, of course, a necessary feature of everyone's devotional life. But do we confine the practise of our faith to Sundays and other days of Obligation, or do we work hard to try to show others the face of Christ at all times wherever we are?

In our prayers: thanks for the life, example and intercession of Saint Francis de Sales; for those who confine practice of their faith to the Holy Days of Obligation; for all spiritual directors and counsellors.

Saint Francis, pray for us, for all writers and for the proper use of all private oratories.

January 25   The Conversion of Saint Paul *(Apostle and Martyr)*

Saul, a Roman citizen and Jew, born in Tarsus and educated in Jerusalem, was a persecutor of Christians, who was converted by a blinding revelation from God on the road to Damascus, recorded in Luke's Acts of the Apostles. Renamed Paul, his missionary work took him, inter alia, to Greece, Asia Minor and Cyprus. He left established communities of Christianity throughout the Mediterranean and farther afield, ready for subsequent development and expansion. Paul was put to death in about 64.

But Saul, still breathing threats and murder against the disciples of the Lord, went to the high priest and asked him for letters to the synagogues at Damascus, so that if he found any belonging to the Way, men or women, he might bring them bound to Jerusalem. Now, as he journeyed he approached Damascus, and suddenly a light from heaven flashed about him. And he fell to the ground and heard a voice saying to him 'Saul, Saul, why do you persecute me . . . I am Jesus, whom you are persecuting.' (Acts 9.1–5)

Paul was an enthusiastic destroyer and informer transformed by the realization of the power of God's grace in Christ the Saviour. In newspaper terms it was a 'dramatic U-turn'. Our imperfections are opportunities to repent, to turn away from one shameful aspect and turn to Christ. We are complex, however, and our lives are made of so many facets; one cut edge will reflect the light, another will be cast in shadow and darkness. If we keep the radiant vision of Christ crucified before us, we gather strength by putting on 'the armour of light'. Paul is a good example of how God can fundamentally change us so that we can fulfil our vocations.

In our prayers: thanks for the life, example and intercession of Saint Paul; for all new converts to the Faith.

Saint Paul, pray for us, for Greece and Malta, and for all places dedicated in your name.

❧❀☙

January 26 Saint Paula
(Also today, Timothy [*Bishop and Martyr*] and Titus [*Martyr*].)

Paula, born in 347, and a widow at 32, was one of those noble women who formed, in Rome under Saint Jerome's (September 30) direction, a Bible study group that developed into a monastic circle. Eventually, Saint Jerome left for Palestine with Paula and others to make pilgrimages to the Holy Places, and to visit the monks in Egypt. They formed convents and monasteries in Bethlehem and the surrounding area. Paula died in 404.

Come, bless the Lord, all you servants of the Lord, who stand by night in the house of the Lord! Lift up your hands to the holy place, and bless the Lord! (Psalm 134[133])

Paula, a widow and mother, was another of those happy saints who completed one vocation and then sought to fulfil a second. This she ably did. By her companionship of Jerome she began to study the Scriptures more deeply, and to pass on her learning to others; in her own right she worked for the development of the monastic life in the Holy Land. What comes down to us through the stories of Paula is that she was a worthy companion to Jerome, a steadying influence, perhaps, enabling him to concentrate on his great work of translation. (At times, almost inevitably, they suffered from taunts, whispers and rumours about their relationship.) Are we sometimes too proud to assist and to be known as an assistant? Do we gossip truth and untruth?

In our prayers: thanks for the life, example and intercession of Saint Paula; for those content to work in the capacity of an assistant; for victims of slander and rumour.

Saint Paula, pray for us, and for all those who assist others in their work.

January 27 Saint Angela Merici *(Foundress)*

Angela was born in 1470 into what now might be regarded as an upper-middle class family, in Lombardy. She was a pious child. As a Franciscan tertiary she gathered around her a group of like-minded women in Desenzano, who wished to be of service and support to young unmarried women in the city. She developed the work in Brescia, moving freely among all the class strata of society. All her distinguished work to the age of 60 was preparatory to her founding the Congregation of Ursulines. She died in 1540 and was canonized in 1807.

Bless the Lord, you servants of the Lord, sing praise to him and highly exalt him for ever. Bless the Lord, spirits and souls of the righteous, sing praise to him and highly exalt him for ever. Bless the Lord, you who are holy and humble in heart, sing praise to him and highly exalt him for ever. (Daniel 3.63–65)

Angela's many years working for the good of young women, with her dedicated team of helpers, were her gradual journey towards her founding, at the great age of 60 (for so it was in the sixteenth century), the Ursulines. She worked unceasingly during her lifetime and left a legacy that stretches through the centuries and reaches our own time. Are we able to follow the example of Angela's devotion to Christian duty, and translate it to our own circumstances?

In our prayers: thanks for the life, example and intercession of Saint Angela Merici; for all vulnerable and lonely women; for those who care for and educate young women.

Saint Angela, pray for us, and for the continuing work of the Ursulines.

January 28   Saint Thomas Aquinas *(Doctor of the Church)*

Thomas was born in 1225 and educated by Benedictines at Monte Cassino, and at Naples University. He entered the Dominican Order and continued his studies in Paris and Cologne. In 1252, he began lecturing at the University of Paris. Thomas was appointed to the University of the Roman Curia; he returned to Paris and then to the Dominicans in Italy in 1272. His principal works include *Summa Theologica* and *Summa Contra Gentiles*. He was a holy man with a deep devotion to the person of Christ and to the Blessed Sacrament exemplified, perhaps, by the *Tantum ergo*. His contribution to our better understanding of Our Lord in the Blessed Sacrament can hardly be overstated. Thomas died in 1274 and was canonized in 1323.

Therefore we before him bending,
This great Sacrament revere;
Types and shadows have their ending,
For the newer rite is here;
Faith, our outward sense befriending,
Makes the inward vision clear.

Thomas, a man who enjoyed many elevated positions in his life, was simply a holy and humble man whose intellect and facility of expression have managed to crystallize for us his profound understanding of the Blessed Sacrament. His writings are set books in all seminaries and theological institutions; his contribution to theological learning and knowledge is enormous. But, just as we do, Thomas prayed those succinct and simple words of adoration before Our Lord in the Blessed Sacrament. Do we thank God for his great gift? Do we regularly kneel before Our Lord in the Most Holy Sacrament?

In our prayers: thanks for the life, example and intercession of Saint Thomas Aquinas; for all theological institutions and seminaries; for those who study the Scriptures; for a greater appreciation of and devotion to the Blessed Sacrament.

O Jesu, in the Most Holy Sacrament, have mercy upon us.
Saint Thomas, pray for us, and for all ordinands.

January 29 Saint Gildas *(Abbot)*

Gildas was a monk of some renown. He settled in a monastery in South Glamorgan. He wrote a diatribe against the laxness of British rulers and clergy. Towards the end of his life he founded a monastery off the south Brittany coast and died in 570 or thereabouts. He was known as Gildas the Wise, and monks travelled from Ireland to receive his good counsel.

For the Lord gives wisdom; from his mouth comes knowledge and understanding; he stores up sound wisdom for the upright; he is a shield to those who walk in integrity, guarding the paths of justice and preserving the way of his saints. (Proverbs 2.6–8)

Gildas was able to put his finger on the nub of a problem: he could see precisely the cause of a trouble. His wisdom, naturally enough, made him sought out by those keen to hear him. Have we asked for the gift of wisdom? Perhaps we think ourselves wise enough: perhaps we are. If so, do we willingly give counsel when asked? Are we too proud to ask those who can give good counsel when we are in need? We can learn from Gildas as we can learn from all the saints. Each is a signpost to heaven; each places the experience of his or her vocation at our disposal to help us on our way.

In our prayers: thanks for the life, example and intercession of Saint Gildas; for all bishops, priests and prophets who point to the errors in Church and state; for all who seek the counsel of the wise.

Saint Gildas, pray for us, and for wise counsellors and those who would be.

January 30 Saint Adelemus

Adelemus was a Frenchman who spent his early years in a monastery in the Auvergne. He later spent some time in Spain working for the recovery of the Catholic Faith based in a monastery built for him by Alphonso VI of Castile. His fame rested on his holiness. Adelemus died in 1070 or thereabouts.

Strive for peace with all men, and for the holiness without which no one will see the Lord. (Hebrews 12.14)

Whatever the life's work of Adelemus and his greatest achievements – and, doubtless, his vocation was fulfilled to perfection in the eyes of the Creator, who gave him his talents, his weaknesses and his vocation – the overriding feature of his life was that of holiness, of sanctity. From a holy life flow all the characteristics of a Christ-like existence. We tend, at best, to be holy in phases, selectively, in fits and starts. Achieving the aim to be thoroughly holy is not easy, but one of our general vocations is to strive for holiness. However, if we live our lives in accordance with our Faith, we shall become holy as a consequence.

In our prayers: thanks for the life, example and intercession of Saint Adelemus; for those who find it difficult to live their lives in holiness; for the faithful, unassuming workers of the Church.

Saint Adelemus, pray for us, and pray for all those with national responsibilities in the Church.

January 31   Saint John Bosco *(Founder)*

John was ordained priest in 1841 and then undertook further theological studies in the Convitto Ecclesiastico in Turin. John began to concentrate on the young in the poverty-stricken areas of the city. His efforts were necessary and successful but he came to realize that he should devote more time to the education of the disadvantaged in society. He invited his mother to assist in a house in a poor district. From this beginning the Salesian Congregation – a religious society within, a secular society without – dedicated to Saint Francis de Sales (January 24) developed and blossomed. There are today many of these congregations throughout the world. John died in 1888 and was canonized in 1934.

Blessed is he who considers the poor! The Lord delivers him in the day of trouble; the Lord protects him and keeps him alive; he is called blessed in the land. (Psalm 41[40].1,2a)

John was a tireless worker, and his work is producing fruit to this day. We give thanks not only for this fact but also for John's saintly example, which is still a guiding light to every Christian. Those to whom he dedicated his life's work are also still with us today, and require our attention in a variety of ways. We are not all called to instruct the young and destitute, but we can assist by supporting Salesian Congregations and their imitators and associated charities, which specialize in this work throughout the world.

In our prayers: thanks for the life, example and intercession of Saint John Bosco; for the impoverished and uneducated; for the Salesian Congregations.

Saint John, pray for us, and for all teachers and workers in Christian education among the disadvantaged.

February

Jerome Emiliani (February 8) is one of the patrons of orphans and neglected children, causes close to my heart. Robert Southwell (21) – at the very least, a religious poet well worth getting to know – had close connections with the Norfolks through his friendship with Saint Philip Howard (October 19) and his wife.

꧁❈꧂

February 1   Saint Henry Morse *(Martyr)*
(Also today, Saint Brigid of Kildare [*Abbess*].)

Henry was born in 1595. Initially, he intended to study law, but became a Catholic and, in 1614, began his studies in Douai. He was part of the mission to England in 1620 and was arrested on landing at Newcastle. He was banished. He began another mission – this time in London – in 1633 and reconciled many to the Church, working as an outbreak of the plague raged about him. Again Henry was imprisoned for his priesthood but only fined and banished on the intervention of Queen Henrietta Maria. He returned to England and ministered in the north where he was eventually captured and sentenced to be hanged, drawn and quartered. The sentence was carried out at Tyburn in 1645, and Henry was canonized in 1970.

'I tell you, my friends, do not fear those who kill the body, and after that have no more that they can do. Are not five sparrows sold for two pennies? And not one of them is forgotten before God. Why, even the hairs of your head are all numbered. Fear not; you are of more value than many sparrows.' (Luke 12.4,6,7)

If only we displayed such resolution and determination in our mission for Christ, undeterred by the probable consequences. Henry had absolute faith in God, whatever the circumstances in which he found himself – saying Mass with lookouts at the door; under guard; in prison; hearing the last confession of a dying plague victim; banished; returning in disguise; reconciling in the north; captured; sentenced; taken to Tyburn. Throughout his life he was in God's hands, the God who creates the sparrow, who numbers the sparrows, who knows for how much they may be sold and by whom and to whom. Henry's vocation was clear to him, and for 25 years he persisted. Our calling is not likely to be as dramatic as the gallows at Tyburn but simply to persist and persevere in the footsteps of Christ, without despair, without complaint.

In our prayers: thanks for the life, example and intercession of Saint Henry Morse; for determination and resolve; for those who live and work under repression.

Saint Henry, pray for us, and for all who fulfil their vocations in constant danger.

February 2 The Presentation of the Lord;
The Martyrs of Vietnam

From the four groups of those beatified in the first half of the twentieth century, 117 priests and lay workers were canonized in 1988. Ninety-six of them were Vietnamese. They were active between the middle of the eighteenth century and the middle of the nineteenth century. Their stories of gruelling hardships, zealous evangelizing, care and attention of the faithful – all under grave penalties – are awe-inspiring.

The apostles said to the Lord, 'Increase our faith!' And the Lord said, 'If you had faith as a grain of mustard seed, you could say to this sycamine tree, "Be rooted up, and be planted in the sea," and it would obey you.' (Luke 17.5,6)

We need hear just a little of the lives and deaths of these holy martyrs to appreciate something of the hardships in the name of Christ that men and women accept without demur. Does this contrast with our reaction to the slightest inconvenience? Was it even worse for the indigenous missionaries, who were received by some of their countrymen but reviled and informed against by others? Probably. The figurative sword of the informant and the steel sword of the official informed both do their grim work with frightening efficiency. And Our Lady felt the first of her Seven Sorrows with Simeon's prediction of the sword-thrust to her heart as she presented God's only-begotten Son to the Father by observing the appropriate rites and ceremonies. How did Mary remain steadfast in love and faith? She had said *yes* to God, and that sacred vow was sufficient. How did those holy martyrs in Vietnam remain steadfast in love and faith as their capture and deaths were executed? How do we compare?

In our prayers: thanks for the lives, examples and intercession of the Holy Martyrs of Vietnam; for victims of cruelty and torture; for those who send others into the mission fields.

Pray for us, O Holy Mother of God, that we may be made worthy of the promises of Christ. Holy Martyrs, pray for us, and for Vietnam and countries of south-east Asia.

⟨❈⟩

February 3   Saint Werberga *(Abbess)*
(Also today, Saint Blaise [*Bishop and Martyr*].)

On the death of her father, King Wulfhere of Mercia, dedicating herself to Christ, Werberga entered Ely Abbey. Her uncle, Ethelred, now on the Mercian throne, ordered her from the abbey to look after three religious houses, including Weedon in Northamptonshire. She was buried at the house in Hanbury in Staffordshire, but her body was later translated to Chester Cathedral. She died around 700. Hers is a simple story of obedience and dedication after her plans had been modified by command of the king.

As Jesus passed on from there, he saw a man called Matthew sitting at the tax office; and he said to him, 'Follow me!' And he rose and followed him. (Matthew 9.9)

A dedication to Christ means that we are available for him to use in whatever manner he chooses. Werberga chose what was a suitable way, in her eyes, of fulfilling that dedication. But, no, God's desires may well require modification of our plans. In this case God's will was made known through the agency of the king, who required his niece to help him fulfil part of his vocation. And so, Werberga's quiet abbey life was taken away and replaced with the responsibility for three religious houses. In Matthew's case, the call to change involved a greater upheaval. But they both were willing to change their plans and tailor them to God's. To respond in this way we have to listen in order to hear what is required of us. To respond positively and immediately to '*follow me*' requires commitment. This call may come from the mouth of Our Lord himself or from another source acting for God knowingly or unknowingly. Do we waver?

In our prayers: thanks for the life, example and intercession of Saint Werberga; for those who modify their own desires in order to conform to your will; for all who are in positions of authority.

Saint Werberga, pray for us, for all those under direction, and for East Anglia.

February 4 Saint Gilbert of Sempringham *(Abbot and Founder)*

As a young man, Gilbert studied in France, returning to England in order to found a school. His father, in whose gift they were, gave Gilbert the livings of two parishes. After refusing an appointment, following his ordination by the Bishop of Lincoln, Gilbert returned to Sempringham where he built a house beside the church for a number of young women who wished to devote themselves to the religious life.

The house was later expanded to house lay brothers and sisters under the spiritual guidance of some Canons Regular. The nuns were Benedictine, the Canons, Augustinian. The Order became known as the Gilbertines. Despite his exhausting workload, his asceticism, his dispute with King Henry II over his support for Saint Thomas Becket (December 29), and his physical disability (he was handicapped from birth), he died in 1189 at the incredible age of around 100 years. Gilbert was canonized in 1202.

Our help is in the name of the Lord, who made heaven and earth. (Psalm 124[123].8)

Trials often beset our endeavours, and Gilbert had his share. But he was a young man, wealthy and well educated, who was given two valuable livings. He might have frittered it all away on loose living. He could have lived a comfortable life, satisfying himself that he was pleasing God as much as himself. Gilbert, however, used his father's gift as a good and faithful servant investing his master's money. The two parishes were lovingly tended, the parishioners correspondingly faithful; furthermore, religious houses were established there and the Order of Gilbertines was born and flourished. How many times have we had the opportunity to build something or to make something for Christ? It may have been nothing more than an opportunity to do good, with a word or a gesture.

In our prayers: thanks for the life, example and intercession of Saint Gilbert of Sempringham; for those who painstakingly build upon sure foundations.

Saint Gilbert, pray for us, and for all who are disabled and carry other great burdens.

༄ ❈ ༄

February 5   Saint Adelaide of Vilich *(Abbess)* (Also today, Saint Agatha [*Martyr*].)

Adelaide was abbess of the two convents founded by her father, the Count of Guelder. She introduced the Benedictine Rule to the convent at Vilich, and was most careful to train the nuns in the proper recitation of the daily offices. Her charitable works included tending the poor in their various needs. She died in 1015 at the age of 55. She has traditionally been one of the patrons of those suffering from troubles of the eye.

The sum of thy word is truth; and every one of thy righteous ordinances endures for ever. Seven times a day do I praise thee for thy righteous ordinances. (Psalm 119[118].160,164).

As was the case with Gilbert (February 4), and Werberga (February 3), Adelaide was given what might be described as *a good start in life*. In fact, if we are honest, most of us have *good starts* these days; but what do we make of these benefits, these talents? The two aspects of

Adelaide's life highlighted in the short biography strike us as the foundations of her life on earth. She concentrated on the detail, the small things: in her worship she saw that perfect praise of Almighty God could not be careless in pronunciation, in pitch of note or in fold of scapula. Once these preparatory matters became second nature, as it were, the worshipper could concentrate properly on the substance of her chanting, her prayer and meditation. And so with the Church; she saw her care of Christ's 'little ones', the lowly, as her clear gospel duty, and the duty of every Christian. She saw in these 'little ones' what were regarded as the unfortunate insignificant details of society, the details that did not really matter in the great scheme of things. Does our attitude and practice compare unfavourably with Adelaide's?

In our prayers: thanks for the life, example and intercession of Saint Adelaide of Vilich; for drug addicts and those who care for them.

Saint Adelaide, pray for us, for the deprived and for those who care for them; for those suffering from eye disorders and for those who tend them.

February 6   Saint Amand *(Abbot and Bishop)*; Saint Paul Miki and Companions *(Martyrs of Japan)*

Amand was renowned as a holy and pious man; he was a significant missionary and evangelist – indeed, the apostle of Belgium and northern France. Born in Aquitaine in about 584, he was ordained in Tours and subsequently consecrated bishop. Amand is credited with having established many monasteries. He died in 676 or thereabouts.

So they went out and preached that men should repent. And they cast out many demons, and anointed with oil many who were sick and healed them. (Mark 6.12,13)

There are a number of similar saintly life stories. Quite simply, Amand lived a saintly life: saintliness was the most remembered feature of Amand's life and character, and this memory is the theme through all the stories about him that make up his biography. As Amand took

37

Belgium and northern France for Christ, his planted monasteries were the garrisons to serve the newly converted people with priests and the sacraments. From this beginning, the future of Christianity in the region was assured. Permeating his work and the whole region was his sanctity, which was recognized by the new Christians. Evangelization was a more hazardous affair in seventeenth-century Japan where, it is estimated, 6,000 died for the Faith within 25 years in that century. But the two vocations required the same dedication, the same holiness.

In our prayers: thanks for the life, example and intercession of Saint Amand and Saint Paul Miki and his Holy Companions; for all missionaries; for Belgium, northern France and Japan.

Saint Amand, Saint Paul and your Holy Companions, pray for us, for all missionaries, for all those who seek to kill them, and for all who would be holy.

February 7 Saint John Lantrua of Triora *(Martyr)*

John, born in 1760, was an Italian Franciscan who joined a missionary expedition to China in 1799. He worked there under arduous conditions for about 15 years and converted many to the Faith. He was eventually captured and taken to Changsha and chained by the arms, legs and neck for six months before being sentenced to death by strangulation. (The lives of all the Martyrs of China from 1750 to 1900 are celebrated jointly on February 17.) John died in 1816 and was canonized in 2000.

For thou art the God in whom I take refuge; why hast thou cast me off? Oh send out thy light and thy truth; let them lead me, let them bring me to thy holy hill and to thy dwelling. (Psalm 43[42].2a,3)

John's vocation not only includes 15 difficult years of evangelizing but also an extreme example of resolution for the work of Christ – six months of torture and a martyr's death. What significance can we place upon our 'trials'? Let us not forget the Far East in our prayers. Let us not forget China of today, for Communism is always an enemy of Christianity, its philosophy rather depends upon atheism.

In our prayers: thanks for the life, example and intercession of Saint John Lantrua of Triora; for those who face torture and the threat of torture; for China and for all who hold the Faith in that country.

Saint John, pray for us, for those who suffer as you did, and for the enemies of the Church.

February 8   Saint Jerome Emiliani *(Founder)*

Jerome was born in 1481. His career as a soldier in the Venetian army ended with his imprisonment by the forces of the League of Cambrai. In prison, he vowed to spend the rest of his life in good works, and he escaped. Jerome was ordained priest and devoted his life to feeding and clothing orphans and instructing them in the Faith. He founded orphanages, rehabilitation houses for prostitutes, and the Congregation of the Clerks Regular of Somasca. Jerome died from disease in 1537. He was canonized in 1767.

For the needy shall not always be forgotten, and the hope of the poor shall not perish for ever. (Psalm 9:18)

Chained to the wall, Jerome began to pray after many years of neglect and begged the intercession of Our Lady. By some means he escaped and resolved to turn to Christ. Jerome's life's work concerned itself with gathering up the lost sheep from the gutters and placing the children in orphanages and the young women in safe houses. There they were given hope, and instruction in the Faith. Jerome did not choose a glamorous priestly life by any means, and he probably died from one of the many plagues and diseases that rampaged throughout the slums where he worked. At whatever stage we are in life, repenting, changing, turning again, is always possible with the help of our Saviour, whether it is in a prison cell, in some disreputable place or even as we travel to work. Jerome's mission was a direct response to his own experience, his own life. He chose the lowliest job, a distinctly glamourless job and dedicated himself to it. Of course, we may already be perfect in every way.

In our prayers: thanks for the life, example and intercession of Saint Jerome Emiliani; for the work of relief for orphans and rehabilitation of prostitutes throughout the world.

Saint Jerome, pray for us, for all orphans and the individuals and organizations who care for them.

૨ઠ✢ઝૂ

February 9 Saint Miguel Febres Cordero

Miguel was born in Cuenca, Ecuador, in 1854. He suffered severe disability in both legs from birth. He attended the Institute of the Christian Schools, and at an early age joined the brotherhood. He began to preach and teach at the age of 15, and was praised for his skill and learning. Miguel worked tirelessly for the brotherhood for the rest of his life in the service of others, often taking appointments under obedience whether or not they were to his liking or made best use of his skills. He wrote many textbooks and Catechetical tracts. He died in 1910 and was canonized in 1984. His deep spirituality and holiness governed all that he did. His special devotion was to the Holy Family.

And when they saw him they were astonished; and his mother said to him 'Son, why have you treated us so? Behold, your father and I have been looking for you anxiously.' (Luke 2.48)

With the ability to teach, Miguel entered enthusiastically into the life marked out for him by his superiors. He thought little of himself and devoted his life to others; to their welfare and wellbeing; to their instruction and salvation. He did this from the absurdly early age of 15 and, later, those who benefited from his instruction included the many farther afield who read and studied his books and tracts. If we do think rather much of ourselves, our self-importance will soon disappear as we begin to devote our lives to the good of others. If we are given a handicap along with a skill, then we may overcome the one by concentrating on the other. Miguel's life points this out to us emphatically.

In our prayers: thanks for the life, example and intercession of Saint Miguel Febres Cordero; for those who patiently assist the uneducated with the written word.

Jesu, Mary, Joseph. Saint Miguel, pray for us, for those who are crippled and physically handicapped, and for those who write for the instruction of others.

February 10   Saint Scholastica *(Foundress)*

Scholastica, the sister of Saint Benedict (July 11), was the prioress of a small community of nuns a few miles from Benedict's monastery at Monte Cassino. Brother and sister used to meet once each year in the area between the two monasteries to discuss spiritual matters. The earliest written account of Scholastica and her brother comes from the pen of Gregory the Great (September 3). Hers was a gentle life of prayer. She died in 547.

I said 'I will guard my ways that I may not sin with my tongue; I will bridle my mouth . . .' (Psalm 39[38].1, quoted in the Rule of Saint Benedict)

It is easy for us to lose control of our tongues: they seem to have a life of their own. One thing said leads to another: if it is an exaggeration, hyperbole, a 'white' lie, it can so easily and with no effort at all become calumny, slander and false witness. Benedict and Scholastica knew that this was a lesson to be learnt inside and outside the monastic wall. Most of us require constant reminders because, perhaps, we enjoy the company of those who enjoy our verbal sport. We enjoy an exchange of gossip, which, generally speaking, is already far removed from the truth by the time we get our tongues on it in order to add a further twist. Scholastica, a holy character, was content to receive spiritual guidance from her brother and to direct her nuns in a life of prayer for others. Prayer for others is one of the good works so neglected. If we pray with our lives, there will be little room for the work of an unrestrained tongue.

In our prayers: thanks for the life, example and intercession of Saint Scholastica; for those who love to gossip and for those who are the victims of slander.

Saint Scholastica, pray for us, for Benedictine nuns, and for all epileptics and convulsive children.

February 11   Saint Gregory II *(Pope)*;
Our Lady of Lourdes

Gregory was a learned theologian who proved to be a strong opponent of the Iconoclastic emperor, Leo III, and of the Lombards. Under Gregory, the papacy was strengthened and, in addition, many churches were built and many ruined ones rebuilt within the city of Rome. Gregory was responsible for sending Saint Boniface (June 5) on his mission as apostle of Germany. He was a quiet and peaceful man. He died in 731.

Blessed is the man who makes the Lord his trust, who does not turn to the proud, to those who go astray after false gods! (Psalm 40[39].4)

The beautiful vision of Our Lady as the Immaculate Conception experienced by Saint Bernadette (April 16) has been the inspiration for many statues – three-dimensional 'snap-shots' of that vision – that have helped, encouraged and prompted us over the years. Gregory cherished the value of the icon and the statue, and was adamant in their defence as aids for teaching and instruction; for contemplation and meditation; for prompts and reminders. We honour and venerate the image we see projected by paint and plaster, by wood and stone. That honour and veneration is conveyed to whomever is depicted, moulded, modelled or carved. Our senses are wonderful gifts. The Iconoclasts' view was always a dangerous one that switched focus from the real problem of idolatry – the worship of those ever-present idols of self, of wealth, health and superficial beauty, those things that stand between us and God, not those things that represent him, his saints and his creatures. From the very beginning we were given the freedom to choose self before God. It was the desire to worship self before God that sealed our fall from grace into our very *DNA*.

In our prayers: thanks for the life, example and intercession of Saint Gregory II; for all artists and sculptors; for missionary societies.

Saint Gregory, pray for us, for all those who beautify worship, and for Germany.

February 12 Saint Saturninus, Saint Dativus and Companions (*Martyrs*)

The priest Saturninus and his congregation were taken to Carthage and there sentenced to imprisonment where they suffered torture until they died. Under his first moves against Christians, Diocletian had ordered Christians to burn all copies of the Scriptures in their possession. The priest Saturninus and his congregation had refused. They died at the beginning of the fourth century.

But at my stumbling they gathered in glee, they gathered together against me. How long, O Lord, wilt thou look on? Rescue me from their ravages, my life from the lions! (Psalm 35[34].15a,17)

Let us not be complacent about our freedom to read and to preach the gospel. We are called to be brave and courageous for Christ in whatever circumstances we find ourselves. When life is still relatively easy for the Christian shall we be judged harshly if we have not taken the opportunities presented to us for the spreading of the gospel? We can spread the gospel simply by showing the face of Christ to others in the way we live our lives.

In our prayers: thanks for the lives, examples and intercession of Saint Saturninus, Saint Dativas and their Holy Companions; for those who live where their faith is the object of persecution by the state.

Saint Saturninus, Saint Dativus and Holy Companions, pray for us, and for all who torture their enemies.

February 13 Saint Ermengild (*Abbess*)

Ermengild was the daughter of the king of Kent, and married to King Wulfhere of Mercia whom she converted to Christianity. Consequently, the Faith spread quickly throughout the kingdom. On the death of her husband, she joined her mother in an abbey her mother had founded on the Isle of Sheppey. Ermengild became abbess after her mother retired to Ely. Ermengild, humble and of gentle demeanour, died at the beginning of the eighth century.

Praise is due to thee, O God, in Zion; and to thee shall vows be performed, O thou that hearest prayer! (Psalm 65[64].1,2)

By her holy demeanour, Ermengild allowed Christ to be revealed to others. Her husband, as a result, converted to Christianity. That simple act of Ermengild's was not a conscious act or something studied, but rather it was the inevitable consequence of her holy life. The Kingdom of Mercia was converted by a glimpse of Our Blessed Lord looking from the face of a young woman. Why do we scoff at Our Lord's assertion that faith can do more important and significant things even than moving a mountain? How many times do we reveal Our Lord's gaze? On the other hand, how many times, by our behaviour, do we actively alienate others from Christ?

In our prayers: thanks for the life, example and intercession of Saint Ermengild; for those who strive to show Christ to others by the way they live their lives.

Saint Ermengild, pray for us, and for all those who would be proud and immodest.

February 14   Saint Cyril and Saint Methodius (*Bishops*)

The brothers Cyril and Methodius were regarded as the apostles of the Slavs. They translated the Scriptures and the Mass into the Slavonic tongue, creating a fresh script for the purpose as the Slavonic language was but a spoken one. They may have been consecrated bishops when they returned to Rome from their mission. Cyril died in 869 in Rome; Methodius's missionary work continued as apostle to the Moravians. Methodius died in 884.

For whatever was written in former days was written for our instruction, that by steadfastness and by the encouragement of scriptures we might have hope. (Romans 15.4)

With Ermengild (February 13) it may have been simply a look; Cyril's and Methodius's vocations involved creating a written structure for the Faith. The brothers equipped the Slavs with what today might be referred to as 'a complete package' upon which future generations would build and develop their faith. The written word is an essential tool in the propagation of the Faith. By means of it we can hear again from the ancient Fathers and Doctors of the Church. We can feel the struggle for orthodoxy in the early Councils of the Church. We can learn. We can immerse ourselves in the Scriptures and in the commentaries of the learned. Do we make enough of our opportunities to learn more about our Faith?

In our prayers: thanks for the lives, examples and intercession of Saint Cyril and Saint Methodius; for all Slavs; for all missionaries; for language teachers and linguists.

Saint Cyril and Saint Methodius, pray for us, for Europe, and for friendly relations among all parts of the Church.

February 15   Saint Claude La Colombière

Claude studied at the Jesuit College at Avignon, subsequently teaching there. He studied theology in Paris. Claude became a renowned preacher and teacher. He strove to combat the spread of Jansenism and dedicated himself for the purpose in the Sacred Heart of Jesus. He met Saint Margaret-Mary Alacoque (October 16) and became her adviser and confessor. For four years he was a chaplain to the Duchess of York, Maria of Modena, at Saint James's Palace. There he instituted the Feast of the Sacred Heart in 1677. Claude was banished to France after having been falsely implicated in the Titus Oates plot. He died in Lyons in 1682 and was canonized in 1992.

So through the death that thou hast suffered
When for me thou didst grow faint,
O Sacred Heart, my heart's desire,
Possess thyself of all my love
And lo, my heart's most sure delight.

The love that emanates from the Sacred Heart of Jesus ameliorates the harshness of Jansenism and its derivatives, and also purges and purifies the laxity of liberalism and its associated waywardness. Claude instituted the Feast of the Sacred Heart over 330 years ago, and since then the statue of the Sacred Heart in the home and in church has reminded us of the immeasurable love of Christ, the love that persuades us to bite our tongues and close our minds when encouraged to unkind or evil words or thoughts; to speak gently and warmly to those who need encouragement and comfort.

In our prayers: thanks for the life, example and intercession of Saint Claude La Colombière; for a faithful adherence to orthodoxy; for those who are falsely accused.

O Sacred Heart of Jesus, have mercy. Saint Claude, pray for us, and for all Royal Chaplains.

February 16 Saint Elias of Caesarea and Companions *(Martyrs)*

Elias and Companions were Egyptian converts to Christianity who were arrested during the persecution of Maximian on their return to Caesarea for having visited other converts condemned to work in the Cicilian mines. Elias and Companions were tortured and beheaded in 310.

Then the King will say to those on his right hand 'Come, O blessed of my Father, inherit the kingdom prepared for you, from the foundation of the world; For . . . I was in prison and you came to me . . . Truly, I say to you, as you did it to one of the least of these my brethren, you did it to me.' (Matthew 25.34–40)

The visiting of those in prison was certainly a dangerous, if not foolhardy, enterprise early in the fourth century if those visited and visiting were Christian. We are called to relieve the plight of prisoners by visiting and counselling, by charitable giving, by prayer. In the world there are innocent prisoners, prisoners who make the streets safer by their absence, prisoners who are sorry, prisoners who are guilty but who have received unreasonably harsh sentences, prisoners who are learning to be cleverer criminals. There are those awaiting deportation; there are those who are political prisoners, and prisoners for the Faith. Do we pray only for the innocent ones and for the penitent ones? Can we be instruments of God's all-merciful love? Elias and Companions were carrying out their Christian duty, but in the eyes of Rome they were criminals visiting other criminals condemned to the mines. The visitors' fate was even crueller.

In our prayers: for the life, example and intercession of Saint Elias and his Holy Companions; for all prisoners throughout the world.

Saint Elias and Holy Companions, pray for us, and for those who visit the imprisoned.

February 17   The Seven Founders of the Servite Order

The seven founders were resolved and agreed to live lives of asceticism and prayer in a small community they built in Monte Sennario. They followed the Rule of Saint Augustine and adopted a black habit. From this small beginning the Servite Order spread throughout the world, at the same time popularizing the devotion of the Seven Sorrows of Our Lady. The seven founders were canonized in 1888. Alexis Falconieri, their leader, died in 1310 at a great age; the other six died during the thirteenth century.

The Seven Sorrows of Our Lady (September 15):
1. *The prophecy of Simeon*
2. *The flight into Egypt*
3. *The loss of Jesus in Jerusalem*
4. *The meeting on the road to Calvary*
5. *The station at the foot of the Cross*
6. *The descent from the Cross*
7. *The burial of Jesus*

The importance for the world of those who dedicate themselves to a life of prayer and intercession is incalculable. The use of the Seven Sorrows as a guide for prayer and meditation can be enormously fruitful. Each one of the articles can fuel countless hours of contemplation, and provide the pilgrim with guidance on those who should feature in our intercessions but so often are neglected. The Seven Sorrows may be used as our Lenten themes – first Sorrow from Ash Wednesday until the first Saturday, second Sorrow from the first Sunday, and so on.

In our prayers: thanks for the life, example and intercession of the seven founders of the Servite Order; for priestly bereavement counsellors; for refugees.

Saint Alexis and Holy Companions, pray for us, and for all Servite Foundations.

February 18   Saint Theotonius *(Abbot)*

Theotonius was born in Portugal and became abbot of the monastery of Canons Regular of Saint Augustine, dedicated to the Holy Cross. He spent a holy life of prayer and intercession, and was known for his advocacy of seemly worship. Theotonius died in 1166 at the age of 80.

And he came to the disciples and found them sleeping; and he said to Peter, 'So could you not watch with me one hour? Watch and pray that you may not enter into temptation; the spirit indeed is willing but the flesh is weak.' (Matthew 26.40,41)

Again, a perfect life of prayer and intercession – a Mary of Bethany life, perhaps, while we in our Martha-like lives bustle about being busy until we retire to sleep. If we do not ignore him, occasionally we catch a glimpse of Our Lord holding up his hand and saying, 'Watch and pray!' We are not all called to a life within the monastic wall, of course, but we can learn from the vocations of others and share their ideas, their experiences, their commitments, and make use of them to complement our own, if we only take the time. For some, however, action and works are the only media through which they can pray. Often we hear that this saint or that saint was known to urge 'seemly' worship. There is no doubt that church worship falls into the trap of following the fashions of the age from time to time into unseemliness and inappropriateness. We must remember the purpose of what we are doing. Are we casual and shallow in our worship?

In our prayers: thanks for the life, example and intercession of Saint Theotonius; for busy people; for those who find contemplation difficult; for those who pray exclusively through action and works.

48

Saint Theotonius, pray for us, and for those who guide others in prayer.

February 19   Saint Conrad of Piacenza

Conrad was instrumental, during a hunt on his land, in devastating a number of houses in a fire. An innocent man was accused and received the death sentence. Filled with remorse, Conrad admitted his involvement in order to save the man from the gallows, and then restored the villagers' possessions using all his wealth. Thereafter, Conrad and his wife sought solitude – she with the Poor Clares and he as an anchorite in Sicily. Conrad died in 1351.

I acknowledged my sin to thee, and I did not hide my iniquity; I said 'I will confess my transgressions to the Lord' then thou didst forgive the guilt of my sin. (Psalm 32[31].5)

Thoughtlessness can devastate. Even an ill-chosen or unkind word here and an intentional or absent-minded snub there are capable of untold damage. If we are fortunate, we realize our error and apologize. Practice in recognizing minor faults and admitting them is the key to improving our general demeanour. God knows what we think we can keep from him, but he loves the last man in the marketplace to be hired as much as the first.

In our prayers: thanks for the life, example and intercession of Saint Conrad of Piacenza; for the victims of carelessness; for those who cannot admit their faults.

Saint Conrad, pray for us, and for all those who devote their lives to prayer.

February 20   Saint Eleutherius *(Bishop)*

Eleutherius was consecrated Bishop of Tournai in 486. He was renowned as a fine preacher and a great and successful converter of souls. He wrote much against the Arian heresies of the day (Arius, inter alia, denied the divinity of Christ) and so was known to be an ardent defender of orthodoxy. Eleutherius died in or around 532.

Seek good and not evil, that you may live; and so the Lord, the God of hosts, will be with you, as you have said. Hate evil and love good, and establish justice in the gate; it may be that the Lord, the God of hosts, will be gracious to the remnant of Joseph. (Amos 5.14,15)

New fads and fancies came and went in those early days as much as they do today. It was extremely serious, however, when such things threatened to affect and infect the Church. The ancient Fathers, and those who came after, were those who were responsible for the present security and purity of the Catholic Faith we own. But it is not only heresy that corrupts and undermines the Faith, the little slackness that develops into a habit, and the little weakness that develops into something more serious are often more sinister because they cannot quickly and easily be detected. Do we notice these things in ourselves? Do we care?

In our prayers: thanks for the life, example and intercession of Saint Eleutherius; for preachers and those who convert others to the Faith; for alertness to weaknesses.

Saint Eleutherius, pray for us, and for all who defend the purity of the Faith.

February 21   Saint Robert Southwell *(Martyr)* (Also today, Saint Peter Damian [*Bishop and Doctor of the Church*].)

Robert was born at Horsham St Faith and schooled in Douai. He was a poet of note. He entered the Jesuit novitiate in Rome in 1578 and was ordained in 1584. In 1586 he was sent on an English mission. (Robert preached at Marshalsea prison and published a leaflet based on the sermon.) He spent six years in the house of Anne Dacre, wife of Philip Howard (October 19), who was confined to the Tower of London. While Anne was sheltering him, Robert compiled the *Epistle of Comfort* – a collection of his letters to Philip Howard. He was arrested and tried for his priesthood and hanged, drawn and quartered at Tyburn in 1595. He was canonized in 1970.

Poets by abusing their talents . . . have so discredited this faculty . . . but the vanity of men cannot counterpoise the authority of God, who delivered many parts of Scripture in verse, and, by his apostle willing us to exercise our devotion in hymns and spiritual songs, warrants the art to be good . . . (From a letter of Robert Southwell to his cousin)

Here is yet another of those faithful men who, regardless of his own safety, served in the English Mission and left us an example of faith and steadfastness. Robert was also a fine poet whose poetry is full of prayer and profound thinking. Let us place ourselves in Robert's shoes, in London, now tired and consequently careless of the pursuivant, the spy, the informant thought to be a friend. Any moment may be our last of freedom before the Tower, the gallows, and the butcher's knife. How would we measure up against this saint?

In our prayers: thanks for the life, example and intercession of Saint Robert Southwell; for poets and those who convey the Faith through art.

If none can 'scape Death's dreadful dart,
If rich and poor his beck obey;
If strong, if wise, if all do smart,
Then I to 'scape shall have no way.
Oh! Grant me grace, O God! That I
My life may mend, sith I must die.
(From 'Upon the Image of Death' by Robert Southwell)

Saint Robert, pray for us, and for all enemies of the Catholic Faith.

February 22   Saint Papias *(Bishop)*

Papias was the Bishop of Hieropolis in Phrygia. He was certainly acquainted with the preaching of the disciples of the Apostles. Possibly he heard the Apostle John preach, but it is, perhaps, doubtful. He wrote a book giving us a little insight into the composition of the Gospels, and a collection and explanation of Our Lord's sayings. However, most of his written work does not survive. Papias belonged to the generation of the disciples of the Apostles. He died early in the second century.

If any disciples of the Apostles happened by, I was wont to enquire for the saying of the Apostles – what Andrew and Peter said, or what Philip, Thomas or James said, or John and Matthew, or any of the Apostles . . . (From the introduction to Papias's The Sayings of the Lord Explained*)*

A moment or two spent in contemplation of Papias's ministry will be repaid many times. Let us visualize his straining eagerly from the middle of a dense crowd to hear the experiences and reminiscences of, say, a disciple of John. After the tales are over, Papias moves forward to meet the man, and enthusiastically to collect more snippets of information about the man into whose hands Our Lord placed the care of his mother. He squirrels away what he has learnt so that one day he can write his *The Sayings of the Lord Explained*. Every time a disciple of the Apostles is nearby, Papias hurries to hear him. He rejoices that the man is but an arm's length in time from Peter or Andrew or James or John. Eventually, he writes his book. Papias is able to bring home to us that Christ is there in the word of the Gospels, in the narrative, stretching out his hand to us through the disciples of his followers, through men like Papias and those who followed, to appear today in the beggar and many others; to be truly present in the Blessed Sacrament; to be visible in the priest at the altar; to long to dwell within us.

In our prayers: thanks for the life, example and intercession of Saint Papias; writers who assist others towards an understanding of the Faith; for teachers.

Saint Papias, pray for us, and for all those who spread the gospel.

February 23   Saint Polycarp *(Bishop and Martyr)*

Polycarp was Bishop of Smyrna, and perhaps best known of the Apostolic Fathers. He was a disciple of John the Apostle (December 27), and an important figure in the spread of the early Church in the years following the death of the Apostles. Polycarp was burnt at the stake in 155.

If we pray for forgiveness from the Lord, we too must be forgiving. We live under the gaze of our Lord and God, and everyone . . . will have to give account of himself. Let us have a real desire for goodness . . . (Polycarp to the Philippians)

If Papias (February 22) inspires us when we give our imagination free rein, Polycarp must also do so for he was, in all probability, one of the men eagerly sought out by Papias. Here was a man who shook the hand of a man who became the adopted son of Our Lady standing there at the foot of the cross. Polycarp was one of the early martyrs, one of the Apostolic Fathers taking the baton from the Apostles and carrying it forward to the future generations of the Church. Let us dwell on that early explosion of the Faith, burning, sometimes smouldering, sometimes erupting in enthusiastic outbreaks, sometimes all-consuming, sometimes spreading abroad like wildfire. We are heirs of these men. Do others know that we are?

In our prayers: thanks for the life, example and intercession of Saint Polycarp; for enthusiasm for the gospel.

God the Father of our Lord Jesus Christ, increase in us faith and truth and gentleness, and grant us part and fellowship among the saints of heaven. (From a prayer by Saint Polycarp)
Saint Polycarp, pray for us, and for those who do not have a real desire for goodness.

February 24   Saint Ethelburt of Kent

Ethelburt was King of Kent when Saint Gregory the Great (September 3) sent Saint Augustine (May 27) to these shores. He was baptized on Whit Sunday 597, his wife Betha already a Christian. He assisted in the peaceful evangelization of Kent, and founded a number of cathedrals and abbeys including Saint Paul's in London. Ethelburt died in 616.

Thy word is a lamp to my feet and a light to my path. I have sworn an oath and confirmed it, to observe thy righteous ordinances. (Psalm 119[118].105,106)

Christ appeared in the face of Betha and Ethelburt was moved to accept baptism at the hand of Augustine. Christianity was in its infancy in these shores, though it could date its origins from late in the Roman period. The Church lacked order, and if Kent was to hold the seat of Augustine, the conversion of that county was essential. Peaceful evangelization was Ethelburt's way, and his establishment of churches and monasteries was patient and Christ-like.

In our prayers: thanks for the life, example and intercession of Saint Ethelbert of Kent; for enablers and those who prepare the way; for those who send and those who are sent.

Saint Ethelburt, pray for us, and for all Christian monarchs.

February 25 Saint Nestor *(Bishop and Martyr)*

Nestor was bishop and leader of the Church in Pamphylia. Emperor Decius began his reign by issuing an edict commanding all citizens to sacrifice to the Roman gods. Under Nestor, the Church in Pamphylia stood firm, although Nestor had sent many away to hide in safety. Nestor was tortured and crucified in 251.

Even though I walk through the valley of the shadow of death, I fear no evil; for thou art with me; thy rod and thy staff, they comfort me. (Psalm 23[22].4)

Christianity was a terrifying prospect for the Roman Emperors. Its message was so simple yet so strange. It frightened them as it augured the breakdown of the tight grasp the authorities had on the many different populations that comprised the Empire. However, refusal to sacrifice to the Roman gods and the serious implications of such a refusal would always spell the end for the Christian in one way or another. The Roman gods have been replaced in our lives by other gods – wealth, celebrity, and instant gratification, to name but three. (We know the others well; we have our favourites.) We seek out these gods and worship them. These are the demons of sin to which we have given form, raising them in our eyes to the status and stature of gods. All this breathes life into Satan, to whom we give cause for his self-satisfied smile.

In our prayers: thanks for the life, example and intercession of Saint Nestor; for the strength to resist the appeal of man-made gods; for spiritual directors.

Saint Nestor, pray for us, and for those who suffer for their faith.

February 26   Saint Porphyry of Gaza *(Bishop)*

Porphyry spent five years as a hermit in the desert, and then five in a cave beside the River Jordan. At his instigation, the proceeds from the disposal of his family's estate were given to the impoverished citizens of Jerusalem. The Bishop of Jerusalem ordained him priest in 393 and he was subsequently consecrated Bishop of Gaza, where he set about building churches and removing pagan temples. Porphyry was known for his care of the poor. He died in 421.

Jesus said . . . 'If you would be perfect, go, sell what you possess and give to the poor, and you will have treasure in heaven; and come, follow me.' (Matthew 19.21,22)

Ten years of contemplation was required by Porphyry. He lived in solitude so that he could hear God's call when it came; so that he could respond and then focus upon the goal of fulfilling the vocation given. There is no doubt that we require silence and solitude from time to time in order to collect our thoughts and listen for God. (Sometimes God will then tell us to go and show the face of Christ to others, somewhere else; sometimes in the work he then gives us to do, or in the work we are already doing.) Porphyry sought to fulfil his vocation by seeking perfection in establishing churches throughout his area of influence, and there he found God; and he sought out the destitute and there too he found him.

In our prayers: thanks for the life, example and intercession of Saint Porphyry of Gaza; for benefactors of churches and Catholic institutions; for those who listen and those who do not.

Saint Porphyry, pray for us, and pray that all bishops be good shepherds and that all the Church's shepherds be good bishops.

February 27 Saint Baldomerus

Baldomerus lived in Lyons trading as a locksmith. He was a simple man, devout and frugal with himself. He gave most to those less fortunate than himself. The Abbot of Saint-Just offered him a cell in his monastery and there Baldomerus devoted his life to prayer and was ordained sub-deacon. Baldomerus was renowned for his simple piety and goodness. He died in 660, or thereabouts.

In the name of the Lord, let us always give thanks. (Baldomerus's invariable greeting to others)

Not a bishop, not a priest, not a man who had the luxury of time to spare, not a man of wealthy stock, Baldomerus was a simple tradesman. He readily understood the will of Christ in his work; he gave away much of his earnings to those he saw as having fewer blessings than those bestowed upon him. He kept what he needed to keep body and soul together. He worshipped no other god of his own manufacture; he was single-minded in his love for Christ. He was recognized, by the abbot of a nearby monastery, for his simple and pure faith, and given a cell to encourage his desire for a life of prayer and service. His goodness must have been extraordinary. Are we famed for our goodness?

In our prayers: thanks for the life, example and intercession of Saint Baldomerus; for generosity; for those who are generous; for abbots, abbesses, priors and prioresses.

Saint Baldomerus, pray for us, for all those who respond to Christ simply and faithfully and for those who work with their hands as locksmiths and mechanics.

February 28 Saint Oswald of Worcester *(Bishop)*

Oswald was made Bishop of Worcester by appointment of King Edgar in 961. He founded a monastery at Westbury-on-Trym; rebuilt Worcester Cathedral and began a fine musical tradition. He was responsible for monastic establishments at Ramsey, at Pershore and Evesham. From 972, Oswald was both Archbishop of York and Bishop of Worcester. He died in 992 in the act of washing the feet of 12 poor men, an act he performed daily during Lent.

Praise God in his sanctuary; praise him in his mighty firmament! Praise him with trumpet sound; praise him with lute and harp! Let everything that breathes praise the Lord! Praise the Lord! (Psalm 150.1,3,6)

How important were those early builders, who established, re-established, reinforced and built upon – literally and figuratively – the work of their illustrious predecessors. In time, the work of these men proved to be the firm foundations of the Church that would stretch through the succeeding centuries, through turmoil and division and into our own time. There would be breaks with tradition and martyrs would be made, but those martyrs would connect us to the Church of the first millennium through all the animosity, destruction and death. No matter how elevated Oswald's position, his calling was always to be the servant of all, and his humble act in the footsteps of Christ reveals that he took the command to heart. And the fact that we even mention it to this very day confirms that every deed we perform for Christ has consequences for the Church as a whole. Perhaps we should prefer not to have such a significant part to play. Should we simply bury our talent and await the master's return?

In our prayers: thanks for the life, example and intercession of Saint Oswald of Worcester; for those who despair of themselves; for builders and contractors.

Saint Oswald, pray for us, and for all those who beautify the worship of God.

February 29   The Holy Patriarchs and Prophets

The Patriarchs were those who gave structure to the great saga of Israel and who were the fathers of God's chosen people of Israel; the Prophets were those who conveyed the word of God to the people, who prepared the people for the fulfilment of God's plan. The Patriarchs and Prophets connect, by means of a long chain of events and traditions, the time man first recognized the Creator's hand then strove to put himself in place of God and use God's prerogative against his fellows and so infect all future generations with this potential, to the birth of the Israelite nation and the slow dawning and revelation of the nature of God's plan.

Blessed art thou, O Lord, God of our fathers, and to be praised and highly exalted for ever . . . Bless the Lord, you priests of the Lord, sing praise to him and highly exalt him for ever . . . Bless the Lord, spirits and souls of the righteous, sing praise and highly exalt him for ever. (Daniel 3.29,62,64)

It is by looking at God's movement through history that we see clearly the gradual revelation of our Faith. Study of the Scriptures is, therefore, essential work. The compilers of the books of the Old Testament brought together their wealth of written and oral traditions, and presented us with a seamless saga through which and beyond which God reveals his hand and prepares us for what is to come. We now have the happy advantage from our standpoint 2,000 years after the birth of Christ, but the Patriarchs and Prophets were 'doing the spadework' and were the essential agents of God, and key figures around whom this seamless saga was woven. The true humanity of the Patriarchs and Prophets, their successes and failures and their understanding and misunderstanding of God's will, were so significant to the Hebrews and later, the Israelites, that they became embedded in the national consciousness and, consequently, the framework of the storytellers' art.

In our prayers: thanks for the lives, examples and intercession of the Patriarchs and Prophets; for those who study and teach Old Testament theology; for those confused by the sagas of Scripture.

Holy Patriarchs and Prophets, pray for us, and for Jerusalem and the Holy Land.

March

The selflessness of Matilda (March 14) in her 30-year-old widowhood, which she devoted to the service of the poor, is inspiring; so too is the life of the humble priest Clement Mary Hofbauer (15). Nicholas Owen (22) was cruelly done to death, but his dangerous life constructing secure and secret 'priest holes' must have saved the lives of many priests.

March 1   Saint David *(Bishop)*

David was born probably in the first quarter of the sixth century, and died in the last. After his ordination as priest and further study, he founded a monastery at Menevia in Pembrokeshire. He is credited with the founding of a number of other monasteries, all of which were renowned for their asceticism. David was consecrated bishop and his seat seems to have been his seat at Menevia. David ruled his diocese by example. He was meticulous about the detail of his monastic way of life.

Be full of joy, my brethren! Keep the Faith and copy the little things you have heard and seen me do. (Attributed to Saint David by Geoffrey of Monmouth)

There is, if you like, a branch of asceticism all of us can practise. Not for us, perhaps, the severity of a strict regime, but a simple daily rule to follow, a little prudent abstinence, and a freedom from the pressures of one-upmanship and the 'must have and throw away' society. If we were to pay attention to those few details, as David paid attention to the detail of his more stringent monastic rule, we should be released immediately from some of the pressures of modern society and able to be 'full of joy'. The biographies of many of the holy men and women emphasize their concentration on the 'little things' – the detail, the fine points. It is true to say that if we tend to bother about those things, the larger things probably take care of themselves; but if our lives are crammed with transitory pleasures, there is no possibility of spending time on the 'little things' and certainly we have little capacity for joy. Joy tends to accompany the living of our lives in faith, as David was anxious to testify.

In our prayers: thanks for the life, example and intercession of Saint David; for the freedom to be joyful; for strength against acquisitiveness and covetousness.

Saint David, pray for us, for the principality of Wales, its Assembly and its people, and for all places dedicated in your name.

ᏝᎨᏝᎨᏝ

March 2 Saint Chad *(Abbot and Bishop)*

Chad trained under Saint Aidan (August 31) on Lindisfarne, lived in a monastery in Ireland for a few years, and then returned to England. Eventually, he was consecrated Bishop of Lichfield. Chad was considered a learned and wise man who lived faithfully in the spirit of the gospel. He succumbed to the plague in 672.

I will sing of thy steadfast love, O Lord, for ever; with my mouth I will proclaim thy faithfulness to all generations. For thy steadfast love was established for ever, thy faithfulness is firm as the heavens. (Psalm 89[88].1,2)

Chad lived his life of learning 'faithfully in the spirit of the gospel'. He was hailed as a saint soon after his death. He had made a lasting impression on the people around him – fellow monks, fellow clergy, the faithful laity. Of course, all saints are called to live 'in the spirit of the gospel', but what precisely is meant by that phrase? After all, the phrase does not seem to be very far away from an excuse for not obeying the letter of the law – 'I park on the double yellow lines but I make sure that my car is not an obstruction.' The *spirit* of the gospel is the life that flows through the gospel. And the *gospel* is not only the good news as delivered in the writings of the New Testament, but it is also, quite simply, the way of life in Christ. To live 'in the spirit of the gospel' is, therefore, to live in Christ who is 'the way, the truth and the life'.

In our prayers: thanks for the life, example and intercession of Saint Chad; for those who strive to live in the spirit of the gospel; for those who suffer in plagues, and epidemics.

Saint Chad, pray for us, for all theologians and places dedicated in your name.

৫❀৩

March 3 Saint Marinus and Saint Asterius *(Martyrs)*
(Also today, Blessed Katherine Drexel [*Foundress*].)

Marinus was about to be promoted centurion when an envious colleague reported him as a Christian. After questioning, Marinus admitted as much, saying that Holy Scripture was more important than the sword. He was immediately put to death. Asterius, a high-ranking politician present at the execution of the sentence, used his own cloak to wrap the body. He was put to death for the act. The two saints died in about the year 260.

Take courage, my children, cry to God, and he will deliver you from the power and hand of the enemy. For I have put my hope in the Everlasting to save you, and joy has come to me from the Holy one, because of the mercy which soon will come to you from your everlasting Saviour. (Baruch 4.21,22)

Marinus felt himself able to serve in the Roman army as a newly converted Christian. He would have executed his tasks as a centurion in the spirit of the gospel (*see* Saint Chad, March 2), in other words, he would have worked as if through the eyes of Christ, the hands and the feet of Christ. Would that we were equipped with the self-discipline to perform all our duties in this way! Asterius was probably converted by Marinus's general demeanour during questioning; if so, the simple act of wrapping the body was the sign of his acceptance of the Faith, of Christ. On the other hand, Asterius, like Marinus, may have been a Christian secretly, who could contain the secret of his faith no longer, and with the sacrifice of his cloak sentenced himself to death. Actions often speak louder than words. Do our actions expose our Christianity?

In our prayers: thanks for the lives, examples and intercession of Saint

61

Marinus and Saint Asterius; for those who live their Christian lives secretly; for those who work in prisons and places of execution.

Saint Marinus and Saint Asterius, pray for us, and pray for the imprisoned and the condemned throughout the world.

♣

March 4 Saint Casimir

Casimir was one of the sons of the King of Poland. He was born in 1458 and, much to the distress of his father, after making a sensible decision not to lead forces against overwhelming odds, resolved not to take up arms again. He became an advocate of the poor, urging his father to defend them, the oppressed and the imprisoned. Casimir died from tuberculosis in 1484 aged 23. He was interred with the hymn *Omni die die Mariae* in his hands, and was canonized in 1521.

'But when you give a feast, invite the poor, the maimed, the lame, the blind, and you will be blessed, because they cannot repay you. You will be repaid at the resurrection of the just.' (Luke 14.13,14)

Casimir's deep devotion to Our Lady is made clear by his love of Saint Bernard's (August 20) hymn – a valuable text for fruitful meditation on the life of Mary. Clearly a prudent young man who had taken to heart Our Lord's parable, Casimir was given the impetus in that life-changing incident to spend the rest of his pitifully short life in service to the less fortunate. His great achievement was to make others think about the plight of the poor and to apply Christ's teaching to their circumstances. Casimir reminds us too, as he has reminded generations of Christians who fall short and turn a blind eye. So often we do not see the Lazarus at our gate.

In our prayers: thanks for the life, example and intercession of Saint Casimir; for the victims of hunger and for those who sustain them; for the ability to see Lazarus at our gate.

Saint Casimir, pray for us, pray for the poor and hungry, and pray for the people of Poland and Lithuania.

♣

March 5   Saint Gerasimus

Gerasimus was a desert hermit held in high esteem for his holiness. He built around him a cluster of 70 cells in which to house the disciples who had gathered in the Jordanian desert to absorb something of his holiness. Gerasimus and his community were renowned for their asceticism. Gerasimus died in 475.

In those days came John the Baptist, preaching in the wilderness of Judea. Now John wore a garment of camel's hair, and a leather girdle around his waist, and his food was locusts and wild honey. Then went out to him Jerusalem and all Judea and all the region about the Jordan. (Matthew 3.1,4,5)

An ascetic and living a life of extreme self-discipline, Gerasimus was frugal with his food and spent much of the day in prayer and contemplation. He became well known. There were, of course, many such Christian desert dwellers at the time, but some stood head and shoulders above the others. Most were ascetic – after all, life in the desert rather leant itself to this way of life. Visitors did not flock to him in order to gauge his asceticism; they gathered around him – indeed, stayed with him in a community of huts and cells – to learn from him but, above all, to be infected by his holiness. He possessed an aura of sanctity, something that was almost tangible. His followers probably said to themselves and each other, 'If only we could stay in his presence, some of it would "rub off" on us.' Holy places and holy lives do have their effect. (We know for certain that the opposite is true.) Desire for holiness rather than a desire for the reputation for holiness is laudable.

In our prayers: thanks for the life, example and intercession of Saint Gerasimus; for Trappists, ascetics, and solitaries; for those who succumb to gluttony.

Saint Gerasimus, pray for us, and for all those who seek solitude in which to pray.

March 6 Saint Julian of Toledo *(Bishop)*

Julian was consecrated in 680 and appointed Bishop of Toledo. He was noted as a champion of the weak, and a devout man. Julian revised the Mozarabic liturgy and wrote the *Prognostics* trilogy, which dealt largely with the Four Last Things. Julian died in 690.

Why do you boast, O mighty man, of mischief done against the godly ... ? But God will break you down for ever ... But I am like a green olive tree in the house of God. I trust in the steadfast love of God for ever and ever. I will thank thee for ever, because thou hast done it. I will proclaim thy name, for it is good, in the presence of the godly. (Psalm 52[51].1a,5a,8,9)

Death is conquered and Christ has won salvation for us. Nevertheless, we are free to reject Christ and decide against the saintly life in favour of one without God. After all, God gave this freedom to his first human creatures along with their everlasting souls when man looked up into the sky and the reality of the Creator, through revelation, dawned upon him. However, he then shook his fist at the handiwork of the Creator and believed himself able to place himself before God in the eyes of his fellows. The seed of evil was sown. The internal struggle between good and evil often ends in a triumph for the mighty, boastful one who subdues the godly one within us. But the godly does, from time to time, rise up again and threaten him with good, and immediately we are able to admit our trust in and reliance on God. So we give thanks and a channel of communication is opened again for God to exploit, for us to maintain. Doubtless Julian struggled as we all struggle, and in the wrestling within himself, he became a champion of the weak because he knew the effect of the mighty man against the small, weak but godly man.

In our prayers: thanks for the life, example and intercession of Saint Julian of Toledo; for the weak and downtrodden; for humility.

Saint Julian, pray for us, for Spain and for all bishops.

March 7 Saint Perpetua, Saint Felicity and Companions *(Martyrs)*

Perpetua and Felicity, the former with infant, the latter heavily pregnant, were arrested in Carthage with three other catechumens. Perpetua and Felicity recorded their plight in prison and a contemporary account of their deaths was made. The procurator, Hilarian, sentenced the five, on account of their Christianity and for failing to sacrifice to the Roman gods, to be thrown to the wild animals in the arena. They were attacked by bear, boar and lion, and finished with the sword as necessary, in 203.

Offer right sacrifices, and put your trust in the Lord. There are many who say 'O that we might see some good! Lift up the light of thy countenance upon us, O Lord!' In peace I will both lie down and sleep; for thou alone, O Lord, makest me dwell in safety. (Psalm 4.5,6,8)

It is difficult to understand this cruelty, this senseless destruction for the fleeting pleasure of the crowd. There would be those who could see nothing beyond the spectacle, could see nothing beyond their enjoyment of the deaths of two young mothers and three others. Had they been created to die for their pleasure or that of the Roman gods? The Roman gods would have no answer to that question, nor to any question, of course. However, this saintly witness sowed seeds among others associated with the imprisonment and the deaths. The plight of the holy five was noised abroad and sickened those without the stomach for blood sports, even among those who had not yet been touched by the hand of Christ. Why did they not deny their God in order to save their lives? What made them so adamant? Is there really something in this new Faith called Christianity?

In our prayers: thanks for the lives, examples and intercession of Saint Perpetua, Saint Felicity and Holy Companions; for the victims of man's inhumanity.

Saint Perpetua, Saint Felicity and Companions, pray for us, and for all those who suffer for their faith.

March 8   Saint John of God *(Founder)*

John was born in Portugal in 1495. After an early life of mixed fortunes, he was taken to a lunatic asylum following a disturbance in church. There he began to understand his vocation to care for the sick, and his confessor, John of Avila (May 10), advised a pilgrimage to Our Lady of Guadalupe (December 12). It was now clear to John that he had to clothe the naked Christ in the persons of the sick poor. In 1538, he rented a property and began his work. The Bishop of Túy gave him the habit, and the Congregation of Brothers was so successful in its work that the Archbishop of Granada provided a monastic building for the hospital. John of God died in 1550. He was canonized in 1690.

Then the King will say to those at his right hand . . . 'Inherit the kingdom prepared for you . . . I was naked and you clothed me, I was sick and you visited me . . .' (Matthew 25.34–36)

Many saints have received vocations to relieve the sick poor; many have founded Orders and Religious Communities for this purpose. John of God was one such saint but one who received his vocation a little later in life, after he had fully grasped what he had to do. John was not given an early insight into what he had to do; rather, he had to work at it. John had been rather a nuisance to the authorities in his youth – not for him a holy childhood and the saintly path stretching ahead of him to the heavenly realms. He had to work at the germ of an idea, the germ of a vocation, rubbing shoulders with and being overshadowed by other interests, other distractions. Once he had settled on his course, he touched others with his enthusiasm – both the Bishop of Túy and the Archbishop of Granada were attracted by John's intentions, as were the countless brethren who joined him. Who is ever influenced in this way by anything we do?

In our prayers: thanks for the life, example and intercession of Saint John of God; for all foundations dedicated to clothing the naked; for directors of religious foundations and of charitable organizations.

Saint John, pray for us, for all hospitals, the sick who enter them, and for all booksellers.

March 9   Saint Dominic Savio
(Also today, Saint Frances of Rome [*Foundress*].)

Dominic was an unusual saint dying in 1857, a 15-year-old, from disease and, probably, from medical bad practice. He was the son of a peasant under the care of John Bosco (January 31). An unusually holy and devout boy, Dominic declared that even the most insignificant duty must be carried out for the glory of God. Dominic was canonized in 1954.

His master said to him, 'Well done good and faithful servant; you have been faithful over a little, I will set you over much; enter into the joy of your master.' (Matthew 25.21)

Attention to detail is a familiar theme among some of the saints – Saint David and Saint Thérèse of Lisieux are good examples whose lives were so very different – and Dominic was an insistent advocate. It is, perhaps, an unusual characteristic to manifest itself in a boy, an adolescent. Let us look more deeply at Dominic's maxim. The most insignificant duty must be performed for the glory of God. How do we work 'for the glory of God'? How different is our approach? Do we carry out the duties with a prayer or as a prayer? Perhaps. How do we dedicate a task to God? By performing the task well and to the best of our ability? Perhaps we pray for those who made the spoon tarnished in our hands, for those who mined the silver, for those in similar work, for those who do not have spoons. Perhaps we associate the tarnish with the tarnish on our souls, and so on. If we adopt and develop this maxim, our lives and demeanour will have no room left for anything that could not be done for the glory of God.

In our prayers: thanks for the life, example and intercession of Saint Dominic Savio; for those who give guidance to adolescents; for the desire to perform all duties to the glory of God.

Saint Dominic, pray for us, and for all boys and adolescents.

March 10   Saint John Ogilvie *(Martyr)*

John was brought up a Calvinist in Scotland but on receiving his education on the continent, converted to Catholicism. He became a novice in the Society of Jesus in 1610, and was ordained priest. In 1613, John was sent on a missionary journey to Scotland, which he saw as one to 'unteach heresy', among other things. In less than a year he was captured and imprisoned, cruelly tortured and tried for treason. He was hanged in 1615 and canonized in 1976.

My mouth will speak the praise of the Lord, and let all flesh bless his holy name for ever and ever. (Psalm 145[144].21)

John saw his mission as a mission easily explained. He was in Scotland for no other reason than to remove confusions and conflicts in people's minds brought about by the influence of Calvin and those whom Calvin influenced. He had joined the Scottish Mission in order to 'unteach heresy', as he succinctly put it. This has been the mission of many saints throughout Christian history; for 1,500 years or more before John the saints had been urging orthodoxy in the Faith against new errors and fashions. The circumstances for John were rather different because the politicians had to win, and it would not be through reasonable argument. Paradoxically, the death of John, and others like him, did indeed 'unteach heresy' for many were reconciled on account of their sacrifice.

In our prayers: thanks for the life, example and intercession of Saint John Ogilvie; for those imprisoned for their faith.

Saint John, pray for us, for all missionary priests, and for Scotland.

March 11   Saint Sophronius *(Patriarch of Jerusalem)*

Sophronius became the Patriarch of Jerusalem in 634. He was ardent for the purity and orthodoxy of the Faith. His writings, prayers and tropes are of note. In early life he, with John Moschus, gathered information and tales about the lives of the Desert Fathers. Sophronius died in 639.

We have accepted Christ in faith as he came to us out of Bethlehem . . . he is the salvation given to us by God our Father Almighty. (From a sermon by Sophronius)

It is to Sophronius and Moschus, and collectors like them, that we owe our knowledge of the Desert Fathers. The information they collected coloured the outlines for us and gave us special insight into their lives out of which, ultimately, arose the forms of solitary and monastic lives we know today. It is important to read and learn from the Desert Fathers and the early centuries of the Faith. Sophronius contributed a wealth of material for the use of generations of the faithful, and so continued to teach long after his death. To this day his tropes are used.

In our prayers: thanks for the life, example and intercession of Saint Sophronius; for writers and historians.

I did scourge Egypt with her first born for thy sake: and thou hast scourged me, and delivered me up. I led thee forth from Egypt, drowning Pharaoh in the Red Sea: thou hast delivered me up to the chief priests. I did open the sea before thee: and thou hast opened my side with a spear. I gave thee a royal sceptre: and thou hast given unto my head a crown of thorns. I exalted thee in great power: and thou hast hanged me upon the gibbet of the cross. (Tropes by Saint Sophronius) O Sacred Heart of Jesus, have mercy. Saint Sophronius, pray for us, for Jerusalem, orthodoxy in the Faith, and for those who strive to make worship seemly.

March 12   Saint Peter and Companions *(Martyrs)*

These martyrs were of Diocletian's own household. Indeed, Peter was his principal manservant – his butler, if you like. He was most cruelly tortured, being whipped until his bones protruded. Salt was then rubbed into his wounds. Eventually he was roasted on a spit. Peter and companions were martyred in 303.

'. . . *the ploughers ploughed upon my back; they made long their furrows.' (Psalm 129[128].3)*

These early martyrs were even more cruelly treated if they were in the

69

Roman army or in some elevated position in society or in the bureau-
cracy of the Empire, but houseservants in the palace of the man responsible for the shedding of so much blood among Christians could expect
to be most horribly used beyond most people's imagination. (What to
do? Diocletian ponders. They will have to be killed, of course. Perhaps I
shall give them to their fellows to do what they will. That will serve as a
warning and discouragement to those who would turn Christian.) Are
we likely to be discovered?

In our prayers: thanks for the lives, examples and intercession of Saint
Peter and Holy Companions; for those who direct the staff of house-
holds, guesthouses, inns and hotels.

Saint Peter and Holy Companions, pray for us, and for our enemies.

March 13   Saint Leander of Seville *(Bishop)*
(Also today, Blessed Agnellus of Pisa.)

Leander became Bishop of Seville in 578 and, during the following 20
or so years, was able to bring relative tranquillity and orthodoxy to the
Catholic Church in Spain. Through the Third Council of Toledo, he
introduced the practice of the recitation of the Nicene Creed at Mass, a
custom that was later taken up by the Church as a whole. Leander
died in 600.

*I believe in One God, the Father Almighty, maker of heaven and earth,
and of all things visible and invisible; and in one Lord Jesus Christ, the
only-begotten Son of God. Begotten of his Father before all worlds . . .
Begotten, not made, being of one substance with the Father . . . (Nicene
Creed)*

The Nicene Creed is a succinct statement of our Faith, our belief. It
repays deep meditation article by article and concentrates the mind
when it is apt to wander. Leander hit the nail on the head with his submission to the Council: familiarity with the Creed was necessary for
priest and layperson alike, for the Church as a whole. We contemplate
one God and remember that phenomena attributed to other gods when
man's mind was dawning are all in the power of the Holy and Blessed
Trinity. We love God as Father even though he is also the Creator of all

we know and do not know, of all we see and do not see. We know Jesus Christ because he came to us and is the Son of the Father. He shows us the Father and is the only way to the Father.

In our prayers: thanks for the life, example and intercession of Saint Leander of Seville; for Spanish-speaking populations throughout the world; for those who instruct others in the elements of the Faith.

Saint Leander, pray for us, and for all bishops and priests in Spain.

March 14   Saint Matilda

Matilda was the mother of Emperor Otto I. After the death of her husband she began a 30-year widowhood. She was noted for her generosity to the poor, which was the cause of conflict with two of her sons from time to time. But her duty to the poor prevailed. She founded two convents, retiring to one of them towards the end of her life. Matilda died in 968.

Blessed are those who hunger and thirst for righteousness, for they shall be satisfied. Blessed are the merciful, for they shall obtain mercy. Blessed are the pure in heart, for they shall see God. (Matthew 5.6–8)

Her wifely duties ended, Matilda, the widow of King Henry of Germany, embarked even more zealously upon the vocation she had been given to feed the poor. Not only that, but she became well known for her concern for the poor and, therefore, an example that others followed. Her sons disliked the idea of her frittering away their inheritance. What a human failing! How easy it is to fall into the trap of envy for good done to others, jealousy of one's standing and position, and the perceived insults to that standing and position. How many other venial and mortal sins flow from these beginnings? The situation was resolved and not to the detriment of the poor in Matilda's care: a lesson had been learnt among her fractious and quarrelsome sons.

In our prayers: thanks for the life, example and intercession of Saint Matilda; for those who would follow the example of Matilda; for the advertisers of charitable organizations.

Saint Matilda, pray for us, and for all who feed the poor.

March 15 Saint Clement Mary Hofbauer

Clement established the Redemptorists in Warsaw, caring for the sick and poor. He also founded an orphanage and schools. The last 12 years of his life were spent in Vienna, where he founded a college for boys and became a renowned counsellor and confessor for rich and poor alike. Clement died in 1820 and was canonized in 1909.

Hear this, all peoples! Give ear, all inhabitants of the world, both low and high, rich and poor together! My mouth shall speak wisdom; the meditation of my heart shall be understanding . . . (Psalm 49[48].1–3)

And nearly 100 years after Matilda (March 14), Clement was tending the sick and poor. The poor, we know, are always with us. How do we ignore them so easily when they are not only at our feet but also gazing pleadingly at us through the ages? Clement saw the need to remove orphans from the squalor of their existence and to educate them. His experience with the lowly enabled him to become a sought-after spiritual director in the common ground of the confessional. God grant that we learn from the execution and fulfilment of our vocations, whatever they are, as we progress through life. We must intercede for the poor and think carefully and pray about the causes of their poverty, whether in our society or in other parts of the world.

In our prayers: thanks for the life, example and intercession of Saint Clement Mary Hofbauer; for men and women who work in orphanages throughout the world; for those who live in the slums.

Saint Clement, pray for us, for all priests who work in the slums, for Warsaw and Vienna, and the Redemptionists.

March 16 Saint John de Brebeuf *(Martyr)*

John entered the novitiate of the Society of Jesus in Rouen in 1617, and was ordained priest five years later. In 1625, he joined a mission to Canada – in particular to the North American Indians. After some success with the Huron tribe, John and his co-missionaries met with a horrible and agonizing death at the hands of the Iroquois tribe in 1649. John was canonized in 1930 as one of the Martyrs of North America, whose general feast day is October 11.

. . . Save thy servant who trusts in thee. Thou art my God; be gracious to me, O Lord, for to thee do I cry all the day. (Psalm 86[85].2b,3)

John was sent out to those who had no knowledge of the gospel. His mission was what we see in our mind's eye as the traditional, typical work of a missionary. Seeds of Christianity were surely sown there in great and grave difficulties. Armed with a few books, preaching through the mists of rare and curious tongues, traditions and cultures, John's obstacles were many. How challenging his duty to show the people to whom he was called, the face of Christ in his daily life. Our duties are the same, our calling identical. Our difficulties are fewer, however. How much more, then, should we be able to live our lives, fulfil our callings and show the face of Christ to all those with whom we have contact? Do we?

In our prayers: thanks for the life, example and intercession of Saint John de Brebeuf; for those who face almost insurmountable obstacles in their work; for those responsible for organizing missionary expeditions at home and abroad.

Saint John, pray for us, and for the aboriginal men and women of North America and for the government and people of Canada.

March 17 Saint Patrick *(Bishop)*

Patrick, the Apostle to Ireland, was probably brought up in a Christian family in Carlisle when this outpost of the Roman Empire was crumbling fast. It is said that the property was raided and Patrick, along with the manservants, was kidnapped and taken to north-west Ireland. After six or so years, Patrick returned to his home where he prepared himself for a mission to Ireland. This he did as bishop halfway through the fifth century. He is known for a number of written works, including *Confession* – an autobiographical work concerning, inter alia, the difficulties he encountered in his ministry, written at the end of his life. He died towards the end of the fifth century.

I saw the Lord sitting upon a throne, high and lifted up; and his train filled the temple. Above him stood the seraphim . . . And one called to another and said, 'Holy, holy, holy is the Lord of hosts; the whole earth is full of his glory.' And I heard the voice of the Lord saying, 'Whom shall I send, and who will go for us?' Then I said, 'Here am I! Send me.' (Isaiah 6.1b,2a,38)

Patrick's mission to Ireland was rather different from John de Brebeuf's (March 16) to North America. The beginnings of Patrick's encounter with Ireland were more dramatic; the end of his mission rather less so. He reveals that his life's work was not always plain sailing. Is any vocation? Is ours? Do we never feel frustrated, depressed or even faithless? Of course we do; these things are necessary for our reflection and self-examination as aids to a firmer and fuller faith. Failures, difficulties and problems can truly be treated as challenges to which we must rise with the help of Christ.

In our prayers: thanks for the life, example and intercession of Saint Patrick; for those who are burdened by fits of depression; for victims of kidnapping.

I bind unto myself this day
The strong name of the Trinity.
By invocation of that name,
The Three in One, and One in Three
I bind today to me for ay. (Saint Patrick's Breastplate)
Father, Son and Holy Spirit, have mercy. Saint Patrick, pray for us, and for Northern and Southern Ireland.

March 18 Saint Salvator of Orta; Saint Cyril of Jerusalem *(Bishop and Doctor of the Church)*

Salvator was born in 1520 and, as an orphan, moved to Barcelona and worked in a shoemaker's workshop. In 1540, he was received as a

Franciscan of the Observance in the Santa Maria Friary. His duties were humble if not mundane, but he became known as one with a healing touch, and famous for his cures. High and low, people flocked to the friaries wherever he was sent. Salvator died in 1567 and was canonized in 1738.

Are all apostles? Are all prophets? Are all teachers? . . . Do all possess the gift of healing? (1 Corinthians 13.29,30)

Salvator's position in the friary was the lowliest position, so why should he have become so famous? Why did people flock to him? Quite simply, Salvator had a gift that was rare and that few others possessed. Why should this simple cobbler have been granted the gift of healing? Why indeed? The rich and the aristocrat were not too proud to kneel before him; poor and humble peasants did not scoff resentfully at him and say he had become too big for his boots. Gifts and talents are God-given, and God can surprise us. Do we equate poverty with stupidity, or simplicity with foolishness? Do we find it difficult to believe that Christ cannot possibly shine from the faith and face of a simple cobbler? Do our minds stray that way from time to time? Our Lord was clear in his instruction to us. After all, it was he who, after his birth, gurgled happily in the hay of a manger – surely the humblest of beginnings – as Mary and Joseph looked on.

In our prayers: thanks for the lives, examples and intercession of Saint Salvator of Orta and Saint Cyril of Jerusalem; for all superiors who have responsibility for the specially talented and gifted; for all unpretentious, simple folk.

Saint Salvator, pray for us, and for those who require healing. Saint Cyril, pray for us, and for those who work in the Vatican, in whatever capacity.

March 19 Saint Joseph, the husband of Mary

Joseph is honoured today as the protector of the Holy Family. In response to the revelation that he must take Mary as his wife and assume the responsibilities of guardianship of Jesus, Joseph becomes the epitome of the dutiful and obedient servant of God.

But as he considered this, behold, an angel of the Lord appeared to him in a dream, saying, 'Joseph, son of David, do not fear to take Mary your wife, for that which is conceived in her is of the Holy Spirit; she will bear a son, and you shall call his name Jesus . . .' When Joseph woke from sleep, he did as the angel of the Lord commanded him . . . (Matthew 1.20,21,24)

What duty could have been more onerous for a man, that he should protect the Mother of God and her Son? Joseph accepted the will of God and was responsible for Our Lord's care during the first years of his life, from Bethlehem to Egypt, to Nazareth where the carpenter's workshop was re-established. As Jesus' ministry begins, Joseph seems to fade into the background; Joseph, the honourable man, the quiet, unassuming man, the man of gentle acquiescence, the man who knew how to work with olive wood, with sycamore, and who knew the grain of the acacia. Are we the sort who thrusts himself forward when he is simply not required?

In our prayers: thanks for the life, example and intercession of Saint Joseph; for those who quietly accept their calling.

Jesu, Mary, Joseph! Saint Joseph, pray for us, for all who protect others quietly and effectively, and for all families.

March 20   Saint Cuthbert *(Bishop)*

Cuthbert, born in 634, was a monk at Melrose where he was a popular guestmaster and, later, prior. He was given the task of introducing the Rule of Saint Benedict (July 11) at Lindisfarne, or of modifying the Rule of Saint Columba (June 9) so that it conformed to that of Saint Benedict. Cuthbert travelled in the north of England preaching, converting and distributing alms. He ended his days as Bishop of Lindisfarne, and died in 687.

God is everywhere present . . . particularly when we celebrate the holy mysteries and say the Divine Office in chapel . . . We ought to consider carefully how to present ourselves in the presence of God and his angels. (Based upon 'On prayerful demeanour' from the Rule of Saint Benedict)

A holy and gentle priest, Cuthbert epitomizes those early saints from the north-east. He can be summed up in a few sentences, but that hardly does justice to his life on earth. What more is necessary? He worked hard and achieved what was asked of him, and remains an example and focus for us in this age – whether priest or lay. Cuthbert was a well-loved guestmaster at the Melrose monastery. He was, therefore, full of joy with infectious happiness (for no one can do the job successfully without); he was charming and helpful; he was equipped with a fine wit and a lively sense of humour. Certainly no popular guestmaster could lack these attributes. We could do worse than aspire to this impressive list of virtues. Is this not showing the face of Christ to others?

In our prayers: thanks for the life, example and intercession of Saint Cuthbert; for all men and women who serve others; for those who aspire to be the least among their fellows.

Saint Cuthbert, pray for us, and for all priests and bishops in England and Scotland.

๏๏๏

March 21 Saint Nicholas of Flüe *(Hermit)*

Nicholas was a happy, family man who served in the army, and was magistrate for his canton in the Swiss Federation. He left his wife and ten children to respond to what he felt was a vocation to the life of a hermit, but was called out of solitude to assist in negotiating a lasting peace among the factions. This peace treaty served Switzerland well in the succeeding years, and encouraged a natural tolerance of ideas. Nicholas died in 1487 at the age of 70, and was canonized in 1947.

'And every one who has left houses or brothers or sisters or father or mother or children or lands, for my sake, will receive a hundredfold, and inherit eternal life.' (Matthew 19.29)

His was a life of curious diversity – a family man, a man of the army, a man of law and administration, a champion of his country. In all these things Nicholas was successful: that he should require the spiritual uplift that often comes with retreat is unsurprising. However, these things must be balanced, and a desire for solitude for spiritual reasons must not be an excuse for early retirement from our vocations! The ability to create an environment in which there is tolerance is the best environment in which to reveal Christ. Do we take that opportunity to heart?

In our prayers: thanks for the life, example and intercession of Saint Nicholas of Flüe; for peacemakers and arbitrators.

Saint Nicholas, pray for us, and for all negotiators and those who broke peace.

୧୧୨୨

March 22   Saint Nicholas Owen *(Martyr)*

Nicholas was a handyman who may well have been a servant to Saint Edmund Campion (December 1) during the latter's mission until 1581. Nicholas himself was in prison in 1581. From 1586 until 1606, Nicholas was a servant to Henry Garnet, the Jesuit. Nicholas must have saved countless priests and laymen from capture, torture and the gallows by means of his ingeniously constructed hiding places. For some time he must have been under scrutiny and watched carefully by government informers. He was eventually taken prisoner and tortured to death in 1606 without trial. He was canonized in 1970.

. . . As he spoke by the mouth of his holy prophets from of old, that we should be saved from our enemies, and from the hand of all who hate us. (Luke 1.70,71)

What a useful right-hand man for those priests on the English Mission, and for those old families who invited the priests into their homes! What a faithful man, who could have carried out his skills as a handyman and builder without attracting any attention, by towing the line. He was a faithful layman who saw his vocation as one to assist and aid the mission of the Catholic priests. He used his skills to create absurd, unlikely, ingenious secret places for the priests to hide in relative safety. We are able to turn our everyday skills and talents to the special purposes of God should we wish to respond to his special directions. Do we listen enough? We are not all called to these dangers, of course, but Nicholas shows us what can be done even in extreme circumstances. How much easier it is for us!

In our prayers: thanks for the life, example and intercession of Saint

Nicholas Owen; for those who work in hazardous conditions; for those who work to protect others.

Saint Nicholas, pray for us, and pray for all handymen and builders.

૱૯ജ૩૭

March 23 Saint Joseph Oriel
(Also today, Saint Turibius of Mogrovejo [*Bishop*].)

Joseph was born in Barcelona of humble stock in 1650, but through the agency of his priest, he was eventually ordained. He existed on meagre meals of bread and water, and although many – high and low, rich and poor – would seek his counsel in the confessional, his gentle demeanour seemed to capture especially the minds of children, soldiers and prisoners. Joseph died in 1702 and was canonized in 1909.

All this is from God, who through Christ reconciled us to himself and gave us the ministry of reconciliation; that is, God was in Christ reconciling the world to himself, not counting their trespasses against them, and entrusting to us the message of reconciliation. (2 Corinthians 5.18,19)

Joseph was another of those simple priests who led an ascetic life. Of humble stock, he might have decided, as a priest and on account of the respect in which he was held, to enjoy a little of the better things in life. He would receive gifts from the faithful. Why not enjoy the comfort of those things? No, bread and water was sufficient to sustain the body and to enable him to serve the Church in the confessional. His vocation was to the penitent. A penitent man was a penitent man whether rich or poor; Joseph did not discriminate, though he was loved particularly by the three groups close to his heart. There was nothing affected in Joseph's manner. Can the same be said of us? There is much that Joseph can teach us if we simply reflect upon what was probably his daily routine.

In our prayers: thanks for the life, example and intercession of Saint Joseph Oriel; for all penitents and confessors.

Saint Joseph, pray for us, and for all penitents, especially for children, soldiers and prisoners.

March 24 Saint Hildelith *(Abbess)*

Hildelith succeeded Saint Ethelburga (October 12) as abbess of the convent in Barking founded by the Bishop of London, Saint Erkenwald (April 30), the brother of Saint Ethelburga. Hildelith was known for her tidy management of the convent and her passion for order and method. Study and an orderly, reverent recitation of the Office were to her essential features of the monastic life. Hildelith died around 712.

I rejoice at thy word like one who finds great spoil. I hate and abhor falsehood, but I love thy law. Seven times a day I praise thee for thy righteous ordinances. Great peace have those who love thy law; nothing can make them stumble. (Psalm 119[118].162–165)

The saints, these signposts and lighthouses for our notice, are able to give us something from their lives and the fulfilment of their vocations to edify our lives, to correct our faults, to suggest another approach. For us the light may pinpoint one aspect of their lives, or floodlight the whole of their lives. Reverence and orderliness in worship is an essential feature of the Rule of a convent or monastery. It is understood that with Hildelith there was something more. She knew that orderliness in worship could easily become 'mechanical' and a matter of course. She knew that lip service could be paid in the recitation of the Divine Office and nothing else, and that is why study went hand in hand with devotion. Proper preparation of the daily portions of Scripture and a profound knowledge of what was being recited were essential features of worship. Do we succumb to laziness from time to time?

In our prayers: thanks for the life, example and intercession of Saint Hildelith; for those who spend their days praying for others; for those who encourage others in living a godly life.

Saint Hildelith, pray for us and for the faithful to engender a sense of holiness in worship.

March 25   The Annunciation of the Lord; Saint Dismas

Our Lady's humble and selfless acceptance of God's plan gives us the very moment in time of the conception of Christ. Our Lord was 'made flesh and man at that very moment within the all-Holy Virgin', as Saint Sophronius (March 11) put it.

Dismas, traditionally named the 'Good Thief', was crucified with Our Lord and merited those absolving words of comfort from Jesus. He had confessed his sin and was sorry; he acknowledged that he was deserving of punishment. Furthermore, he recognized Jesus as his King and Saviour.

One of the criminals who were hanged railed at him, saying, 'Are you not the Christ? Save yourself and us!' But the other rebuked him, saying, 'Do you not fear God, since you are under the sentence of the same condemnation? And we indeed justly; for we are receiving the due reward of our deeds; but this man has done nothing wrong.' And he said, 'Jesus, remember me when you come into your kingly power.' And he said to him, 'Truly, I say to you, today you will be with me in Paradise.' (Luke 23.39–43)
'The Holy Spirit will come upon you, and the power of the Most High will overshadow you; therefore the child to be born will be called holy, the Son of God.' And Mary said, 'Behold, I am the handmaid of the Lord; let it be to me according to your word.' (Luke 1.35,38)

Both Our Blessed Lady and the Good Thief were present beside Jesus at the end. The Good Thief must have heard all the sayings of Jesus from the cross and must have wondered deeply. His was the finest and most beautiful deathbed confession and conversion; he was the last man in the marketplace to be hired, a lost sheep that was found and over which the very angels in heaven would rejoice. The miracle of the cross was at work before the death of the Saviour. As Our Lady stood at the foot of her Son's cross, her encounter with the angelic messenger must have seemed a lifetime away, but there were no angry cries at God, no regrets at the 'yes' she gave God through Gabriel. Do we ever regret our promises to God?

In our prayers: thanks for the life, example and intercession of Saint Dismas; for those who are living their last moments before execution.

Holy Mary and Saint Dismas, pray for us, and for all prisoners and captives.

March 26 Saint Ludger of Münster *(Bishop)*

Ludger was born in 742 and studied in Utrecht, England and at Monte Cassino. He was a missionary of note in Friesland and Saxony. He was consecrated bishop in 804, and settled in Münster in a monastery he had previously founded. He was known for his gentle demeanour and charm. His devotion and complete attention to his duties at Mass and during the Offices were noteworthy. Ludger died in 809.

For we never used either words of flattery, as you know, or a cloak for greed, as God is witness; nor did we seek glory from men, whether from you or from others, though we might have made demands as apostles of Christ. But we were gentle among you, like a nurse taking care of her children. (1 Thessalonians 1.5–7)

The unswerving love of Christ creates in us a desire to give special attention to our devotions. For example, if we love Our Lord, how can we give his real presence in the Blessed Sacrament scant attention? We cannot. But Ludger smiles at us and points out that we all fall prey to the failing of negligence despite our best endeavours; he goes on to suggest that we ought to practise on our family and friends. After all, if we cut dead our family and friends and harbour a grudge against our brother, we surely cannot, really and truly, give our devoted love to the Lord unless we first seek out those whom we have offended and those who have offended us. Enjoying the wit and gentle admonitions of Ludger, we resolve to do better. What an important lesson for us to learn. We hear that lesson an awful lot ringing in our ears as we say, 'I cannot forgive so-and-so for that!' We make excuses for ourselves and convince ourselves that even God would not forgive that grievous slight against us.

In our prayers: thanks for the life, example and intercession of Saint Ludger of Münster; for the spirit of forgiveness; for those who find forgiveness difficult.

Saint Ludger, pray for us, and for servers at the altar.

March 27   Saint Rupert *(Bishop)*

Rupert has been called the apostle to Bavaria. He built the church and monastery in Saltzburg and based his episcopal seat there. Both this monastery and the convent he subsequently built followed the Rule of Saint Benedict (July 11). Rupert, with his monks and companions, travelled throughout the region spreading the gospel and building churches. Rupert died in the first quarter of the eighth century.

The seventy returned with joy saying, 'Lord, even the demons are sub-ject to us in your name.' And he said to them, 'Behold, I have given you authority . . . over all the power of the enemy. Nevertheless, do not rejoice in this . . . but that your names are written in heaven.' (Luke 10.17–20)

Rupert's missionary zeal is an extreme example for us, but extreme exemplars are often required to bring home to us where we fall short. For most of us a magnificent evangelizing progress through a country, building church and monasteries to the right and to the left as we go, is not likely to be our calling. It was not as easy and as splendid as it sounds for Rupert. It was hard, unstinting service for God – day and night, rain or shine. Sometimes the work seemed easier and more fruit-ful; sometimes it was gruelling and depressing. Our spreading of the gospel in our work, in our lives, in our demeanour, is spasmodic at best, but we can experience the same joys as Rupert even though we inevitably will experience the same distress. We all require the discipline of the daily adjustment our devotions can bring.

In our prayers: thanks for the life, example and intercession of Saint Rupert; for all evangelists; for the men and women who show Christ in their lives.

Saint Rupert, pray for us, and for the people of Bavaria.

March 28   Saint Hesychius of Jerusalem

Hesychius was a priest of Jerusalem. Little is known of the detail of his life and ministry, but his teaching revealed through the writings of his that are known to this day show him to have been a holy man of scrupulous orthodoxy, whose teaching on Scripture and the sacrifice of the Mass are of great merit. Hesychius died in 450 or thereabouts.

In the beginning was the Word and the Word was with God, and the Word was God. And the Word became flesh and dwelt among us full of grace and truth. (John 1.1,14)

By Hesychius's words we know him: his writings are orthodox and profound. His exploration into the theology of the Incarnation binds that mystery securely into the creation of the world, into the firm belief that the Word was God in the beginning. He invites our contemplation of this mystery – the Incarnation of the Word, the Word becoming flesh. This Mystery, the Divine Intention of God, is realized in the person of Jesus and, in the light of the Incarnation, God begins his creation. Into God's cupped hands we now peer; we see the effects of our bitterness, our jealousies, our hates. We see our conflicts and aggressions, so small in the scheme of things, so large and significant in their effects. There, but for the grace of God, we see darkness and gloom of our making; there, but for the salvation of mankind, we see perpetual misery of our generation; there, but for God's saving goodness, we see nothing. Hesychius, the holy priest of Jerusalem, bids us wake and ponder.

In our prayers: thanks for the life, example and intercession of Saint Hesychius; for all who study and teach the writings of the Fathers and Doctors of the Church.

Saint Hesychius, pray for us, for all who study, and for the people of Jerusalem.

☙✢❧

March 29 Saint Jonas and Saint Barachisius *(Martyrs)*

Jonas and Barachisius were monks in Persia, who attended the last moments of fellow Christians before execution of their death sentences. They themselves were brought before the judges and were horribly tortured to encourage them to deny the Faith. They would not, and were both burnt with pitch and crushed in a press. They died in about 326.

There, my beloved brethren, be steadfast, immovable, always abound-
ing in the work of the Lord, knowing that in the Lord your labour is not
in vain. (1 Corinthians 15.58)

There is much most of us find difficult to comprehend in the matter of
terror and man's inhumanity. We can certainly imagine them, because
we are aided by what we see televised from all over the world. Generally
speaking, personal experience eludes us and only at arm's length do we
experience these things. Most of us are reluctant to visit the imprisoned
in normal circumstances, but under a government whose edicts preclude
the profession of Christianity, should we, as Christians, expose ourselves and visit those of our number under sentence of death? Should we
not keep well away, and keep our heads down in the hope that no one
would notice our faith or our practice of it?

Jonas and Barachisius were called to this unenviable duty. A psalm
was sung and a Gospel was quoted; perhaps a hymn was sung. Goodbyes
were said, and Christians were returned to their Creator. Then a guard,
or an official of some sort, detained Jonas and Barachisius, who were
taken before judges and promised much in exchange for their apostasy.
Let us set ourselves against these examples of immovability and steadfastness. Or worse, let us imagine ourselves before those judges, who
laugh at us and say, 'Get on with you, you aren't Christians!' They enjoy
the joke and send us packing with a bag of gold for amusing them so
much.

**In our prayers: thanks for the lives, examples and intercession of Saint
Jonas and Saint Barachisius; for prisoners and captives and those who
are sorely tested.**

*Saint Jonas and Saint Barachisius, pray for us, and for all who need
support in their faith.*

March 30   Saint Leonard Murialdo *(Founder)*
(Also today, Saint John Climacus [*Abbot*].)

Leonard studied in Turin and was ordained priest in 1851. He was in
contact with John Bosco (January 31), who begged him to take care of
the Oratory of San Luigi in Turin. He visited France and concerned
himself with the plight of young workers. He returned to Turin and

became a driving force in the education of the young. Leonard died in 1900 at the age of 72, and was canonized in 1970.

You shall not oppress a hired servant who is poor and needy, whether he is one of your brethren or one of the sojourners who are in your land within your towns; you shall give him his hire on the day he earns it, before the sun goes down ... (Deuteronomy 24.14,15)

Leonard founded the Congregation of Saint Joseph for the purposes of the care and education of the abandoned and exploited. He was instrumental in urging others to do what they could for the young who worked, often in unsuitable conditions, in factories and unhealthy workshops. What is Leonard's signpost? Upon what road does he direct us? Most of the problems of nineteenth-century Turin are no longer with us in Europe in regulated establishments; they do exist out of sight of the authorities and elsewhere in the world, of course. If practical help is impossible, the support of worthy Catholic organizations is not, and, most important, intercession requires only thought and a little time. However, there is more to it. All human life is a precious gift, which we pay scant regard to from the moment of conception. If we do not care if the unborn survive, why should we care if workers are exploited?

In our prayers: thanks for the life, example and intercession of Saint Leonard Murialdo; for those responsible for the treatment of migrant workers; for the young workers of the world; for those who are oppressed and enslaved.

Saint Leonard, pray for us, and for all young workers and those who train them.

༄༅

March 31   Saint Stephen of Mar Saba

Saint Sabas (December 5) had founded the monastery of Mar Saba in Palestine in the fifth century. Stephen removed himself from this monastery where he had lived from an early age, to a semi-solitary life nearby, accepting visitors for counsel from time to time. He returned, in his fifties, to the monastery, where he was admired for his care of the brethren, his good counsel and for his easy way with visitors from far afield. He was guestmaster at Mar Saba well into his seventies.

Stephen was known also for his special rapport with animals and birds. He died in 794.

Above all hold unfailing your love for one another, since love covers a multitude of sins. Practise hospitality ungrudgingly to one another. As each has received a gift, employ it for one another as good stewards of God's varied grace. (1 Peter 4.8–10)

We have seen Saint Cuthbert's (March 20) message to us as guestmaster. What can Stephen add? To those under his care – and to everyone else – he is the same. He is charming, witty and of gentle demeanour. His duties are varied but always his disposition is cheerful and of great comfort to all he meets. Christ himself must be able to peer from his face and catch the eye of his guest. Good counsel is natural to him, as is the ability to acknowledge the customs of the foreigner and to communicate with him despite ignorance of his guest's tongue. Perhaps Stephen extends the guestmaster message for us, and embraces patience and understanding of those who are different from ourselves.

In our prayers: thanks for the life, example and intercession of Saint Stephen of Mar Saba; for those who make others feel at ease; for those in alien environments; for those who are officially responsible for others.

Saint Stephen, pray for us, for those who care for others and those who care for animals and birds.

April

George's (April 23) martyrdom was a potent example to Roman Christians and his holiness was later of great significance to the Crusaders. He is the patron of soldiers and of England. Stephen of Perm (26) is the patron of interior decorators and designers, something of special interest to me. And Catherine of Siena (29) encourages us in her wide range of benevolent works from tending the poor to writing letters of good counsel to Pope Gregory XI.

April 1   Saint Hugh of Grenoble *(Bishop)*

Hugh was made Bishop of Grenoble in 1080. He spent his life as a reformer on finding the diocese in a parlous state. Apart from his effectiveness in this respect, he was a priest with fine qualities as a confessor and as an example to others. He helped Saint Bruno (October 6) establish the Carthusians within the diocese. Hugh died in 1132 and was canonized in 1134.

Set the believers an example in speech and conduct, in love, in faith, in purity. (1 Timothy 4:12)

Hugh was an enabler, a doer, an exemplar. It is as an exemplar we focus on Hugh. His diocese was much in need of care and attention. We can imagine the administration in poor order; the buildings, too; some of his clergy were found wanting, perhaps. Hugh put the diocese on its feet and there, for many, the matter would have rested. To be renowned as an example to others the individual must surely have a reputation for thorough goodness, a man who practised what he preached. This was certainly so in Hugh's case. As a priest he was called to be a confessor; as a bishop to transform his diocese and accommodate Saint Bruno's monastery. But as a Christian he already had the vocation we all share –

to be 'other Christs'. That he fulfilled this vocation as well shone through his work as a priest and as a bishop enabling him to do all that he did in purity of thought, in generosity of spirit, in gentleness of tongue. The manner in which he lived was the example he gave to others that they could translate to their own lives and occupations.

In our prayers: thanks for the life, example and intercession of Saint Hugh of Grenoble; for all bishops and diocesan administrators.

Saint Hugh, pray for us, and for all who lack purity of thought, generosity of spirit, and gentleness of tongue.

❧✣❧

April 2 Saint Francis of Paola *(Founder)*

Francis was born in southern Italy in 1416. Already renowned for his humble holiness as a teenager, Francis was the founder of the Order of Minim Friars, largely under the Rule of Saint Francis (October 4). But his modifications to the Rule drew heavily from the lives of the Desert Fathers. Francis was concerned at the moral laxity within the Church at large and urged self restraint and self discipline at all times. The Order opened houses in France, Germany and Spain in his lifetime. Francis, a layman all his life, died in France in 1507 and was canonized in 1509.

For it has seemed good to the Holy Spirit and to us to lay upon you no greater burden than those necessary things; that you abstain from what has been sacrificed to idols and from unchastity. (Acts 15.28,29)

It does trouble us when we hear of 'moral laxity' among the priests and others of the Church. It ought not afflict the Church, of course, and yet, time and again we note that one saint or other 'was concerned at moral laxity among the clergy'. The Church has always needed to devote special attention to itself in this matter, and these saints were given that duty. Whether the problem was unorthodoxy or 'moral laxity', it required a determined and courageous man (or woman) to point to these things and eradicate them. We are all subject to human failings (and we know the remedy well enough) but leading the Church into disrepute and others astray elicits the harshest words from our Lord in the Gospels. Let us allow our hands to be the hands of Christ, our feet the feet of Christ and our eyes, his eyes.

In our prayers: thanks for the life, example and intercession of Saint Francis of Paola; that we might become worthy dwelling places for Christ; for those who fall short of the ideal.

Lord Jesus Christ, Son of the living God, who came to us from the Father, and bore five wounds on the wood of the cross, and who shed blood for the forgiveness of sins, grant that we may be worthy to hear the words 'Come into the kingdom of my Father'. Amen.
Saint Francis, pray for us, for those who fall short of the ideal, and for all Italian seafarers whose patron you are.

෴

April 3   Saint Richard of Chichester *(Bishop)*

Richard was born in 1197. After an academic life culminating in the chancellorship of Oxford University, Richard became diocesan chancellor to the Archbishop of Canterbury. He was ordained priest in 1243 and consecrated Bishop of Chichester in 1245. Richard was a great reformer particularly concerned with proper instruction of the laity, and that the behaviour of his clergy should be beyond reproach. Richard died in 1253 and was canonized in 1262.

For I have kept the ways of the Lord, and I have not wickedly departed from my God. For all his ordinances were before me, and his statutes were before me. I was blameless before him and I kept myself from guilt. (Psalm 18[17].21–23)

And Richard too was determined to instil in his clergy a purity of mind, a purity of purpose. Earnest as he was about these matters, as was Francis (April 2) 200 years earlier, Richard saw the need for the Church to pay greater attention to the instruction of the laity in the Faith. The laity must be able to understand the preaching and teaching from the pulpit: the homily that travels literally and figuratively over the heads of the congregation is worthless and a waste of time, even though it may satisfy the ego of the preacher! Equally, there must be a desire by the laity to learn and study, and so experience more fully the joy of the knowledge of the Lord. But it is not possible or desirable for everyone to become eminent theologians. Today, there is, perhaps, more scope for the instruction of the laity, but every man, woman and child must make an effort to the appropriate level of their ability. We are all called to instruct others in the Faith by the way we live, by word and deed.

In our prayers: thanks for the life, example and intercession of Saint Richard of Chichester; for all seminaries and places of training; for those who devise courses of instruction.

Daily, O Lord, these things I ask: to see thee more clearly; to love thee more dearly; to follow thee more nearly. (From a prayer by Saint Richard)
Saint Richard, pray for us, for all catechists, and for all taxi drivers and bus and coach drivers whose patron you are.

April 4 Saint Isidore *(Bishop and Doctor of the Church)*

Isidore was born around 565 and has left us a large quantity of his diverse writings. He became Bishop of Seville in 600. He saw his role as bishop to be a good shepherd of the flock and all that that entailed. He was particularly concerned with developing in his clergy and people a faithful, spiritual life. Isidore died in 636 and was declared Doctor of the Church in 1722.

Those who wish to be with God must pray and read often: in praying we may speak with God, in reading God may speak to us. (Saint Isidore)

After Richard (April 3), we also find Isidore achieving precisely what a bishop is called to do. He is a shepherd (and a shepherd is, quite obviously, not someone who is employed to lead his flock astray) who is precise in his theology, pure in his orthodoxy and meticulous in his moral teaching. He does not sway and bend to the society in which he finds himself, adopting society's standards and desires by allowing society to influence and evangelize the Church. Heaven forbid! Much of that which is acceptable in society can never be acceptable in the Church. Isidore experienced similar problems undoubtedly, and his goal was to develop in his clergy and people a faithful, spiritual life. And within this spiritual framework, the faithful have, by the grace of God, the happy and uplifting remedies of penitence and absolution.

In our prayers: thanks for the life, example and intercession of Saint Isidore; for all shepherds of the flock; for all bishops in Europe.

Saint Isidore, pray for us, and for all authors and journalists.

April 5   Saint Vincent Ferrer

Vincent, a learned Dominican and popular peripatetic preacher and missionary, was instrumental in influencing the Church towards a resolution of the Great Schism (though he died in 1419 before any matter was finally resolved). The few years before he died were dedicated to preaching and teaching in Brittany and Normandy. Vincent was canonized in 1455.

Blessed are the peacemakers, for they shall be called Sons of God. (Matthew 5.9)

Wise counsel is a great gift, and Vincent's use of it illustrates, in an extreme way perhaps, its power. In any arbitration we need to ponder and observe from the firm base of understanding fully the circumstances of the rift. A wise counsellor does not blurt out the first thing that comes to his tongue: he is careful and prudent in his speech and in his preparation. We are not all called to be wise counsellors, though many who are not think that they might be. If there is doubt, a quiet tongue will often allow sense to prevail.

In our prayers: thanks for the life, example and intercession of Saint Vincent Ferrer; for those who seek wise counsel; for those who give wise counsel; for those who give careless advice.

Saint Vincent, pray for us, for all peacemakers and for pawnbrokers whose patron you are.

✿

April 6   Saint William of Eskill *(Abbot)*

William was born in 1125 in France. He became a canon of the house of Canons Regular, which had been founded at Saint Genevieve in Paris. Such was his renown for holiness that he was asked to reform monastic life in Denmark, which, with the assistance of three fellow canons, he began in 1170. William died in 1203 and was canonized in 1224.

Thy decrees are very sure; holiness befits thy house, O Lord, for ever-more. (Psalm 93[92].5)

To be asked to reform the monasteries of Denmark, you need more than simple piety and saintliness – both of which William had in abundance. Clearly, William was appropriately equipped. Reformation is defined in a number of ways, but the reformation required in most of us, and in the monasteries of twelfth-century Denmark, is the removal of faults and abuses that have sullied – a return to the original form, a form that existed before the need for reform became apparent. Reformation returns someone or something to the point from which he (or it) strayed. Reformation does not mean – as it has appeared to mean so often – straying yet farther from that point.

In our prayers: thanks for the life, example and intercession of Saint William of Eskill; for those who know their need for reform.

Saint William, pray for us, for Paris and for Denmark.

April 7 Saint John Baptist de la Salle *(Founder)*

John Baptist was born in 1651 at Rheims. He established throughout France Congregations of the Brothers of Christian Schools devoted largely to the education of the disadvantaged, though not exclusively. The brethren number in their thousands to this day. John Baptist was a tireless worker for God and his Church. He died in 1719 and was canonized in 1900.

When he ascended on high he led a host of captives, and gave gifts to men. And his gifts were that some should be . . . pastors and teachers . . . for the building up of the body of Christ. (Ephesians 4.8b–12)

For 30 years or so, these Congregations and their many good imitators have been working to give a Christian education to the destitute and to others. This essential work often goes unnoticed in pockets here and there, in this obscure little school, in that one; as so much good work does. That John Baptist was a *tireless* worker for Christ indicates to us his unswerving dedication to his vocation. By his tirelessness he achieved what was required; by his tirelessness he encouraged others to assist and to work alongside; by his tirelessness he enabled others to work elsewhere by his example. We ought to be tireless in our praise giving and thanksgiving, in our intercession and in all we do in the name of Christ.

In our prayers: thanks for the life, example and intercession of Saint John Baptist de la Salle; for those who work with the poor and sometimes unlovely; for those who train teachers.

Saint John Baptist, pray for us, for headmistresses, headmasters and for all teachers of the young.

᯽

April 8   Saint Julie Billiart *(Foundress)*

Julie was born in 1751 in France. A pious girl, she taught the catechism to children and farm workers when she was in her early teens. In her twenties she became increasingly invalid, unable even to stand. She made a miraculous recovery, however, when she was in her fifties, after she had begun to prepare the ground for what would become the Institute of Notre Dame – a congregation formed for the training of school teachers and for the education of the poor. Julie founded many schools throughout France and Belgium, the effect of the Revolution on the Catholic Church concerning and motivating her. She died in 1816 and was canonized in 1969.

The righteous shall flourish like a palm tree, and grow like a cedar in Lebanon. They are planted in the house of the Lord, they flourish in the courts of the house of our God. They still bring forth fruit in old age, they are ever full of sap and green to show that the Lord is upright. (Psalm 92[91].12–15)

Julie's is a curious story – certainly with regard to her incapacity. Like John Baptist de la Salle (April 7) Julie worked tirelessly, broadening the skills she developed as a simple catechism teacher to cope with the training of teachers for her foundations, for the better education of those less fortunate. The Church in France suffered badly during the revolutionary period, and Julie strove to assist in the Church's gradual recovery. Working against these difficulties she achieved much in the preparation of the young for their future in France and for the good of the Church. She refused to allow her incapacity to inhibit her work. There is Julie's signpost for our journey when we become disconsolate.

In our prayers: thanks for the life, example and intercession of Saint Julie Billiart; for those who work despite suffering from debilitating disease; for those who work in our Catholic schools.

Saint Julie, pray for us, for those who suffer in body, and for those who work for the good of the Church.

April 9   Saint Waldetrude *(Foundress)*

After bringing up a family of four children, Waldetrude withdrew to a life of austerity in prayer and thanksgiving. Eventually, she founded a convent in Mons where she gained the reputation for her charitable works and spiritual counsel. Waldetrude died in 688.

And everyone who has left houses . . . for my name's sake, will receive a hundredfold and inherit eternal life. (Matthew 19.29)

In the days when a monastic life was not such an extraordinary way of life to consider, a vocation to austerity later in life was by no means unusual. Waldetrude had raised a family successfully, and that task was now over. She retreated to consider her next step, and resolved to bring into being a religious foundation out of which would spring good works. Furthermore, her carefully thought about approach to her second vocation, and the wisdom she displayed in its creation, developed yet another strength latent in Waldetrude, born, perhaps, in the experience she had gained while bringing up her family. As a spiritual counsellor she excelled. We should leave time in our lives to listen to the Master. Indeed, how many times in our youth were we told 'When you have completed the task, ask for another'?

In our prayers: thanks for the life, example and intercession of Saint Waldetrude; for those who are planning a positive response to God's call; for those who direct religious foundations dedicated to those in need; for all governments.

Saint Waldetrude, pray for us, and for those who would help the impoverished.

❧❀❧

April 10   Saint Fulbert *(Bishop)*

Fulbert has left us a number of written works, including hymns and poems. He was a learned man who was made Bishop of Chartres in 1007. He was recognized as a holy man who was particularly conscious of the need for the Church's clergy to be good examples to the faithful. Fulbert had a special devotion to Our Lady. He died in 1029.

Right gloriously he triumphs now,
Worthy to whom should all things bow;
And joining heaven and earth again,
Links in one commonweal the twain.
And we, as these his deeds we sing,
His suppliant soldiers, pray our King,
That in his palace, bright and vast,
We may keep watch and ward at last.
(Saint Fulbert, trans. J. M. Neale)

As another good, worthy shepherd, Fulbert was recognized throughout his diocese and beyond. Through his writing he became further known in his own time and during the thousand years that have since elapsed. Through good verse and poetic utterance, orthodoxy can be instilled in those who sing the praises of the heavenly Father; through good verse and poetry, worship can be enhanced and made seemly and reverent. We may travel farther picking out only a phrase or even one word to see where it takes us.

In our prayers: thanks for the life, example and intercession of Saint Fulbert; for the discipline to consider carefully what we read, hear and sing.

O God, whose Holy Word was made flesh in the womb of Our Blessed Lady, at the message of an angel: grant that we, who believe her to be the Mother of God, may benefit from her intercession for us. Through the same Jesus Christ our Lord. Amen.
Saint Fulbert, pray for us, for all writers, publishers and sellers of Catholic books, and for the diocese and city of Chartres.

April 11   Saint Gemma Galgani
(Also today, Saint Stanislaus of Cracow [*Bishop and Martyr*].)

Gemma was born near Lucca in 1878 and suffered as an invalid for the whole of her short life. Her correspondence with her spiritual directors reveals a deeply pious young woman who saw her suffering as a pale reflection of the Passion of Christ. She occasionally exhibited the stigmata in her hands and feet. Gemma died in 1903 and was canonized in 1940.

But he said to them, 'Unless I see in his hands the print of the nails . . . I will not believe' . . . Jesus came and stood among them, and said . . . to Thomas, 'Put your finger here, and see my hands . . . Blessed are those who have not seen and yet believe.' (John 20.26–29)

This young woman, crippled by unfathomable disease and, from time to time, the physical pain of the stigmata, devoted her life to correspondence with her priests and those with whom she could enter upon a particular theological world for her spiritual benefit, for theirs, for ours. There was unadulterated beauty in her nonchalant brushing aside of her physical trials, dismissing them as nothing more than a beneficial (to her) hint of Christ's Passion. We need hardly point out to ourselves how unfavourably we compare with this selfless attitude. Many have the bravery and fortitude to suffer in silence, but for Gemma pain and discomfort could be turned into a starting point in a quest for theological exploration. In this way, Gemma can make a profound difference to our lives; a tiny fingerpost to the heavenward road.

In our prayers: thanks for the life, example and intercession of Saint Gemma Galgani; for those who suffer from incurable disease; for priests and comforters of the invalid; for those in despair.

Saint Gemma, pray for us, and for all those who wait to die on a bed of pain.

April 12 Saint Teresa of Los Andes

Teresa was born in Chile in 1900. She was brought up with a daily Mass in the family chapel. From 15 she saw herself as destined for the religious life. She spent time in works of charity among the poor, and in 1918 entered the Carmelite house in Los Andes. She reveals herself in her letter writing and in her spiritual diary. Teresa died from typhoid fever in 1920 and was canonized in 1993.

And we know that the Son of God has come and has given us under-standing, to know him who is true; and we are in him who is true, in his Son Jesus Christ. This is the true God and eternal life. Little children, keep yourselves from idols. (1 John 5.20,21)

Even younger than Gemma Galgani (April 11) when she died, Teresa committed her thoughts, experiences and notes on her spiritual develop-ment to her letters and diary. She examined herself in the light of what she had done. Her experience in good works before her entry into the Carmelite house was her apprenticeship, her prelude to the religious life. Our experiences are, for most of us, greater and more varied than those of Teresa, but her example is often overlooked. Our lives are full of valuable things – lessons we have learnt and not learnt, and so on – from youth until now, to be thought about and made use of at any time. We can use these things for our own spiritual benefit by examining our spiritual progress, and for the benefit of others if we can give wise coun-sel in the light of our own experiences. We ought to give time to this careful consideration in case, for example, we are not quite on the road we thought. Teresa's self-examination was deep and searching. Can we discover in our lives that we have made many idols, some of which we still regularly worship without being conscious that they are idols? Can we discover where we may have ignored Christ in the beggar or, indeed, remember with love when we encountered him in some other?

In our prayers: thanks for the life, example and intercession of Saint Teresa of Los Andes; for openness to the criticisms and observations of others; for a willingness to learn from our experiences.

Saint Teresa, pray for us, and for all Carmelite houses.

April 13 Saint Martin I *(Pope and Martyr)*

Martin was elected pope in 649. The Emperor Constans II refused to recognize the new pope and when Martin held a Council in Rome to condemn the Monothelitism of the Emperor and his imperial court, there was an attempt to have Martin arrested. He was eventually arrested in 653 and imprisoned on a charge of treason. He was condemned to torture and death. He suffered brutal treatment in prison and then was exiled to the Crimea when his sentence was commuted. He died in prison in 655, broken in body.

Teach me thy paths. (Psalm 25[24].4)
Teach thy way, O Lord, and lead me. (Psalm 27[26].11)
Teach me thy statutes. (Psalm 119[118].12)
Teach me good judgements. (Psalm 119[118].66)

Martin was passionate about the purity of the Faith and the expulsion of the heresies of the age. (The Monothelites, for example, admitted the divine nature of Christ and his human nature but claimed that the two natures possessed a will common to both. The matter was not resolved until this heresy was condemned at the Sixth General Council in 681, 26 years after the death of Martin.) It was the meticulous work of men like Martin that enabled the Church gradually to rid itself of the cancerous heresies of the time. The Church must remain vigilant against the heresies of the modern age. Martin urges us to know our Faith well. If something sits ill with the teaching and tradition of Holy Church, is it not undeniably heretical?

In our prayers: thanks for the life, example and intercession of Saint Martin I; for the Holy Father, the Cardinals, Archbishops and Bishops.

Saint Martin, pray for us, and for the Holy Father and his advisers.

April 14 Saint Bénézet

Bénézet was born in Belgium in about 1163. He was a shepherd until his late teens. After being guided by a vision, he moved to Avignon to build a bridge across the Rhône. He began the work in complete ignorance of the principles of engineering and architecture necessary for the project, but armed instead with the confidence of God's good care. In response to his enthusiasm the bishop financed the project. Bénézet died in 1184 shortly before the bridge was complete.

The apostles said to the Lord, 'Increase our faith!' And the Lord said, 'If you had faith as a grain of mustard seed, you could say to this sycamine tree, "Be rooted up, and be planted in the sea!" and it would obey you.' (Luke 17.5,6)

Based solely on his vision and, later, partly on the bishop's financial support, Bénézet began his work in total ignorance and absolute faith. The project was nearing its completion when he died. Here was a young man with a single purpose – to build the bridge. (This was a difficult but most necessary project for those either side of the Rhône. Indeed, the building of a bridge opened the possibilities of so much more twelfth-century expansion and development.) It is a strange story, and Bénézet's saintly example is not easy to follow or emulate. We are not often guided by vision – or are we? In this case it was not, however, the vision itself that was remarkable, unusual though it was, so much as Bénézet's absolute faith in God from whom his vision had come. Our multifarious vocations and callings are directed at us not so that we should fail but so that we should succeed. All we need is Bénézet's confident reliance upon God.

In our prayers: thanks for the life, example and intercession of Saint Bénézet; that we may be alert to the promptings of the Holy Spirit; for those whose vocation it is to respond to the zeal of others.

Saint Bénézet, pray for us, for bridge builders and for Avignon.

❦

April 15 Saint Paternus of Avranches *(Abbot and Bishop)*

Paternus was born in Poitiers in 481. He founded a monastery at Granville, and several daughter houses nearby. Paternus was abbot for many years. In 551 he was made Bishop of Avranches. He died in 564, a holy and respected bishop.

The saying is sure: If any one aspires to the office of bishop, he desires a noble task. Now a bishop must be above reproach . . . (1 Timothy 3.1,2)

Often those who do not aspire to the office of bishop make the best bishops. They are sought out for their holiness, modesty and humility. They are often raised to the episcopacy with some reluctance. Paternus was certainly a humble abbot concerned with the spreading of his monastery by means of houses founded throughout the region. Their purpose was, inter alia, to assist in the spreading of the gospel by example and by daily prayer. The setting aside of time for devotion and intercession is the backbone of the monastic day. If we are not all monks and nuns we are unlikely to be able to devote so much time to our devotion and intercession. Of course, that is understood because we are not all called to the monastic way of life. However, we can learn by extreme example – and the lesson is simply that daily prayer and daily intercession for others is an important feature of our lives. We can pray in many ways throughout the day: we need not be on our knees in chapel. Paternus was seen to be faithful in his monastic duties. Does the heavenly Father hear us daily?

In our prayers: thanks for the life, example and intercession of Saint Paternus of Avranches; for all parish priests and chaplains.

Saint Paternus, pray for us, and for all who live a monastic life.

April 16 Saint Bernadette of Lourdes

Bernadette was born in 1844. The family was poor and lived in the basement of a house in Lourdes. For five months at the age of 14, she experienced visions of Our Lady, who declared 'I am the Immaculate Conception.' Never did Bernadette exploit the interest in this phenomenon; she remained entirely modest and matter-of-fact about the episode. She entered the Sisters of Charity in 1866 and lived there in poor health but in a dutiful life of prayer and obedience until her death in 1879. Bernadette was canonized in 1933.

In the sixth month, the angel Gabriel was sent from God to a city of Galilee named Nazareth, to a virgin betrothed to a man whose name was Joseph, of the house of David; and the virgin's name was Mary. And he said, 'Hail, full of grace, the Lord is with you.' (Luke 1.26–28)

Eight years after the extraordinary visions she was granted, Bernadette embraced a life of prayer with the Sisters of Charity. These visions were undoubtedly of a different genus to the vision, if that is the word, experienced by Bénézet (April 14). They were of enormous encouragement to the faithful at large and, indeed, still remain so, but to Bernadette they simply guided her into a life of devotion. Perhaps Bernadette was merely a vehicle for these visions. She is an example of openness, modesty and prayerfulness. Do we cultivate these attributes ourselves?

In our prayers: thanks for the life, example and intercession of Saint Bernadette of Lourdes; for simplicity, modesty and humility.

Jesu, keep me this day under the standard of thy Holy Cross. (Saint Bernadette)
Holy Mary and Queen conceived without original sin, pray for us. Saint Bernadette, pray for us, and for the sick and suffering who visit Lourdes.

April 17 Saint Robert of Chaise-Dieu *(Abbot)*

Robert was born in 1000 in central France and was ordained priest in 1026 at Brioude. He left the community of canons at St Julian's for Rome and Monte Cassino, and on his return decided to settle in a life of prayer, preaching and charitable work for the impoverished with a few companions. This attracted many disciples and pilgrims, and so the monastery of Chaise-Dieu was begun in 1043. Further houses were subsequently established, all following the Rule of Saint Benedict (July 11). Robert died in 1067 and was canonized in 1070.

Any guest ought to be received as Christ himself because he promises to say on the last day, 'I was a stranger and you welcomed me.' (Matthew 25.35) (On the reception of guests, the Rule of Saint Benedict)

Robert's solitude was an essential preparation for his late work. Perhaps he was not fully aware of what God had in mind for him because he seems to have embarked upon what was going to be a simple life caring for others with a little help from a few fellows. However, he was, in addition, destined to receive vast numbers of pilgrims and guests as though he were receiving Christ, which surely is receiving Christ. Many saints give us these examples of showing Christ to others and to receiving others as Christ. In doing these things we become guides to others.

Hospitality extends well beyond the odd occasion when we give up a bed for the night; it can mean as much or as little as simple, friendly encouragement and acknowledgement in the most ordinary of places, be it bread queue or waiting room.

In our prayers: thanks for the life, example and intercessions of Saint Robert of Chaise-Dieu; for novice masters and those who train others for higher positions; for men and women who offer comfort and rest to pilgrims in their journey through life.

Saint Robert, pray for us, and for all those who show kindness and hospitality.

April 18   Saint Ursmar *(Abbot and Bishop)*

Ursmar became Abbot of Lobbes in Belgium at about the age of 49. He is credited with enlarging the abbey church and dedicating it to Saint Peter and Saint Paul (June 29), and for introducing the Rule of Saint Benedict (July 11). Ursmar established many other churches and foundations in Flanders. His fame for simple holiness and dedication to the gospel made him an important figure in the conversion of Flanders. He died in 713.

Blessed is every one who fears the Lord, who walks in his ways! You shall eat the fruit of the labour of your hands; you shall be happy and it shall be well with you. (Psalm 128[127].1,2)

Dedication to the gospel is a phrase that accords happily with the psalmist's first sentence. Ursmar's successful work in spreading the gospel and founding monasteries and building churches was his vocation. He achieved it through his simple holiness and his dedication to the gospel. We are successful in our vocations if we conform to Christ and are dedicated to the gospel. This is Ursmar's signpost for us – here is the way, the simple life in Christ, in the spirit of the gospel, under the direction of Holy Church. The way is clear, sometimes easily strayed from by putting self first, but always visible and, by God's grace, readily resumed.

In our prayers: thanks for the life, example and intercession of Saint Ursmar; for moral counsellors; for the people of Holland and Belgium.

Saint Ursmar, pray for us, for those who strive to keep to the way of Christ; for children who cannot walk or who have difficulties and handicaps, whose patron you are.

ᕫᕬ

April 19   Saint Alphege of Canterbury *(Bishop and Martyr)*

Alphege, an austere man, was abbot in Bath before his consecration as Bishop of Winchester in 984. There he gained a reputation for his charitable works among the disadvantaged. In 1005 he became Archbishop of Canterbury but was taken prisoner and murdered by the Danes who raided Canterbury in 1011. Alphege was a holy and self-effacing man.

... The righteous man is generous and gives ... The wicked watches the righteous, and seeks to slay him. (Psalm 37[36].22,32)

Someone once said that the cross is the capital letter 'I' crossed out. It is a demonstration of self-abnegation. Alphege subscribed to that view and acted it faithfully in his life by denying himself the pleasure of food and drink, using them only to sustain the body. He was ungenerous to himself and the opposite to the poor of late tenth-century and early eleventh-century Winchester. Over them his generosity poured and he blessed them with what he had over and above his meagre requirements. There is no doubt that the same applied in Canterbury. Alphege asks us to look carefully at our excessive intake of food and drink. Perhaps our intake is modest. Do we pass on what we do not use for our own well-being to worthy charities for the hungry? Perhaps we do. The saintly exemplars should be constantly before us. Perhaps they are.

In our prayers: thanks for the life, example and intercession of Saint Alphege of Canterbury; for those who direct charities for the relief of famine; for those who suffer in famine; for those who are susceptible to gluttony.

Saint Alphege, pray for us, for all charities dedicated to the relief of hunger, and for all churches dedicated in your name.

April 20   Saint Agnes of Montepulciano

Agnes was born about 1268 near Montepulciano and joined the Sisters of the Sack when very young. She became the superior of a daughter house at Proceno in 1283. Agnes then returned to her hometown and was made prioress of a new Dominican convent. She died in 1317, highly thought of for her sanctity and simplicity of life. Agnes was canonized in 1726.

Behold the eye of the Lord is on those who fear him, on those who hope in his steadfast love. (Psalm 33[32].18)
The eyes of the Lord are toward the righteous, and his ears toward their cry. (Psalm 34[33].15)

The single-mindedness of an ascetic living her simple life, directing her fellow sisters in holiness of living and deep devotion in prayer is worthy of our contemplation from time to time. How does the way we live compare with the holiness and perfection of Agnes? How does our prayer life compare with that of Agnes's, which was born of the way she lived? That gives us our answer, perhaps, without any further thought. It is the indirect answer to the questions we need to hear. No, my life is not as pure, holy and simple as Agnes's; and, no, my prayer life cannot be equal with hers. Of course not, but how I live my life might determine how I pray – whether or not I thank God; how I confess; whether or not I bother to think enough of others to pray for them.

In our prayers: thanks for the life, example and intercession of Saint Agnes of Montepulciano; for those who would be pure and prayerful.

Saint Agnes, pray for us, and for all who strive to lead a simple life in the spirit of the gospel.

April 21 Saint Anselm *(Bishop and Doctor of the Church)*

Anselm was Abbot of Bec in 1078 when nominated for the See of Canterbury by King William Rufus in 1093. Through disagreements with King William and King Henry I, Anselm was twice exiled. He was keen to ensure his clergy were pure and faithful, and that they had surrendered themselves entirely to God for the sake of Holy Church. Anselm died in 1109 and was declared Doctor of the Church in 1720.

Blessed is the man who walks not in the counsel of the wicked, nor stands in the way of sinners, nor sits in the seat of scoffers; but his delight is in the law of the Lord, and on his law he meditates day and night. (Psalm 1.1–2)

Anselm's priests were to be living examples to the faithful – as all priests ought to be. They were to be pure and faithful to the gospel and to Holy Church – as all priests ought to be. They could be these things only if they had surrendered themselves entirely to God for the sake of Holy Church. That is obvious to us when we see it in black and white. If priests are living examples to the faithful laity, it follows that the faithful laity must emulate and copy their examples. By living the life of the gospel, inevitably we surrender ourselves entirely to God. From that will flow all that is good in our lives. We have contemplated this from many angles, from many aspects of saintly lives, but the problem is always how to achieve it. There is no doubt that Anselm's own simple words of prayer can help us towards this achievement.

In our prayers: thanks for the life, example and intercession of Saint Anselm; that we might surrender ourselves entirely to God for the sake of Holy Church.

O God of Truth, let my mind contemplate you; my mouth speak about you; my heart love you; my soul hunger for you; my flesh thirst for you until I enter into the joy of the eternal Lord, who is God, Three in One, and for ever Blessed. Amen. (Saint Anselm)
Saint Anselm, pray for us, and for secular clergy.

April 22   Saint Leonides *(Martyr)*

Leonides was the father of the theologian and writer, Origen, and an instructor of philosophy and theology at the Alexandrian School of Theology. He was an evangelist of the Christian Faith, was arrested under the orders of Emperor Septimus Severus, and beheaded for his faith in 202.

'Rejoice and be glad, for your reward is great in heaven, for so men persecuted the prophets who were before you.' (Matthew 5.12)

Here is an early saint, only a few generations after those who heard the Apostles, who lived in notorious times when many were tested beyond endurance. God will have forgiven them for denying him under torture. After all, they may have denied with the tongue but earnestly held him in their hearts. Some, the martyrs, had the strength and the calling to hold firm until the end, no matter the ingenious methods employed to encourage a change of mind. God seems to have harvested the souls of the righteous at a time and a place, which, in our eyes, was most unfortunate and injurious to the Church. But it was not so. The faith and blood of the martyrs is most precious to Christ and his Church. God's ways are not our ways, and our great wisdom is his foolishness. Without any further detail of this worthy saint, Leonides' life of study and training of others was a life devoted to the gospel. He yearned to pass on and share his knowledge and understanding. His faith and steadfastness to the end confirmed the importance and veracity of that which he taught. If we are not all called to be tested in the way Leonides was, we are tested in many other ways. Do we fail without realizing it? How many ways are there in which to say, 'I do not know the man!'?

In our prayers: thanks for the life, example and intercession of Saint Leonides; for those who are tested beyond endurance; for those imprisoned for their faith; for all teachers of theology.

Saint Leonides, pray for us, and for those who strive to learn.

April 23 Saint George *(Martyr)*

George was a martyr who was tortured and put to death for his faith, in Lydda during Diocletian's persecution of Christians. It may have been that George was a Roman soldier who held the Christian Faith, in which case the penalties and punishments before death would have been even more severe. The date of George's death was about 307.

Here is a call for the endurance of the saints, those who keep the commandments of God and the Faith of Jesus. And I heard a voice from heaven saying, 'Write this: "Blessed are the dead who die in the Lord henceforth."' (Revelation 14.12,13)

Many fantastical stories have been woven around the life of George. Some of them may well have their feet in fact in order to illustrate the holiness and faithfulness of George. He may well have saved a maiden from some evil or other, or, perhaps, a whole village, for the purity of the Faith. We do not know precisely, but all these stories show a faith of such conviction that it could be tested under humiliating torture and the threat of death. George's death was of such significance that his life and death fed and engendered the stories that wrap around his life: his was from the earliest times a life and death of note. He was readily adopted as the patron of England (along with many other lands). His faith he deemed worth fighting for, worth dying for. In a land whose new laws and constitutional modifications gradually reveal the handiwork of the atheist and the denial of our reliance on God, let alone our belief in him, we value the example of George.

In our prayers: for the life, example and intercession of Saint George; for the men and women who seek to persuade others against the moral evils of this present age; for those who strive to live God-centred lives; for the governments and authorities operating under the sovereign.

Saint George, pray for us, for England, and for the Queen and all the Royal Family.

April 24 Saint Fidelis of Sigmaringen

Fidelis (born Mark Roy) was a learned man who, after years of study, began to practise law in Alsace. The dishonesty of his fellow lawyers distressed him to the extent that he became a priest and a Capuchin. Many testified to his holiness and steadfastness in the Faith. He was known also for his charity to the poor. Fidelis was murdered during a mission to re-establish the Catholic Faith in Switzerland in 1622. He was canonized in 1746.

Holy, Holy, Holy, Lord God of Sabaoth . . . The noble army of martyrs praise thee. (Te Deum 5,9)

Fidelis's calling was not, after all, to be the honest lawyer but something even more difficult and, ultimately, dangerous. He was martyred by an anti-Catholic mob at the age of only 42. His dedication to the task given is the example he sets those who live and work in the secular world. Our lives must be as blameless as his, removed as it was, in one sense, from the secular world; and yet, in another sense, he worked right at the heart of the secular world from which the mob that killed him arose. We live and work at the heart of the modern secular world and we know the dangers and temptations, where sin is expected and even encouraged, and, in some cases, given a specially protected status by law. We realize that we, like Fidelis, are not to be *of* the world: we turn to the crucifix, to the face of Christ, and we are pleasantly surprised when we see that face again in others in a wicked world. The joy of the Lord will over-whelm the ungodly tendencies in the world if we help spread it.

In our prayers: thanks for the life, example and intercession of Saint Fidelis of Sigmaringen; for those who make laws and those who enforce them.

Saint Fidelis, pray for us, and for all lawyers.

April 25 Saint Mark the Evangelist

Mark the Evangelist was probably the cousin of Saint Barnabas (June 11) and the Mark referred to by Saint Peter and Saint Paul (June 29). The tradition that, in Rome, Mark wrote his Gospel based upon what

Peter had told him or dictated to him is fairly well accepted. Perhaps he was also the young man who fled naked in Mark 14.51,52. He may have been martyred – certainly he was venerated as a martyr in the early centuries.

Aristarchus my fellow prisoner greets you and Mark the cousin of Barnabas. (Colossians 4.10)
She who is at Babylon [Rome], who is likewise chosen, sends you greetings; and so does my son, Mark. (1 Peter 5.13)

Peter's testimony may have been supplemented by another or other source(s) by Mark. Among other things, the writer of the Gospel of Mark aims to reveal and stress the source of the *authority* of Jesus. The chief priests, scribes and elders ask Jesus, 'By what authority are you doing these things?' 'Who gave you authority to do them?' (Mark 11.28). Mark answers these questions emphatically in the Gospel by showing us that Jesus' authority emanates from God and therefore is nothing other than God's own authority. The Evangelists had the responsibility of setting down the essentials of the gospel for the future, and these writings were carried with Holy Church as it grew and developed over the centuries and countries and continents. Our responsibility, in turn, is to savour and learn and know the Gospel of Mark.

In our prayers: thanks for the life, example and intercession of Saint Mark the Evangelist; for those who instruct the young and old in Holy Scripture; for the people of Venice.

Saint Mark, pray for us, for Venice, Egypt, and for all who make and fashion glass.

April 26   Saint Stephen of Perm *(Bishop)*

Stephen was a well-educated monk in the Saint Gregory Nazianzen (January 2) monastery in Rostov. He set about preparing himself to evangelize the Zyryani. He learnt the language and produced an alphabet so that the language might be written and the Holy Bible and the Liturgy translated. Stephen became the first Bishop of Perm, building schools, training priests and feeding the hungry. He died in Moscow in 1396 and was canonized in 1549.

So Solomon made all the things that were in the house of God . . . the lamp stands and their lamps of pure gold to burn before the inner sanctuary . . . the flowers . . . the dishes for incense. (2 Chronicles 4.19–22)

This brilliant man gave the people to whom he ministered their first journey into Holy Scripture and the Mass. Concurrently he established schools and seminaries and, above all, churches. He passionately advocated beauty in worship, from the manner in which the rite was sung or spoken, to the surroundings in which it was performed, to the candles, the icons and the vestments. Stephen had great gifts, one of which was as a painter of icons. The heightened beauty of holiness at Mass is such an important ingredient that lifts us beyond the material world. Icons, paintings and statuary can aid us in our worship in church and at home in our private prayer. The love and devotion lavished upon the prayerful painting of an icon can be released before our eyes as we contemplate the images before us. Stephen's life underlines the importance of art and heightened language in our response to God.

In our prayers: thanks for the life, example and intercession of Saint Stephen of Perm; for men and women who use their talents to show us something of God's infinite beauty.

Saint Stephen, pray for us, and for painters of icons.

April 27 Saint Zita

Zita was a maid in the household of a wealthy cloth manufacturer and merchant of Lucca. She was passionately industrious and faithful, and became a model of pious dutifulness, which her fellows sought to emulate. Furthermore, she exercised enormous generosity by giving away what little she had to those less fortunate. Zita had remained in the same household for nearly 50 years when she died in 1278.

Jesus said: '. . . but whoever would be great among you must be your servant, and whoever would be first among you must be slave to all. For the Son of Man came not to be served but to serve, and to give his life as a ransom for many.' (Mark 10.43b–45)

Can we pay scant regard to our responsibility at work, be dishonest with time and materials and in the manner of the execution of our duties, and be a faithful and honest servant of Christ? In these circumstances can we approach the altar of God with a clear conscience? It is difficult to envisage. Zita gives us a lesson in our relations with employers and superiors, co-workers and friends; a lesson in faithfulness in small things. Hers was a humble post for a lowly girl. What did that matter? The message is the same for scullery maid, personal assistant and managing director. Zita shows us the way to be 'great' among our fellows – by becoming the least. Applying the gospel to her employment and ordinary way of life, she fulfils all the requirements made of her by Christ.

In our prayers: thanks for the life, example and intercession of Saint Zita; for all who serve others; for those who find humility difficult.

Saint Zita, pray for us, for all domestic staff, and for the town of Lucca.

April 28 Saint Peter Chanel *(Martyr)*

Peter was born in 1807 in France and ordained priest in 1827. In Crozet where he became the parish priest, he was popular for his great care of the sick. He joined the Society of Mary in order to carry out the foreign missionary work he felt called to. Peter and companions settled in Futuna in the South Pacific Ocean in 1837. In a few years he began to make progress, but in 1841 a gang of thugs battered him to death. Peter was canonized in 1954.

Out of the depths I cry to thee, O Lord! Lord, hear my voice! Let thy ears be attentive to the voice of my supplications! (Psalm 130[129].1,2)

Peter proved himself a fine parish priest of great sanctity and warmth in the care of the sick. This was, in effect, his training for his all-too-brief sojourn in Futuna, where he spent only four years taking the gospel to those whose land it was. Slowly but surely he sowed the seeds of the Faith, which had begun to sprout and develop by the time he was done to death. We wonder if God made proper use of him. Would he not have been more useful to God spending, say, 20 more years at Crozet? Our heavenly Father probably does not count what we might regard as 'success' in years and in size of crop. One little mustard seed sown in a moment would have been sufficient – sufficient for the gardeners later to tend and care for. Precisely what good (or harm) we do with a gesture, a look, a word, we never know. God knows.

In our prayers: thanks for the life, example and intercession of Saint Peter Chanel; for the people of the South Pacific islands; for all Societies and Orders dedicated to Our Lady.

Saint Peter, pray for us, and for all who work in foreign mission fields.

April 29 Saint Catherine of Siena *(Doctor of the Church)*

Catherine was born in Siena in 1347 and joined the Third Order of the Dominicans in 1363, in which capacity she cared for the poor and the sick, and gathered round her a team of devoted assistants – clerical and lay, men and women. Catherine wrote a great number of letters of guidance to influential people, including no less a person than Pope Gregory XI himself, in order to assist with the healing of wounds within the Church caused by the Great Schism. She wrote, among many other things, the *Dialogue*, a highly thought of mystical work. Catherine died in 1380, was canonized in 1461, and declared Doctor of the Church in 1970.

If thou triest my heart, if thou visitest me by night, if thou testest me, thou wilt find no wickedness in me; my mouth does not transgress. I call upon thee, for thou wilt answer me, O God; incline thy ear to me, hear my words. Wondrously show thy steadfast love, O saviour of those who seek refuge from their adversaries at thy right hand. (Psalm 17[16].3,6,7)

Catherine's written works are of enormous importance and repay study. Catherine is able to transport us to other realms and levels of contemplation of the great theological Mysteries, not in any arrogant manner as though the Mystery under scrutiny were a mystery to be solved by deduction, but in a humble, searching manner we know God rewards with wisdom and understanding. We can adopt this method, revealed rather beautifully in the quotation below, and apply it in our contemplation of the great Truths. We shall find it of assistance to address our musings, our searchings, our meditations, our wonderings and wanderings, to our heavenly Father, as Catherine did.

In our prayers: thanks for the life, example and intercession of Saint Catherine of Siena; for the Congregation of Saint Catherine of Siena; for all mystics and theological writers.

Our nature reflects yours as your nature reflects ours on account of the union of the eternal Godhead with the flesh of human substance. How did this happen? Your inexhaustible love for your creatures was the cause. (From Dialogue, *Saint Catherine of Siena)*
Saint Catherine, pray for us, for all Catholic women, for Italy, and for all churches dedicated in your name.

❦

April 30   Saint Pius V *(Pope)*

Pius was elected pope in 1565. His particular quality of asceticism was urgently required in the Church at the time, and he set about reforming the clergy and implementing the reforms of the Council of Trent. His reforms in the Church – and particularly in Rome – strengthened the practice of the Catholic Faith. Pius died in 1572 and was canonized in 1712.

The discipline of the Sacraments . . . requires the skill and industry of the Priest; and that by the diligent and frequent use thereof, the faithful may be fitted worthily and savingly to be made partakers of these most excellent and most holy things. (From Part II of 'The Catechism for the Curates' by the Decree of the Council of Trent)

Pius could see what was necessary to purge the Church of laziness, laxity and corruption of worship, and set about the task immediately with firmness tempered with generosity. So often, sadly, through the Church's history this appears necessary. We should not despair because we are not despaired of, and we can be picked up and set down on our faltering feet again and again. A symptom of the Church's difficulties throughout history has been the sloppiness and indifference of the clergy and the people in the manner in which they offer Mass. A holy, reverent and dignified demeanour in church will enable us to offer Mass in the appropriate manner. The language – whether it is good English or Latin – and the music we sing are important ingredients in heightening our worship above the ordinary. We must associate ourselves with time-honoured traditions and with our fellow pilgrims throughout the world and through the ages.

In our prayers: thanks for the life, example and intercession of Saint Pius V; for masters of ceremonies, servers, organists and choirmasters; for liturgists, translators of hymns and hymn writers.

Saint Pius, pray for us, and for all priests, deacons, those in minor Orders, and servers.

May

May is Mary's month – our chapel here at Arundel is dedicated to Our Lady – a month when spring and summer meet. It ends with the celebration of the Visitation of Mary to her cousin Elizabeth. In addition to Joseph the Carpenter's feast on May 1, we celebrate the life of Peregrine Laziosi: he is the patron of those suffering from cancer. And one must be struck by the simplicity of Isidore's (15) life – humble, prayerful and holy.

✧✦✧

May 1 Saint Joseph the Carpenter; Saint Peregrine Laziosi

Joseph's guardianship of the Holy Family is considered on March 19; now we think of the man behind that most responsible of duties. He was a carpenter and, as such, would have been in constant demand. We cannot doubt his skills and that he passed them to Our Lord himself. We know little enough of Joseph but what we do know reveals to us the fulfilment of two distinct, God-given vocations, which merged successfully in the life of the man.

Peregrine is brought to our attention by famously striking the Servite and Papal Legate, Saint Philip Benizi (August 22), who was on a peace mission on behalf of the pope. Philip immediately offered Peregrine the other side of his face. The remorseful Peregrine joined the Servite Friars himself in 1292, became a priest and was noted for his reverence and his holiness. The diseased foot with which he had been suffering for many years miraculously healed one night after a prayerful vigil. The foot was to have been amputated in the morning. Peregrine died in 1345 and was canonized in 1726.

'Is not this the carpenter's son?' (Matthew 13.55a)

'Go and tell John what you have seen and heard: the blind receive their sight, the lame walk, lepers are cleansed . . .' (Luke 7.22)

Joseph was skilled in fashioning wood into all manner of articles, jointing and joining timber, and constructing the framework of houses. Furthermore, he made the house in Nazareth a home for the Holy Family. His successful work was a metaphor for our circumstances, our perpetual endeavour to make and maintain a dwelling place within ourselves, suitable for Christ to call his home. Peregrine, on slapping the face of Saint Philip, was discomfited at Philip's turn of the cheek. At that point did Peregrine catch a glimpse of Christ gazing sadly from Philip's face and saying, 'Peregrine, why do you strike me again?' We know that Peregrine soon prepared himself as a well-garnished home. We wonder at his chronic affliction: we marvel at the faith that removed it.

In our prayers: thanks for the lives, examples and intercession of Saint Joseph and Saint Peregrine; for those who have cancer and for those who look after them; for all who adopt children.

Saint Joseph, pray for us, and for all guardians of the young. Saint Peregrine, pray for us, and for all those who suffer from cancer.

May 2   Saint Athanasius *(Bishop and Doctor of the Church)*

Athanasius was a bishop for over 40 years and hailed as the father of orthodoxy in his successful battles against the heresy of Arianism. He was Bishop of Alexandria from 328 until his death in 373, and was a writer of note. His work on the doctrines of the Incarnation and the Holy Trinity hold good to this day. The Athanasian Creed is a later work but is firmly based upon the work of Athanasius.

For there is one Person of the Father, another of the Son, and another of the Holy Spirit. But the Godhead of the Father, of the Son, and of the Holy Spirit is all one, the glory equal, the Majesty co-eternal. Such as the Father is, such is the Son, and such is the Holy Spirit . . . So, likewise the Father is Almighty, the Son Almighty, and the Holy Spirit Almighty. And yet there are not three Almighties, but one Almighty . . . there are not three Gods, but one God . . . there are not three Lords, but one Lord. (Athanasian Creed)

God slowly revealed himself to early man, allowing his creature gradually to absorb and understand, so that succeeding generations were imbued with a growing acknowledgement of the Divine and a yearning for wisdom and understanding. Then, in more recent times, he called faithful theologians to piece together for the benefit of mankind Christ's actual relationship with the Father. The Spirit of Truth descended upon the Church as promised. We are called to think and understand, and to discern to the extent of our capabilities and of our calling.

In our prayers: thanks for the life, example and intercession of Saint Athanasius; for teachers of doctrine.

Saint Athanasius, pray for us, and for all who seek for understanding.

ᙅᙓᙚ

May 3   Saints Philip and James *(Apostles)*

Philip introduces Nathanael Bartholomew to Jesus. When Jesus is contemplating the five thousand, Jesus asks Philip, 'How are we to buy bread, so that these people may eat?' And Philip asks Jesus at the Last Supper, 'Show us the Father.' In each case Philip initiates important teaching from the mouth of Our Lord.

This James – the son of Alphaeus and, possibly, the brother of Matthew (September 21) – can be conveniently referred to as James II to differentiate between him and James the Great (James I, July 25), who was the brother of John (December 27), son of Zebedee and cousin of Our Lord. The relics of Philip and James were venerated together in a church in Rome dedicated to the two saints.

The next day Jesus decided to go to Galilee. And he found Philip and said to him, 'Follow me!' (John 1.43)
And when it was day, he called his disciples, and chose from them twelve, whom he named apostles; Simon, whom he named Peter and Andrew his brother, and James and John, and Philip and Bartholomew, and Matthew, and Thomas, and James the son of Alphaeus . . . (Luke 6.13–15)

Philip is a prompt. 'Show us the Father,' he says. Perhaps up to that point all the others were willing themselves the courage to ask the same question. 'Have I been with you so long, and yet you do not know me,

118

Philip? He who has seen me has seen the Father . . . Believe me that I am in the Father and the Father in me . . .' Philip has asked the question for us and we have our answer: clear, straightforward and definitive. What more do we require? The other disciples heard the answer and they with Philip bore that out into the world in the joy of the Resurrection a little later.

In our prayers: thanks for the lives, examples and intercession of Saint Philip and Saint James; for all places dedicated in the names of Philip and James.

Saint Philip, pray for us, and for all bakers and confectioners whose patron you are. Saint James, pray for us, and for all manufacturers of cloth and workers with textiles whose patron you are.

৩ৡ✢৸৩

May 4 The Blessed Martyrs of England and Wales; Saint Florian *(Martyr)*

Florian was yet another victim of the persecutions of the Roman emperor, Diocletian. Florian was an officer in the Roman army, who confessed to the governor, Aquilinus, that he was a Christian. Florian was flayed and cast into the River Emms at Lorch in about 304. The feast of the Blessed Martyrs is additional to that celebrated on October 25, but embraces those named on November 22 and many others martyred between 1535 and 1680.

I gave my back to the smiter, and my cheeks to those who pulled out my beard; I hid not my face from shame and spitting. (Isaiah 50.6)

Florian was a senior man in the Roman army. There were many such men trying, probably, to keep quiet about their faith at first; then, when cornered, perhaps, confessing their faith openly, boldly, unashamedly. The penalties in the Roman Empire in the fourth century were severe, and varied with the depravity of those into whose hands was given the task of ending the Christian's life. The butchery to which many of the martyrs of England and Wales were subjected before they died was almost as vile and merciless. Removal of the head and general disfigurement of the body and the mocking of the remains were the common themes. In the Roman Empire, Christianity was blasphemy and treason;

in England and Wales, the martyrs were generally found guilty of treason either because evidence was manufactured or (later in the sixteenth century) the definition of treason became so wide as to embrace the most innocent of activity. Often we do precisely this. We manufacture reasons for our hate and our petty dislikes so that they sit more comfortably on our consciences.

In our prayers: thanks for the lives, examples and intercession of Saint Florian and the Blessed Martyrs of England and Wales; for those cruelly treated for their faith.

Saint Florian, pray for us, for Poland, for the Polish people who live in Britain, and for those who struggle with the effects of fire and flood. Holy Martyrs of England and Wales, pray for us.

May 5 Saint Angelo *(Martyr)*

Angelo was a Carmelite who lived as a hermit on Mount Carmel for a few years. He travelled to Sicily where he preached and taught to great acclaim. In 1220 as he preached, Angelo was attacked and stabbed to death by a gang of criminals, whose way of life he had condemned. As he lay dying, Angelo prayed for his killers and for those others to whom he had been preaching.

. . . Let the bones, which thou hast broken, rejoice. Hide thy face from my sins, and blot out all my iniquities. Restore to me the joy of thy salvation and uphold me with a willing spirit. Then will I teach transgressors thy ways, and sinners will return to thee. (Psalm 51[50].8,9,12,13)

By means of a daily manual we may be disciplined into daily intercession. We spend only a short time doing so in order that we have plenty of time for our work, our play, our living. That is perfectly in order because we can use our daily living as a vehicle for prayer, or from which to collect experiences to commit to more formal prayer. To transform an act into prayer may be quite easy, or quite difficult. To transform our dying breaths into prayer for our murderers and for those others around us is quite another matter. Our natural instincts would embrace terror, sorrow, self-preservation, anger at ourselves, anger and hatred at our attackers and those who failed to help us. Angelo prayed out loud for his congregation, for his murderers; he forgave his murderers and commended them to God. He had no time for the emotions noted above: his duty was to love his enemy and to forgive him readily. Angelo died perfectly. Should we not live every moment as though it were our last? We do not know the hour.

In our prayers: thanks for the life, example and intercession of Saint Angelo; for those who travel a great distance to work; for commuters.

Saint Angelo, pray for us, for all preachers and for Sicily.

May 6   Saint Evodius of Antioch *(Bishop)*

Evodius was the first Bishop of Antioch, who was succeeded by Saint Ignatius (October 17). There is a tradition that Evodius was one of the 70 disciples sent on a missionary journey by Our Lord (Luke 10.1). He died in the early 60s, in all probability.

Now those who were scattered because of the persecution that arose over Stephen, travelled as far as Phoenicia and Cypress and Antioch ... and in Antioch the disciples were for the first time called Christians. (Acts 11.19,26)
A little leaven leavens the whole lump. (Galatians 5.9)

Let us accept the early and strong tradition that Evodius was one of those who were sent out and joyfully returned to regale Our Lord with tales of their successes. Jesus may have had his tongue in his cheek when he greeted them and responded to their excitement; there is no doubt he was pleased with them. After Stephen's (December 26) death, Evodius settled in the place where Christianity readily took root; he became the bishop there, and from these early beginnings, the gospel spread west to Rome. Evodius, like all Christians, was fired with overwhelming enthusiasm for Christ: he passed on the message of the gospel, he preached, he became an example that others longed to follow, he converted others by the way he lived his life. Why do we seem to be rather less excited than these men? There is no reason to be and every reason not to be!

In our prayers: thanks for the life, example and intercession of Saint Evodius of Antioch; for the men and women who carry the gospel to other lands; for those who endeavour to show Christ to others by the way they live their lives.

Saint Evodius, pray for us, and that we might be filled with the enthusiasm of the early Church.

꧁✿꧂

May 7 Saint John of Beverley *(Bishop)*

John was a holy and learned monk in the monastery at Whitby where he ministered to the destitute. He became Bishop of Hexham in 687. He is credited with teaching a boy with a severe impediment to talk. John was Bishop of York in 705 and died in 721 in the monastery he founded at Beverley.

As they were going away, behold, a dumb demoniac was brought to him. And when the demon had been cast out, the dumb man spoke; and the crowds marvelled, saying, 'Never was anything like this seen in Israel.' (Matthew 9.32,33)

Thank God for holy and learned monks. From their priories and abbeys they taught and learnt. Their libraries became repositories of the written word. Their destiny was to educate the future. There were few learned men outside these environs: their importance for the Faith and for the quality of first-millennium life cannot be overstated. And yet, a boy is produced who is dumb, has a cleft palate, a hair lip, a deformed tongue. Why does the Bishop of Hexham bother with such a child? Some nursemaid would probably care for him. Why, the king wants to see the bishop next week! Do we overlook the seemingly small opportunities?

In our prayers: thanks for the life, example and intercession of Saint John of Beverley; for those with speech and hearing impediments; for the desire to seize the opportunity to do good when it arises.

Saint John, pray for us, and for all who are deaf or dumb.

꧁✿꧂

May 8   Saint Victor the Moor *(Martyr)*

Victor, the black patron of Milan, was a member of the Praetorian Guard, who admitted his Christianity and was put to death in Milan in about 303 during Maximian's violent persecution of Christians in the reign of Diocletian.

For behold, the Lord is coming forth out of his place to punish the inhabitants of the earth for their iniquity, and the earth will disclose the blood shed upon her, and will no more cover her slain. (Isaiah 26.21)

The flow of faithful souls from this unhappy period on earth was rapid. There were children, men and women. The women were sometimes young maidens, sometimes old. Some were pregnant, some nursing. The men were boys, married men, old men. Victor hailed from the North African region of the Roman Empire, and was a member of Rome's elite force. How had he come to know Christ? Can we imagine an environment so hazardous to our lives? Perhaps we can. Victor's death was as many other martyrs' deaths, but the Christians of Milan were so captivated, encouraged by the power and infectious enthusiasm of Victor's witness, that his cult was quickly born. Victor's death was a happy prize for Milan.

In our prayers: thanks for the life, example and intercession of Saint Victor the Moor; for the men, women and children of Milan; for the people of the countries of North Africa.

Saint Victor, pray for us, and for the civil authorities of Milan.

May 9   Saint Pachomius *(Abbot)*

Pachomius was the father of the monastic community. Becoming a Christian on leaving the Roman army in 316, he served as a hermitic disciple for a number of years before building a community of houses whose occupants devoted themselves to manual work and regular worship throughout the day. Pachomius died in 346 leaving a dozen such monastic communities.

He led them to safety, so that they were not afraid; but the sea over-whelmed their enemies. And he brought them to his holy land, to the mountain, which his right hand had won. (Psalm 78[77].53,54)

The desert was the womb of the monastic way of life and the womb of much carefully considered theological thought. There in the desert – away from the army, away from everyday life – there was a chance to order the mind and ponder the next step. John the Baptist certainly pre-pared himself in the desert; Our Lord himself probably did so. Later, Pachomius – and he was not the first to do so – saw that some need this release from society in order to take a step back, to pray for the world, for the spread of the Faith. It was in this environment that some could receive instruction and others could think and put into words many theological concepts that would find acceptance in the early Councils of the Church.

In our prayers: thanks for the life, example and intercession of Saint Pachomius; for more vocations to the religious life; for those on retreat; for those who study and teach in monasteries and religious communities.

Saint Pachomius, pray for us, and for all desert dwellers.

May 10　Saint John of Avila

John was a law student, and then a student of philosophy and theo-logy. He was ordained in 1525. John earned a reputation as a preacher and teacher in southern Spain where he helped to restore the Faith. His long letters give us a flavour of what must have been a well-earned reputation. He died in 1567 and was canonized in 1970.

'For it will be as when a man going on a journey called his servants and entrusted to them his property; to one he gave five talents, to another, two, to another, one, to each according to his ability.' (Matthew 25.14,15)
In the fullness of his knowledge the Lord distinguished them and appointed them different ways; some of them he blessed and exalted and some of them he made holy and brought near to himself. (Sirach 33.11,12)

Where the Faith has suffered from paganism, suffered from lapses by bishops, clergy and laity, Christ himself has suffered again. The opportunity to re-evangelize was given to John and many others. They had to discover hints of the old Faith, a desire for the Faith, a yearning for the Faith, and work in those little side streets into the hearts of the people. They had to engender an excitement, a thrill, a joy at the sound of the gospel of Resurrection and the saving of mankind among those who had never known or inherited knowledge of the Lord. They had to refute error. Would the landscape of our hearts remind John of southern Spain? How are our enthusiasms for Christ and his Church? Are others easily infected by our enthusiasm? Have we made idols of our desires and placed them upon the altar before Christ in the Most Holy Sacrament?

In our prayers: thanks for the life, example and intercession of Saint John of Avila; for those who instruct and encourage others by the written word; for those who receive the missionary with joy.

Saint John, pray for us, and for those who are sent out to work in other lands.

May 11 Saint Francis Girolamo

Francis was a Jesuit who spent his ministry in the slums of Naples, preaching, teaching and converting. His work was largely among the hospitals, the hostels, and among prisoners and prostitutes, even though all strata of society seemed to be represented at his confessional. Francis trained others for the mission field. He died in 1716 at the age of 74, and was canonized in 1839.

And Jesus said to him, 'Today salvation has come to this house, since he also is a son of Abraham. For the Son of man came to seek and to save the lost.' (Luke 19.9,10)

Imaginations can cope with the picture of the squalor, vice and hopelessness. Indeed, similar slums are everywhere to this very day, and require either our direct help or help through the many good Catholic charities. We can so easily look in disparagement at those who, perhaps through poverty, perhaps not, live lewd and immoral lives because we can show that our paintwork is cleaner and our immorality better disguised. More commonly, even if our lives are relatively 'good' our hearts, minds and tongues are often open sewers of deceit, dishonesty, of malice, of envy and jealousy, of covetousness, of adulterous thoughts, of blasphemy, of callousness, of reflections of every sin of the Naples slums known to Francis.

In our prayers: thanks for the life, example and intercession of Saint Francis Girolamo; for the authorities and officials responsible for slums and deprived areas; for those who live in slums.

Saint Francis, pray for us, and for all institutions that care for the less fortunate.

❧

May 12 Saint Nereus and Saint Achilleus *(Martyrs)*

Nereus and Achilleus were second-century martyrs. They were of the Praetorian Guard and, inevitably, persecutors of Christians. They were converted and professed Christ, leaving their duties and the army. They were caught and beheaded.

'Or what woman, having ten silver coins, if she loses one coin, does not light a lamp and sweep the house and seek diligently until she finds it? And when she has found it, she calls together her friends and neighbours, saying, "Rejoice with me, for I have found the coin which I had lost." Just so, I tell you, there is joy before the angels of God over one sinner who repents.' (Luke 15.8–10)

Here are two martyrs who, together, prepared themselves for a Christian future. They were wise enough to agree that they should first leave the Roman army. Were they able to purchase their discharge? Perhaps they were not. Many were martyred for confessing the Faith in uniform, and the preludes to their deaths were often more terrible. Did they simply abandon their posts, as Matthew did his seat of custom? Life as a Christian in this period was dangerous whatever one's occupation. Nereus and Achilleus had reasoned together, had reached conclusions, had been assisted by other Christians. They had committed themselves to the Faith and had decided that they would exercise their

126

Christianity elsewhere. Their commitment is the important feature of their conversion: they knew what they had to do. But was it in their martyrdom that the strength of their witness lay?

In our prayers: for men and women who live in fear in totalitarian regimes.

Saint Nereus and Saint Achilleus, pray for us, and for all those who suffer at the hands of others.

May 13 Saint Andrew Fournet of Maillé *(Founder)*
(Also today, Our Lady of Fatima.)

Andrew was born in 1752, a pleasure-seeker, lazy in his youth and adolescence, who seemed to do nothing worthy for the first 20 years of his life. In 1776, under the influence of his uncle, he was transformed and was ordained priest. He was a generous almsgiver and his preaching was much sought after. Andrew found relative safety in Spain during the French Revolution, but was pursued by agents of the state as he had refused the oath demanded of him and all priests. On his return, he founded the Daughters of the Cross. Andrew died in 1834 and was canonized in 1933.

'If a man has a hundred sheep, and one of them has gone astray, does he not leave the ninety-nine on the hills and go in search of the one that went astray?' (Matthew 18.10–12)

It is odd that the failings of others should be of comfort to us. In this case it is a positive reaction we have, because we see hope for our present state. (In other cases we might, less honourably, gloat over people's naughtiness and see that ours compares quite favourably!) Indeed, as there is joy in heaven at a conversion, we too must rejoice. Andrew's life was a life of repentance, of turning to Christ, of changing, of realigning his sights, of rejecting certain aspects of his life that gave him transitory pleasure and short-lived gratification. Andrew shows us that we must constantly examine ourselves and begin to rid ourselves of what idols we have made to stand on the altar.

In our prayers: thanks for the life, example and intercession of Saint Andrew Fournet of Maillé; for those who need help to extricate themselves from lives of crime; for all work of rehabilitation.

Saint Andrew, pray for us, for all young people and for the work of the Daughters of the Cross.

༼༺✤༻༽

May 14   Saint Matthias *(Apostle)*

Matthias was chosen as the twelfth apostle, to replace Judas Iscariot. It is clear that Matthias was one of Our Lord's disciples during the whole of his ministry. It is thought that he was crucified.

'So one of the men who have accompanied us during all the time that the Lord Jesus went in and out among us, beginning from the baptism of John until the day when he was taken up from us – one of these men must become with us a witness to his resurrection.' And they put forward two; Joseph called Barsabbas, who was surnamed Justus, and Matthias. And . . . the lot fell on Matthias, and he was enrolled with the eleven apostles. (Acts 1.21–26)

What a mixture of emotions would have been experienced by Matthias! First, he is preferred to Joseph Barsabbas (and that would have done something for the ego), second, he joins the special group, the 12 (he had probably been one of the 70 disciples sent out on a missionary journey by our Lord), and, third, he steps into the place vacated by the traitor, Judas (would he always be known simply for the notoriety of his predecessor?). Our position in the great scheme of things is always dependent upon what went before and who went before. We learn by their experiences and failings. We are given our vocation, and the talents with which to achieve success in that vocation, together with our handicaps. Handicaps may be congenital, of our own making or caused by the position in which we find ourselves. If the fulfilment of our duty is the aim of our lives we are halfway towards overcoming the difficulties that lie in between.

In our prayers: thanks for the life, example and intercession of Saint Matthias; for those who strive to overcome their handicaps in order to fulfil their vocations; for those who are overwhelmed by their difficulties and for those who counsel them.

Saint Matthias, pray for us, and for the faithful workers in the Church.

May 15   Saint Isidore the Farmer

Isidore was a peasant farmer in Madrid, who carried out his work prayerfully and visited the church daily. His life was simple and good – he loved nature, God's handiwork, his wife and his fellow man. Isidore died in 1130 and was canonized in 1622.

Blessed is every one who fears the Lord, and walks in his ways! You shall eat the fruit of the labours of your hands; you shall be happy, and it shall be well with you. (Psalm 128[127].1,2)

Can we imagine anything more perfect? We hardly need anything further from Isidore. His signpost lists: prayerful simplicity, gentleness, generosity and gratefulness. And that largely sums up a Christian way of life. Is there room for anything else? Is there room for selfishness? Is there room for making idols of our desires and pleasures? If there is no room for these things, perhaps Isidore gives us a clue.

In our prayers: thanks for the life, example and intercession of Saint Isidore the Farmer; for those who are distracted by transitory pleasures.

Saint Isidore, pray for us, for farmers and for the civil authorities and citizens of Madrid.

May 16   Saint Alexander of Caesarea *(Bishop and Martyr)*

Alexander, at first a pagan, was converted to the Faith, trained at Alexandria, made Bishop of Cappadocia, then of Jerusalem. He founded a school where converts were taught the rudiments of the Faith. Alexander died in chains for his faith in about 250.

Give to the Most High as he has given and as generously as your hand has found. For the Lord is the one who repays, and he will repay you sevenfold. (Sirach 35.10,11)

Alexander's example was one of steady progress, learning as he travelled through life. On the way he saw the urgent need to cater for those newly converted, to ensure that they were well schooled in the gospel and the traditions of the Faith. The custom of learning and of seeking further knowledge after conversion is well established today, then, the matter was potentially far more perilous. Alexander ended his valuable witness in prison, where, no doubt, he gave succour to his fellow prisoners before he died. If our lives do not quite run the course we have mapped out for ourselves, do we become disgruntled and disaffected? Do we give comfort to others in our chains?

In our prayers: thanks for the life, example and intercession of Saint Alexander of Caesarea; for all catechists, for those newly converted to the Faith; for the imprisoned.

Saint Alexander, pray for us, and for all bishops of the Middle East.

May 17 Saint Paschal Baylon

Paschal was a shepherd who, at the age of 21, entered the reformed Franciscan house of Saint Peter Alcántara (October 19). He led an honest and blameless life of prayer. He paid close attention at Mass and his serving was meticulous. He was highly thought of by his fellow brethren for his care for the poor who called at the friary. Paschal died in 1592 and was canonized in 1690.

I give thanks, O Lord, with my whole heart . . . I bow down toward thy holy temple and give thanks to thy name for thy steadfast love and thy faithfulness; for thou hast exalted above everything thy name and thy word. (Psalm 138[137].1,2)

We can imagine Paschal's day at the friary. Perhaps we are envious of his easy way, his simple devotion, his attention to detail at Mass, his patience with those who knock at the door. He is a willing servant. Brother John is sick, would Paschal serve at the low Mass and then look after John? Of course! Simplicity and straightforwardness may not sit comfortably in our modern busy lives but they are worth cultivating and practising if we lack them.

In our prayers: thanks for the life, example and intercession of Saint Paschal Baylon; for the simple men and women who serve faithfully; for church servers and those responsible for them.

Saint Paschal, pray for us, for all lay brothers and for those who serve at the altar.

May 18   Saint Felix of Cantalice

Felix was another peasant farmer – a shepherd and ploughman, who decided to be a Capuchin lay brother. He was sent to Rome in 1548 where he begged for the friary for 40 years. Felix was ascetic in temperament and noted for his thorough goodness. He died in 1587 and was canonized in 1712.

Do not rob the poor, because he is poor, or crush the afflicted at the gate; for the Lord will plead their cause and despoil of life those who would despoil them. (Proverbs 22.22,23)

A single-minded man who responded to God's call to perform a specific task, Felix led a life of frugality in keeping with the character of the friary and was content to remain as a simple beggar for many years. The income of such a friary was largely drawn from unsolicited gifts and from begging. A religious beggar gave devoted service to his friary; his life was his offering. Felix's ploughing and shepherding were now applied to his public, who were the source of support for the friary and the recipients of his good rustic wisdom and humour. Is this openness possible for us? Christ will always be able to shine radiantly from such a face, from such a person.

In our prayers: thanks for the life, example and intercession of Saint Felix of Cantalice; for those who beg for others and those who beg for themselves.

Saint Felix, pray for us, for farmers, shepherds and for friars.

May 19   Saint Dunstan *(Bishop)*

Dunstan was appointed Abbot of Glastonbury in 943 and became, successively, Bishop of Worcester and Bishop of London. In 960 Dunstan became Archbishop of Canterbury. Despite his high rank, Dunstan was known for his pastoral work and for his hobbies of metalwork, painting and music. He died in 988.

I will feed them with good pasture, and upon the mountain heights of Israel shall be their pasture; there they shall lie down in good grazing land, and on fat pasture they shall feed on the mountains of Israel. (Ezekiel 34.14)

Dunstan was a man of some importance who never overlooked the fact that a bishop is a pastor, a shepherd. He cared personally for those of his flock, despite his elevated standing, who lived in the lowly dwellings clustered about his cathedrals. His interests and skills extended to the crafts of the ordinary as well as of the cultured. The appreciation of these arts shows Dunstan's passion for the Creator's work and for the talents he gives to us. Contemplation of the beauty of sacred art and music allows us to glimpse and, perhaps, understand a little of God's creative power.

In our prayers: thanks for the life, example and intercession of Saint Dunstan; for all men and women who honour God with the work of their hands; for the bishops of England, Scotland and Wales.

Saint Dunstan, pray for us, for jewellers, locksmiths, and artists of all kinds.

May 20   Saint Bernardino of Siena

Bernardino was born in 1380 in Siena. As a Franciscan he was ordained in 1404 and gave himself to study until 1417 when he began his life of preaching in Lombardy, Milan and Naples. Bernardino was a good actor, which skill he employed in his open-air preaching. He wrote many learned theological works. He died in 1444 and was canonized in 1450.

'The Pharisee stood and prayed thus with himself, "God, I thank thee that I am not like other men, extortioners, unjust, adulterers – or even like this tax collector . . . "' (Luke 18.10,11)

Bernardino's acting was a successful and popular means by which he was able to deliver sound and orthodox teaching to those who gathered to hear him in the public places. He was no street-corner preacher of little learning: Bernardino had a fine theological mind. Acting can sugar the pill for the reluctant pupil, the reluctant listener. Hand in hand with this ability is always a sense of humour. Bernardino saw in the Gospels evidence of our Lord's ability to act and to be enormously funny. His parables sometimes invite laughter. Sometimes they would invite comment and even cries of 'Rubbish!' from his audience, so he would be able to say to them with a smile, 'Exactly, so if you would not act in that way, why do you do so when it is even more important that you don't?' Following the Master can involve many surprising things. How much more of the Gospels do we overlook?

In our prayers: thanks for the life, example and intercession of Saint Bernardino of Siena; for all preachers; for Franciscans and Dominicans; for all who work in the theatre, and in film and television studios.

Saint Bernardino, pray for us, and for all actors and comedians.

May 21   Saint Godric of Finchale

Godric was a pedlar, and of Norfolk stock, who travelled widely in England, Scotland and the Holy Land. He ended his wanderings in Finchale on the Wear in about 1110, and settled there as a hermit until his death in 1170 at the age of 100. He latterly lived under a Rule and was 'adopted' by the Cistercians. His life was austere and one of private contemplation, but he produced poems and verse set to music.

Preserve me, O God, for in thee I take refuge. I say to the Lord, 'Thou art my Lord; I have no good apart from thee.' As for the saints of the land, they are the noble, in whom is all my delight. (Psalm 16[15].1–3)

What a curious life – a door-to-door salesman in Scotland and in England, a seller of artefacts to the tourists in the Holy Land! During these early years Godric would have gathered priceless experience of people and the ways of mankind. There was more than enough to feed his mind for decades. His subsequent ordered and ascetic life produced the fruits of his meditation – his poetry, prayer and verse. Godric was a simple man who wrote in his clear and unmannered style from the heart. He was attended by many, subject always to the prior's permission, and became known for his simple wisdom. He was ever conscious of his own shortcomings; nevertheless, he enjoyed recounting the extraordinary stories from his past. He developed a firm devotion to Our Lady, whom he saw as someone who could draw him nearer to God if he kept her before him in his meditation.

In our prayers: thanks for the life, example and intercession of Saint Godric of Finchale; for poets and songwriters.

Holy Mary, Virgin Dame,
Mother of Jesu (the Christ of God, his Lamb)
Take, shield and do thy servant bring
To thee where Christ is King.
Our Lady, Maiden, Springtime's Flower,
Deliver me from this hour. (From a prayer by Saint Godric)
Saint Godric, pray for us, and for all poets and songsters.

May 22   Saint Rita of Cascia

Rita, born in 1377, suffered an unhappy marriage. On being widowed, she became an Augustinian nun after three requests for admission. She was known particularly for her gentle care of the sick and elderly in the convent. Rita died in 1457 and was canonized in 1900.

'. . . *and there was a widow in that city who kept coming to him and saying, "Vindicate me against my adversary." For a while he refused; but afterwards he said to himself, ". . . I will vindicate her, or she will wear me out by her continual coming."' (Luke 18.2–5)*

Being compelled to ask for something time and again is, of course, a test of our resolve. Rita saw that her future lay in the convent where she would use the bedside manner she had already acquired visiting the sick. She had achieved all she could in her early life, dutifully remaining faithful in an unhappy house. Released from further obligation she then knew that she had served her apprenticeship and was told, no. She asked again and was told, no. For a third time Rita begged the abbess for admission and her perseverance and importunity were rewarded. Are we ever as anxious to perform good works?

In our prayers: thanks for the life, example and intercession of Saint Rita of Cascia; for the men and women who dedicate themselves to good works; for abbesses, prioresses and superiors.

Saint Rita, pray for us, and for those who persevere.

May 23 Saint John-Baptist Rossi

John-Baptist was born near Genoa in 1698. At 13 he attended the Roman College but succumbed to epilepsy. However, he was ordained in 1721. For the rest of his life he spent time visiting and teaching the poor, the homeless, beggars and prostitutes. John-Baptist was known for his quiet counsel in the confessional, and penitents were many. He died in 1763 and was canonized in 1881.

Jesus looked up and said to her, 'Woman, where are they? Has no one condemned you?' She said, 'No one, Lord.' And Jesus said, 'Neither do I condemn you; go, and do not sin again.' (John 8.10,11)

As he was subject to seizures and fits, John-Baptist was not destined for the higher ranks in the Church of the eighteenth century. No, he would be a useful man in the less than healthy parts of the city. And so he turned out to be. Like so many saints, he worked among those among whom Jesus often worked – the outcast, the unhealthy in mind, body and morals. As he absolved the penitent he was conscious of his own failures and shortcomings. Our own shortcomings are ever before us in others, but it is much easier to express our distaste for their sin.

In our prayers: thanks for the life, example and intercession of Saint John-Baptist Rossi; for those who constantly fall short of the ideal; for all confessors.

Saint John-Baptist, pray for us, and for all epileptics.

May 24   Saint David of Scotland

David, son of Saint Margaret of Scotland (November 16), reluctantly became King of Scotland in 1124 at the age of 39. He took care to modernize and develop his country. He established many monasteries and bishoprics, and sought firmer links with Rome. David fulfilled his vocation as a good and faithful servant. He died in 1153.

Vindicate me, O Lord, for I have walked in my integrity, and I have trusted in the Lord without wavering. Prove me, O Lord, and try me; test my heart and my mind. For thy steadfast love is before my eyes and I walk in faithfulness to thee. (Psalm 26[25].1–3)

There have been many saintly monarchs in our lands. David lived a holy life in an age when such a thing was certainly no easier than it is today. His work of building for the future stability of the Church in Scotland is noteworthy. Out of all that we do consequences follow. They are not necessarily the consequences we intend or envisage, but that is hardly the point. Do we ever know the intention behind God's call? Furthermore, our duty must be to perform whatever task we are given to the best of our ability, no matter the consequences.

In our prayers: thanks for the life, example and intercession of Saint David of Scotland; for the Scottish people; for Her Majesty the Queen and the Scottish Parliament.

Saint David, pray for us, and for Scotland.

May 25   Saint Bede *(Doctor of the Church)*

Bede was born in 673 and spent his whole life – from the age of seven – in the monastery of Wearmouth, and abbey of Jarrow. He was a prolific writer and a fine teacher. Indeed, Bede occupied his time in these pursuits and in studying the Scriptures. Much of his work is extant and known to us. Bede died in 735.

One generation shall laud thy works to another, and shall declare thy mighty acts. On the glorious splendour of thy majesty, and on thy wondrous works, I will meditate. Men shall proclaim the might of thy terrible acts, and I will declare thy greatness. They shall pour forth the fame of thy abundant goodness, and shall sing aloud of thy righteousness. (Psalm 145[144].4–7)

Bede's life of study, teaching and writing gave the Church and society a lasting legacy of piety and information. Against Bede's histories we can assess the subsequent centuries, their culture, their Faith and their men. His life was devoted to these things, to looking back at our country's experiences in order to apprise the present and the future of the wrongdoing and the blind alleys so readily taken in ignorance, for pleasure or for personal gain. As he worked he lived the life of an exemplary monk.

In our prayers: thanks for the life, example and intercession of Saint Bede; for those who show us how to learn from experience; for scholars and teachers.

Be thou our joy and strong defence,
Who art our future recompense:
So shall the light that springs from thee
Be ours through all eternity.
O Risen Christ, ascended Lord,
All praise to thee let earth accord,
Who art, while endless ages run,
With Father and with Spirit, One. (Saint Bede, trans. B. Webb)
Saint Bede, pray for us, for writers, historians and those who study diligently.

May 26   Saint Philip Neri *(Founder)*

Before he left for Rome at 18, Philip had travelled to Monte Cassino to learn something of the life of contemplation and solitude. In Rome he studied and lived on a meagre diet. He was ordained in 1551, and formed the core of the Congregation of the Oratory, with friends and companions. Philip's compelling personality, good counsel and ready wit were great attractions, and no one was refused admission, whether highborn or low. After study of the Scriptures, or some other worthy book, the group would pray, visit a church or listen to music. The followers were expected to spend time in the lowest and lowliest places and there carry out important charitable work. Philip produced something quite wonderful in the formation of the Oratory, which flourishes throughout the world today. Philip died in 1595 and was canonized in 1622.

I wash my hands in innocence, and go about thy altar, O Lord, singing aloud a song of thanksgiving, and telling all thy wondrous deeds. (Psalm 26[25].6,7)
The Lord is my light and my salvation; whom shall I fear? I will offer in his tent sacrifices with shouts of joy; I will sing and make melody to the Lord. (Psalm 27[26].1a,6)

Philip's personality was a great gift, which he used in the service of the Church to good effect. Philip gives us a sharp nudge in the right direction and it is the direction of one's life that must be established first. Gifts are given to us to be employed in the execution of our duties along the way, wisely and not self-indulgently. Philip's life and work and that of the Oratorians embraced the entirety of God's magnificent creation in joy and love. Do we?

In our prayers: thanks for the life, example and intercession of Saint Philip Neri; for those who live in the lowliest places; for artists and architects; for the priests and brethren of the Oratory.

Saint Philip, pray for us, and for all congregations of the Oratory throughout the world.

May 27 Saint Augustine of Canterbury *(Bishop and Apostle of England)*

In 597, Augustine, with his companions, was despatched to England by Pope Gregory the Great (September 3). He successfully evangelized the south of England having established his See at Canterbury. Augustine created a firm base from which, in subsequent years, the

Faith would spread north, the British pagans would be converted, and the British Christians would conform themselves to the Holy See. Augustine died in 604.

'Who then is the faithful and wise servant, whom his master has set over his household, to give them their food at the proper time? Blessed is that servant whom his master, when he comes, will find so doing. Truly, I say to you, he will set him over all his possessions . . .' (Matthew 24.45–47)

In only seven years, Augustine had achieved all that was required of him. His diplomacy among existing Christians was remarkable; his evangelical skill among pagan men and women was effective, and won many friends for the Church. Gregory knew Augustine's strengths and that he was a perfect choice for the task. Our Church is Augustine's Church. His diplomacy and evangelism must now be ours. Our lives, in their very different ways, are as important to the life of the Church as was Augustine's. Our vocations are not necessarily the vocations of archbishops, but the way we are called to fulfil them, the same.

In our prayers: thanks for the life, example and intercession of Saint Augustine of Canterbury; for the Catholic Church in England and for all who profess and call themselves Christian.

Saint Augustine, pray for us, and for the people of England.

May 28 Saint Germanus of Paris

Germanus was born in 500, or thereabouts. As Bishop of Paris, Germanus did much to encourage the honouring of the saints. He was justly noted for his own sanctity throughout his life. He was also something of a healer, offering comfort and cures for the blind, paralytics and epileptics. He died in 576.

'. . . Whenever you enter a town and they receive you, eat what is set before you; heal the sick in it and say to them, "The Kingdom of God has come near to you" . . .' (Luke 10.8,9)

The holy men and women, as we see day by day throughout the year, are all pointing us towards heaven. Their methods and their routes vary, and may not be suitable for all of us. However, each is able to show something of benefit to us from his or her life, a life that was lived on earth as though in heaven. Germanus's path is clear. Of course, he was a holy man, which means that the manner of his living was holy. He was a good bishop who was at pains to point to the saints as models for the Christian. He was a successful healer and comforter of the sick. Some of us are indeed called to cure the sick, but surely all of us are called to comfort them. We are also called to point others to the merits of the saints, and to be holy ourselves.

In our prayers: thanks for the life, example and intercession of Saint Germanus of Paris; for all healers and comforters of the sick and dying; for all disabled men, women and children.

Saint Germanus, pray for us, for all the citizens of Paris and for those who suffer from failing sight and for those who are blind.

May 29   Saint Maximinus of Trier *(Bishop)*

Maximinus became Bishop of Trier in 333. He was an outspoken champion of orthodoxy and champion of those who suffered under the scourge of Arian heresy that denied the divinity of Christ, during the fourth century. For two years he housed and protected Saint Athanasius (May 2). Maximinus died in 347.

When many days had passed, the Jews plotted to kill him, but their plot became known to Saul. They were watching the gates day and night, to kill him; but his disciples took him by night and let him down over the wall, lowering him in a basket. (Acts 9.23–25)

Being an outspoken champion of orthodoxy was often not a particularly comfortable or safe pursuit in the developing Church in the fourth century. The efforts of men such as Maximinus and Athanasius, by their stance and teaching, wrestled the Church away from the followers of Arianism, and eventually the Nicene Creed was re-established as the true statement of belief. The Church throughout these difficult periods emerged the stronger and more secure for all its bitter arguments. It seems to have been a necessary process and one we reflect upon as we read the works of these holy men. We still learn from a study of these disputes and they make us surer in our orthodoxy.

In our prayers: thanks for the life, example and intercession of Saint Maximinus of Trier; for those who stray from the Church's teaching; for His Holiness the Pope, his Cardinals, Archbishops and Bishops.

Saint Maximinus, pray for us, and for all who suffer for their orthodoxy.

⟨❀❉❀⟩

May 30 Saint Hubert of Liège *(Bishop)*

After the murder of Saint Lambert (September 17), Bishop of Maastricht, Hubert replaced him and moved the seat of the diocese to Liège, taking his predecessor's relics with him. He was a devout and ardent worker for the Church. Hubert was believed to have experienced a vision of the crucifix between the antlers of a stag. For this reason, he became the patron of hunters and those in country pursuits. Hubert died in 727.

Make a joyful noise to the Lord, all the earth! Serve the Lord with gladness! Come into his presence with singing! Know that the Lord is God! It is he that made us, and we are his people, and the sheep of his pasture. (Psalm 100[99].1–3)

There are other saints who are recorded as having experienced such a vision. Certainly an optical illusion of this sort is perfectly feasible when the stag's head assumes a particular attitude. Being reminded of Christ's Passion and death, whether by antlers, other objects in our daily life or, more especially, by the crucifix we are likely to have in our halls, bedrooms and studies, can give us a useful jolt when our minds have strayed into unholy territory or when we simply need to re-focus upon the work in hand. Relics too are an important aid in associating ourselves with the lives of the holy men and women through all ages as they intercede for the souls of the departed and for us. Our Christianity touches those who walked with Our Lord and those who died during the persecution afterwards. The relics sealed in every altar connect us in a holy web of faith to those secret Masses on the tombs of the faithful martyrs in the catacombs.

In our prayers: thanks for the life, example and intercession of Saint Hubert of Liège; for all who work on the land; for all landowners.

Saint Hubert, pray for us, and for all who enjoy country pursuits.

૯**ૐ**ૐ

May 31   The Visitation of Our Lady

When Our Lady visited her cousin in Judea, Elizabeth's unborn child kicked and brought home to her the incredible things that had already taken place. The greeting of the two women is not difficult to imagine. As soon as their stories had been exchanged, Elizabeth declared, 'Blessed are you among women and blessed is the fruit of your womb!' She might have continued, 'Blessed are you for hearing the word, for responding to God in a selfless way, for being the Mother of my Lord.'

My soul magnifies the Lord, and my spirit rejoices in God my Saviour, for he has regarded the low estate of his handmaiden. For behold, henceforth all generations will call me blessed; for he who is mighty has done great things for me, and holy is his name. (Luke 1.46–49)

The Visitation is the subject of almost as much art as the Annunciation, perhaps. The embrace of the two women, one the mother of the last of the Old Testament prophets, the forerunner, the preparer, and the first of the New Testament saints, marks the fusion of the two eras. Elizabeth's greeting is our daily greeting to Mary. The fruit of her womb is God's Word made flesh, who, as man, would conquer sin and death once and for all; God's Word made flesh, God's only-begotten Son, God from God, of one substance with the Father, born of Mary, the Mother of God.

In our prayers: thanks for the life, example and intercession of Our Blessed Lady; for friends and relatives.

Hail, holy Queen, Mother of mercy, hail, our life, our sweetness and our hope. To thee do we cry, poor banished children of Eve; to thee do we send up our sighs mourning and weeping in this vale of tears. Turn then, most gracious advocate, thine eyes of mercy towards us; and after this our exile, show unto us the blessed fruit of thy womb, Jesus. O clement, O loving, O sweet Virgin Mary.
Holy Mary, pray for us.

June

Methodius (June 14) was ardent in his belief that icons and images were important aids to honouring the saints, as icons of Our Blessed Lord and crucifixes were in the worship of God. He is the patron of sculptors, and Aloysius Gonzaga (21) is patron of youth. He was but 23 when he died of the plague, having dedicatedly nursed its victims for two years.

༼༅༢༽

June 1   Saint Justin Martyr *(Martyr)*

Justin received a classical Greek education and upbringing. He was well versed in philosophy of various schools, but his philosophical searches and explorations made sense to Justin only after he was introduced to the Prophets and to Christ. Justin embraced Christianity with enthusiasm. His teaching was founded upon the teaching of the infant Church, which he presented with his orderly and logical mind. He was in his element when debating with the enemies of the Church. Some of his written work is extant. Justin was beheaded for his faith in 165, at the time of Aurelius.

My heart overflows with a goodly theme; I address my verses to the King; my tongue is like the pen of a ready scribe. You are the fairest of the sons of men; grace is poured upon your lips. (Psalm 45[44].1,2)

Justin appears roughly halfway between the birth of Our Lord and the terrors of Diocletian. The infant Church recorded in the Acts of the Apostles had developed and spread. It was under constant attack at the vacillating whim of the Roman authorities, but it never had an easy time; it was either under persecution or threat of persecution. The Church strengthened by the day, by the hour. And by the first quarter of the fourth century it had slowly but surely spread west through Greece

143

to pockets in Italy, Spain, in southern France, even London and York. Under the Edict of Milan in 313, Constantine granted liberty of worship to Christians. This was some time in the future. Justin's dedicated work was undertaken at a pivotal time: he was one of the learned men who tested and proved argument about the direction and faith of the early Church. It was upon his work and the work of others that the long process of securing orthodoxy and unifying the formulae of belief began.

In our prayers: thanks for the life, example and intercession of Saint Justin Martyr; for all persecutors of Christians; for those who write and lecture on theology.

Saint Justin, pray for us, and for all philosophers that they might glimpse the truth of Christ.

June 2 Saint Marcellinus and Saint Peter *(Martyrs)*

Marcellinus and Peter were, as so many were, victims of the persecutions instigated in the reign of Diocletian. They were in Holy Orders and were imprisoned for professing the Faith. Their ministry did not end there, however, because they converted many in prison. Marcellinus and Peter were beheaded in 304.

O come, let us worship and bow down, let us kneel before the Lord, our Maker, for he is our God, and we are the people of his pasture, and the sheep of his hand. (Psalm 95[94].6,7)

Towards the end of the period mentioned yesterday, we are given Marcellinus and Peter, as martyred priests. They exercised their ministry in dangerous times to a determined and courageous flock, giving the Church the inbuilt strength and tradition of steadfastness that would stand her in good stead in the future when different circumstances would give rise to different forms of attack. So, filled with enthusiasm for the Faith, Marcellinus and Peter treated their imprisonment in the way a priest would treat a pastoral transfer from one parish to another, in this day and age. Their fellow prisoners were their flock, their fellow citizens to whom they had the same priestly duty as those under their care elsewhere. How well does our faith travel with our changes in circumstances?

In our prayers: thanks for the lives, examples and intercession of Saint Marcellinus and Saint Peter; for those who have lost faith through the difficulties they have faced; for those who give wise counsel to their fellow prisoners.

Saint Marcellinus and Saint Peter, pray for us, and for all political and religious prisoners.

᙭

June 3 Saint Charles Lwanga, Saint Joseph Mkasa and Companions *(Martyrs)*

Charles was the page-master to the King of Baganda in southern Uganda, who was burnt naked on a pyre along with four newly baptized boys on Ascension Day 1886. Joseph, a catechist, was Charles's predecessor and had been beheaded in 1885 for criticizing the king for the murder of an Anglican bishop. These men were among the first fruits of the first Catholic mission to Uganda. On this day all martyrs of the missions are commemorated. They were canonized in 1969.

Who shall separate us from the love of Christ? Shall tribulation, or distress, or persecution, or famine, or nakedness, or peril, or sword? As it is written, 'For thy sake we are being killed all the day long; we are regarded as sheep to be slaughtered.' For I am sure that neither death nor life . . . nor anything else in all creation, will be able to separate us from the love of God in Christ Jesus our Lord. (Romans 8.35,36,38a)

It never ceases to surprise us that so many forms of torture and killing have been found for the punishment and disposal of Christians. That the Christian Faith should engender such venom in others is difficult to fathom. Did the Christians appear arrogant? Surely not! Were the 'authorities' frightened of the consequences of the spread of the Faith? Possibly. Did they hate to be challenged by something new and seemingly rather odd, something that talked of love for enemies, forgiveness of sins, new birth in the man who seemed to have died? Undoubtedly. Here in Uganda the missionaries were late in coming. Protestant and Catholic workers collected their martyrs in abundance, and here, in this story, among the faithful were Ugandans, whose eyes had shone with the newly discovered joy in Christ, unwilling to relinquish their new faith for the sake of a painful journey from this world. God give us this faith.

In our prayers: thanks for the lives, examples and intercession of Saint Charles Lwanga, Saint Joseph Mkasa and their Holy Companions; for those who are sorely tested when new to the Faith; for all secular authorities and governments in Africa.

Saint Charles, Saint Joseph and Holy Companions, pray for us, and pray for Uganda.

⁕

June 4   Saint Francis Caracciolo *(Founder)*

Francis, born in southern Italy and a remote relative of Saint Thomas Aquinas (January 28), was the founder of the Minor Clerks Regular, devoted to serving others in hospitals, prisons, and as missionaries. The Order lived in poverty. Francis began a tradition in the Order that each member should daily spend an hour in adoration before the Blessed Sacrament. Francis died in 1608 at the age of 45. He was canonized in 1807.

'I was naked and you clothed me, I was sick and you visited me, I was in prison and you came to me'. 'When did we see thee sick or in prison and visit thee?' 'Truly, I say to you, as you did it to one of the least of these my brethren, you did it to me.' (Matthew 25.36,38,39)

Throughout the world there are many small cells of religious devoted to this work; there are many secular societies that perform the much needed duties of taking food to patients and settling their short-term affairs of business. Even if only the material need is alleviated, it is, of course, still a good work. However, one of the worthy examples given to us by Francis is his ardent preparation for his work each day before the Blessed Sacrament. Our Lord is there most surely: it is one of his most strengthening gifts. Sadly, we tend to take it for granted. It is a habit we should resume, or begin, when we have the opportunity. If a daily visit is impossible, we can, at the very least, adopt the principal purpose of Francis's visits to the Blessed Sacrament – his desire to prepare himself properly for the day ahead. Daily we ought to ask for the Father's daily guidance, Christ's blessing on the people we are to meet, and the Holy Spirit's power to persevere. If our work is always placed in God's hands in this way . . .

In our prayers: thanks for the life, example and intercession of Saint Francis Caracciolo; for a greater devotion to the Blessed Sacrament.

O God, who in the wonderful Holy Sacrament hast left us a memorial of thy Passion; grant us, we beseech thee, so to venerate the sacred mysteries of thy Body and Blood, that we may ever feel within ourselves the fruit of thy redemption. Who livest and reignest, for ever and ever. Amen.
Saint Francis, pray for us, and for a greater devotion to the Blessed Sacrament among the faithful.

June 5 Saint Boniface *(Bishop and Martyr)*

Boniface was educated in Exeter and became a monk at Nursling in Hampshire. He left in 722 to preach the gospel to the Germans. In 722 he was made bishop and he founded many dioceses and monasteries. Boniface became primate of Germany. He was murdered in Friesland in 754 when in his seventies.

The righteous man perishes, and no one lays it to heart; devout men are taken away, while no one understands. For the righteous man is taken away from calamity, he enters into peace; they rest in their beds who walk in their uprightness. (Isaiah 57.1,2)

Boniface's martyrdom is, perhaps, unexpected. We can trace his career in the Church without difficulty and a summary of it reads well – the life of a most illustrious monk, the rise of a fine bishop. He was clearly an effective evangelist, a good administrator and leader of men. He returned at the end of his life to his first work, his first love – that of the conversion of the warlike tribes of Friesland, many of which had not been sustained in the Faith. There he was martyred as a very old man. The Bridegroom came when and in the manner, we might suppose, Boniface was not expecting. But Boniface's faith was such that throughout his life he had daily prepared for what that day would bring him. He knew the joys of conversion and the dangers that could accompany confrontations with pagan tribes. Both these things Boniface would have placed before God at the beginning of the day during an early Office: he prepared himself for a long, steady journey through life in the service of the Church. With daily devotion, regular receipt of the Blessed Sacrament and the sacrament of Penitence, Penance and Absolution, we are ready should the Bridegroom arrive unexpectedly and without warning.

In our prayers: thanks for the life, example and intercession of Saint Boniface; for the self-discipline to submit to a daily Rule.

O Jesus Christ, just and merciful Lord of the living and dead, before whom we must appear one day to give an exact account of our lives. Enlighten me and give me a humble and contrite heart, that I may recognize my sin and judge myself now so that then thou may judge me with loving kindness and mercy.
Saint Boniface, pray for us, and for all German people.

June 6   Saint Norbert *(Bishop and Founder)*

Norbert was born in 1080. In his youth he enjoyed good living, and was keen to advance in society. In 1115, after a sudden conversion, he was ordained priest and became a peripatetic preacher. He founded the Order of the Premonstratensian Canons and was made Bishop of Magdeburg, where he invited opposition by reforming the dishonest and lazy clergy of the diocese. Norbert died in 1134 and was canonized in 1582.

And when Jesus came to the place, he looked up and said to him, 'Zacchaeus, make haste and come down; for I must stay at your home today.' So he made haste and came down, and received him joyfully. (Luke 19.5,6)

Many of our saints began life in a less than holy manner. We can make good use of our early experiences, whatever they were. (It may be that Norbert, knowing well the ways of the lazy and the dishonest man, was the ideal person for the recovery of Magdeburg.) When we live lives of self-indulgence and transitory pleasure, we know instinctively that we are wasting our time. We try to obscure this realization with even greater self-indulgence, while all the time our eyes tell a different story – a yearning for goodness, for Christ, for us to have the strength to withdraw ourselves from the slavery of sin.

In our prayers: thanks for the life, example and intercession of Saint Norbert; for the victims of selfish living and self-indulgence.

Saint Norbert, pray for us, and for all preachers and teachers of the Faith.

❦

June 7 Saint Willibald *(Bishop)*

Willibald was the nephew of Saint Boniface (June 5), who made a ten-year pilgrimage to the Holy Land, and who spent another ten at Monte Cassino. Willibald placed himself under the care of his uncle and was ordained priest. He became Bishop of Eichstäff in 742, where he remained for 45 years. He founded a double monastery and, as a truly pastoral bishop, was especially concerned with his flock's spiritual needs. Willibald died in 786.

The Lord is my shepherd, I shall not want, he makes me lie down in green pastures. He leads me beside still waters; he restores my soul. He leads me in paths of righteousness for his name's sake. (Psalm 23[22].1–3)

As an exemplary bishop, Willibald gives us an idea of the psalmist's view of God. We are in God's hands as sheep in the hands of the shepherd who cares for them and brings them home. Willibald performed these duties within his diocese, single-mindedly guiding his flock to Christ and to the heavenly banquet. Like Willibald, we endeavour to place our feet in the steps of the Apostles and all the saints so that we can conform ourselves to Christ, and then show him to others by the way we live.

In our prayers: thanks for the life, example and intercession of Saint Willibald; for all faithful pastors.

Saint Willbald, pray for us, and for all who labour painstakingly.

❦

June 8 Saint Médard *(Bishop)*

Médard was not ordained until he was in his early thirties. In his old age he was made Bishop of Saint-Quentin in northern France, where he had lived since his youth. Médard confined his work to that which he knew best, to that which had occupied him since ordination – preaching and converting the heathen. He died in 560.

Come, bless the Lord, all you servants of the Lord, who stand by night in the house of the Lord! Lift up your hand to the holy place, and bless the Lord! (Psalm 134[133].1,2)
The earth has yielded its increase; God, our God, has blessed us. God has blessed us; let all the ends of the earth fear him! (Psalm 67[66].6,7)

A life of spreading the gospel to those who do not know Christ is truly living the gospel. Generally speaking, unless this is our vocation, our efforts are unlikely to be as concentrated and concentrating as Médard's. For us, our duty is to live our daily life in such a manner as to show those who do not know Christ a glimpse of him in the way we act, respond, love, laugh and live. He will surely be visible in our eyes, in our face. But we cannot fulfil this calling by affectation and by a mannered and studied 'holiness': those are the attributes of the Pharisee.

In our prayers: thanks for the life, example and intercession of Saint Médard; for the people of northern France; for owners of vineyards and their employees.

Saint Médard, pray for us, and for good harvest where care is lavished upon the crop.

June 9 Saint Ephraem the Syrian *(Doctor of the Church)*
(Also today, Saint Columba of Iona [*Abbot*].)

Ephraem was born in Nisibia. He was a poet and preacher, and wrote hymns and canticles to be sung by the choir in church. Over 70 of his hymns are known. He also wrote commentaries on the Scriptures. During a famine, he took charge of the fair distribution of the relief supplies. Ephraem died in the 370s. In 1920 he was declared a Doctor of the Church.

The mind of the wise makes his speech judicious, and adds persuasiveness to his lips. Pleasant words are like a honeycomb, sweetness to the soul and health to the body. (Proverbs 16.23,24)

Psalms, hymns and spiritual songs are an important ingredient in the uplifting of worship. They can convey truths and embody theological dogma; they can explain and elucidate; they can illustrate and picture. And clothed in the melodies of ages, they can even more readily attend the senses. Saint Ephraem's intentions and achievements were all these things: like ours should be, his desire was to worship God appropriately and in a fitting manner.

In our prayers: thanks for the life, example and intercession of Saint Ephraem; for all those who convey the gospel in verse, drama and music.

Receive, O Lord, in heaven above
Our prayers and supplications pure;
Give us a heart all full of love
And steady courage to endure.

The holy name our mouths confess,
Our tongues are harps to praise thy grace;
Forgive our sins and wickedness,
Who in this vigil seek thy face.

Let not our song become a sigh,
A wail of anguish and despair;
In loving-kindness, Lord most high,
Receive this day our daily prayer.

O raise us in that day, that we
May sing, where all thy saints adore,
Praise to thy Father, and to thee,
And to thy Spirit, evermore. Amen.
(Saint Ephraem the Syrian, trans. F.C.B.)

Saint Ephraem, pray for us, and for all church composers and poets.

June 10   Saint Ithamar of Rochester *(Bishop)*

Ithamar was consecrated Bishop of Rochester by Archbishop Honorius of Canterbury. He was acclaimed a saint in the early years on account, it must be surmised, of his evident sanctity while in office. Ithamar died in or around 656.

But as he who called you is holy, be holy yourselves in all your conduct; since it is written, 'You shall be holy, for I am holy.' (1 Peter 1.15,16)

The characteristic of a saintly life is a *holy* life; after all, one is a synonym for the other. A holy life is revealed only by the way in which we live; by our conformation to the will of God; by the manner and diligence in which we perform our God-given vocations. We do not first acquire holiness as we might a new pen and then try to find a use to which it might be put. That is, as we have seen, the affectation of the Pharisee, the problem pointed to by Saint Benedict in his cautioning those who would acquire a *reputation per se* for holiness. We are all able to lead holy lives no matter our calling, but first we concentrate on how we live our lives. There is no need to look constantly in the mirror to see if there are any evident signs of holiness creeping into our features. Ithamar's reputation for holiness was won because he was holy.

In our prayers: thanks for the life, example and intercession of Saint Ithamar of Rochester; for the Church in England and all her separated brethren.

Saint Ithamar, pray for us, and for all those who would be holy.

June 11   Saint Barnabas *(Apostle)*

Barnabas was a Cypriot, generous, and with a sense of humour. Without demur he sold his land and gave the money into the common fund. Barnabas worked alone and on many missionary journeys with Paul. It is believed that he was stoned to death in Salamis around 60.

And when he had come to Jerusalem he [Saul / Paul] attempted to join the disciples; and they were all afraid of him, for they did not believe that he was a disciple. But Barnabas took him, and brought him to the

*apostles, and declared to them how on the road he had seen the Lord
... (Acts 9.26,27)*

Apart from Barnabas's passing on Christ's message to us about the care
of those less fortunate than ourselves, about gifts to reputable charities
and good works, he gives us another salutary lesson. How nervous and
wary are we of the convert and the newcomer? In Paul's case, the appre-
hension came with the knowledge that he had been instrumental in the
imprisonment and death of many Christians. Caution was natural. But
do we join those who cold-shoulder, who ostracize? Do we sidle away
embarrassed, or do we, as the good Barnabas did, see the Christ within
and warmly recommend? How do these attitudes translate in our lives?
Are we peacemakers or murmurers?

**In our prayers: thanks for the life, example and intercession of Saint
Barnabas; for those who make themselves responsible for good relations and harmony.**

*Saint Barnabas, pray for us, for Cyprus, and for those who share their
wealth.*

June 12   Saint Caspar Bertoni *(Founder)*

Caspar was born in 1777 of a wealthy family. Eschewing the traditional profession of the family – that of the law – he was ordained in
1800. He was a preacher of note and founded a religious house of the
Holy Stigmatics (now the Congregation of the Holy Stigmatics of Our
Lord Jesus Christ). For many years he gave spiritual direction from
his sick-bed until he died in 1853. His Order is flourishing. Caspar was
canonized in 1989.

*They have pierced my hands and feet – I can count all my bones – they
stare and gloat over me; they divide my garments among them, and for
my raiment they cast lots. (Psalm 22[21].16b–18)*

The Sacred Wounds of Our Lord are the object and focus of many
prayers and devotional exercises. Meditation upon the Wounds brings
home to us the Mystery of the Passion of Christ, and is able to elevate
our thought and prayer. We can imagine similar wounds present in our

body – some are blessed with the physical marks of these wounds – and we can exercise ourselves in the spirit of humility, reverence and penitence. Our injured feet can take us for no purpose where Christ would not go; our injured hands and wrists can perform no un-Christlike deed; our injured side can ache for none but Christ; our wounded head can entertain no thoughts incompatible with those of Christ.

In our prayers: thanks for the life, example and intercession of Saint Caspar Bertoni; for those who continue to work from their sick-bed.

Soul of Christ, sanctify me;
Body of Christ, save me;
Blood of Christ, inebriate me;
Water from the side of Christ, wash me;
Passion of Christ, strengthen me;
O good Jesu, hear me;
Within thy wounds, hide me;
Suffer me not to be separated from thee;
From the malicious enemy defend me;
In the hour of my death call me
And bid me come to thee
That with thy saints I may praise thee
For ever and ever. Amen.
Saint Caspar, pray for us, and for the work of the Congregation of the
Holy Stigmatics of Our Lord Jesus Christ.

June 13   Saint Antony of Padua *(Doctor of the Church)*

Antony is often shown with the child Jesus, on account of the vision he was granted. He was a Friar Minor, a friend of Saint Francis (October 4) known for his gentle sanctity; acclaimed for his sermons (both delivery and content); known for his love of Creation, of trees, flowers, birds and animals of all kinds. Antony died in 1231, and was canonized shortly afterwards. He was declared Doctor of the Church in 1946.

The wolf shall dwell with the lamb, and the leopard shall lie down with
the kid, and the calf and the lion and the fatling together; and a little
child shall lead them. (Isaiah 11.6–9a)

A number of the saints were known for the love of God's lower creatures; this attraction to his handiwork was much a part of their lives. It is difficult to worship God and to see Christ in our fellows and reveal him to others in isolation from the rest of creation. The world is for our use, our care and attention. We arose out of the swirling gases, and then dust and mud of the earth because God willed it that way. We arose slowly and by degrees with other creatures until the Creator saw his intentions realized and saw that the work was correspondingly full of goodness. Was it at this point he gave our special gift – the gift of immortal soul? Is this for us to know? However superior and more precious to God we are, we are the stewards of the earth and we shall have to account for our treatment of it. Antony draws our attention to the power each one of us has in the care of others and of things. Everything in our field of activity is at some time or other in our care. Where we have power to harm with a deed or with our tongues, we also have the power to do the opposite.

In our prayers: thanks for the life, example and intercession of Saint Antony of Padua; thanks for the joy of all creation.

O Holy Child of Mary, have mercy upon us for our sin against the innocence of the world, against the innocence of children, against the hungry, against the unborn child, against the poor, against the sick, against the old.
Saint Antony, pray for us, and for the poor and hungry of Asia, Africa and South America.

᚛ᚄᚔᚄ᚜

June 14 Saint Methodius of Constantinople (*Patriarch*)

With the revival of Iconoclasm early in the ninth century, Methodius was adamant that statues and icons were essential aids to worship, and that their use sat well within the long tradition of Holy Church. He was twice imprisoned and flogged. The Empress Theodora halted the persecution and Methodius became Patriarch of Constantinople. He died in 847.

[We have decreed] that the brave deeds of the saints be portrayed on tablets and on the walls, and upon the sacred vessels and vestments, as

155

hath been the custom of the holy Catholic Church of God from ancient times . . . (Letter to the Emperor and Empress following the VII Ecumenical Council in 787)

The images of the saints – the statues, the paintings, the icons – and, in particular, the crucifixes, are all good and necessary aids to worship, to devotion, to meditation and contemplation. They are an excellent focus for our thoughts when we need to concentrate and not let our minds wander. We can be drawn into the lives of the saints, to a particular episode in a saint's life, to Our Lady's life and the theology of the Mother of God, to Calvary and on to the Mystery of the Passion, Death and Resurrection, to Bethlehem, by means of the crib, to the Mystery of the Incarnation.

In our prayers: thanks for the life, example and intercession of Saint Methodius of Constantinople; for all artists who fashion aids to worship; for those who prayerfully paint icons.

Saint Methodius, pray for us, and for all who assist us to draw nearer to the holiness of God.

June 15   Saint Edburga of Winchester

Edburga, born in about 920, was the granddaughter of King Alfred the Great and daughter of King Edward the Elder. She entered Nunnaminster in Winchester at an early age. She spent her time in simple life and in quiet and humble works of charity within the convent, and in the streets of Winchester. Edburga died in 960.

'Nothing is covered up that will not be revealed, or hidden that will not be known. Whatever you have said in the dark shall be heard in the light and what you have whispered in private rooms shall be proclaimed upon the housetops . . . And I tell you, every one who acknowledges me before men, the Son of man also will acknowledge before the angels of God . . .' (Luke 12.2,3,8,9)

No act of mercy or generosity performed by Edburga in the slums and hovels of tenth-century Winchester would have gone unnoticed by Our Lord. This high-born nun would carry out her tasks with love and gentleness, anonymously. The poor women would not know who was attending their sores, filling their larders, praying over their ailing children and mopping their brows. Generally, we are, perhaps, less inclined to be anonymous and quiet about our good works. We can be sure that God knows; but how many of our other acts would we hide from him if we could?

In our prayers: thanks for the life, example and intercession of Saint Edburga; for those who rely upon charitable organizations; for all Orders and charities dedicated to feeding the hungry.

Saint Edburga, pray for us, and for all religious Orders dedicated to the sick.

June 16 Saint Tychon of Amathus *(Bishop)*

Tychon was a fifth-century bishop of Cyprus and noted for his holiness and easy way with all classes of his flock. He was of humble stock himself. Tychon has always been much honoured in Cyprus. He was an amateur of the grape and so has become the patron of vinegrowers.

'I am the true vine, and my Father is the vinedresser. Every branch of mine that bears no fruit, he takes away, and every branch that does bear fruit he prunes that it may bear more fruit.' (John 15.1,2)

Tychon's presentation of the gospel was such that his flock paid scant regard to the matter of breeding or wealth; he was able to minister with some success to high-born and low. They recognized Christ in his teaching and in his very being – furthermore, they could enjoy a glass of wine with him. Many of the saints – certainly the secular ones – would have enjoyed a hobby or interest that would engage them in their ministry. In growing vines – not an uncommon activity in fifth-century Cyprus – he was able to use the process most knowledgeably in his preaching and teaching. His hobby became a part of his ministry. The vine is one of the most potent and significant symbols in the Christian gospel.

In our prayers: thanks for the life, example and intercession of Saint Tychon of Amathus; for the Turkish and Greek authorities of Cyprus; for the people of Cyprus.

Saint Tychon, pray for us, and for all vine growers.

June 17   Saint Rainerius of Pisa

Rainerius enjoyed a dissolute life in his youth. He was, however, converted by means of an association with the monastery of San Vito. He visited Palestine and the Holy Places, and then returned to Pisa where he lived with the canons of Santa Maria. He was sought after for his preaching and gifts of healing. Rainerius was born in 1117 and died at about the age of 45.

From that time Jesus began to preach, saying, 'Repent for the kingdom of heaven is at hand.' (Matthew 4.17)
And he called to him the twelve and began to send them out two by two . . . so they went out and preached that men should repent. (Mark 6.7a,12)

Rainerius's gift of healing was discovered after he had journeyed from his unsavoury youth to his conversion and on to his ministry of preaching. Was it acquired as he visited the Holy Places? Did it simply develop as his skills at preaching developed? Healing by preaching and touch are often closely associated. The word is able to heal most effectively and the touch can confirm the conversion from some pain and despair. Touch is also instrumental in curing physical distress in the body, and this God-given gift is given to skilled physicians and sometimes to those without any such skill. Whether or not we are so gifted, we are all called to heal by word of mouth.

In our prayers: thanks for the life, example and intercession of Saint Rainerius of Pisa; for those who exercise their gifts of healing by word and by touch; for those who need comfort.

Saint Rainerius, pray for us, for Pisa and for all healers.

June 18   Saint Gregory Barbarigo *(Bishop and Cardinal)*

Gregory was successively Bishop of Bergamo and Bishop of Padua, and was made cardinal. He was a rich man born of Venetian nobility, and he used his riches to endow a college, a seminary and a theological library. In addition to this, he used his wealth for the benefit and comfort of the poor of the diocese. He was known also for his care of the faithful. Gregory died at the age of 72 in 1697.

Therefore I love thy commandments above gold, above fine gold. Therefore I direct my steps by all thy precepts; I hate every false way. Keep steady my steps according to thy promise, and let no iniquity get dominion over me. (Psalm119[118].127,128,133)

The placing of wealth at the disposal of others is one of the good works to which we are all called subject to our means. This is more often achieved through reputable Catholic charities rather than by personal endowment of seminaries, but they are of the same genus. Gregory's wealthy birth was a talent that he was free to use or misuse, just like any other. That he derived pleasure from a proper use of his wealth there is probably no doubt, for we cannot do the work of Our Lord without the appearance of joy in our lives. Joy always accompanies or follows what we do for Christ and his Church.

In our prayers: thanks for the life, example and intercession of Saint Gregory Barbarigo; for seminarians and theological librarians; for those who are testing their vocation to the priesthood.

Saint Gregory, pray for us, and for Venice.

June 19   Saint Juliana Falconieri *(Foundress)*

Juliana was born in 1270 and became a tertiary of the Order of the Servites of Mary. In 1304 she was able to found a community of sisters for work with the sick poor, and she was hailed for her dedication to the great task. She died at 71 and was canonized in 1737.

When the poor and needy seek water, and there is no more, and their tongue is parched with thirst, I the Lord will answer them, I the God of Israel will not forsake them. (Isaiah 41.17)

Juliana's life was one of self-imposed austerity, which often affected her health adversely, though she was not deterred from her life-long dedication to the sick poor. She seemed to balance her intake of nourishment to reflect the diet of those she attended. From an early age she had resolved to dedicate her life to God and to commit herself entirely to him. This was borne out by her unswerving devotion to duty and to hard work. Juliana's single-mindedness is worthy of some contemplation. We are easily distracted from our prayers, from our good works, from our enabling our faces to reveal Our Saviour.

In our prayers: thanks for the life, example and intercession of Saint Juliana Falconieri; for all women of the Order of Servites; for those who dedicate their lives to the sick poor.

Saint Juliana, pray for us, for all women religious and for Florence.

༼ ༀ ༽

June 20 Saint Alban *(Martyr)*

Alban was probably an officer in the Roman army stationed in Verulamium who gave sanctuary to the Christian priest who converted him. By a simple ruse, Alban fooled those who were searching his home for the priest (Alban must have been under suspicion, of course) by leaving his house disguised as his guest. Alban was taken before the magistrate to whom he admitted his identity and his Christianity. He was flogged and beheaded early in the third century.

But the souls of the righteous are in the hand of God, and no torment will ever touch them. In the eyes of the foolish they seemed to have died, and their departure was thought to be an affliction, and their going from us to be their destruction; but they are at peace. (Wisdom of Solomon 3.1–3)

The ingredients of Alban's story are those of a tragic thriller. He was a Christian in an unchristian land; a Christian where Christianity was proscribed. His was the first blood that was shed for Christ in England. There were priests in secret, lay folk in secret but, until this time, no life had been taken. Perhaps in this outpost the more terrible acts had not yet begun to be practised against Christians. However, for an officer in the Roman army to espouse this new religion at the expense of the time-honoured gods, was a very different matter. In his story, Alban reveals a love of danger, a sense of humour and a desire to protect others to the extent of laying down his life.

In our prayers: thanks for the life, example and intercession of Saint Alban; for men and women of the armed forces.

Saint Alban, pray for us, for soldiers and for England.

June 21 Saint Aloysius Gonzaga

Aloysius was born in 1568 in wealthy circumstances in Lombardy. From his extreme youth he was blameless in his life, though, perhaps, a troubled adolescent. Despite opposition from his father, he joined the novitiate of the Society of Jesus in Rome at the age of 17. Rome suffered an epidemic of the plague in 1589 and Aloysius asked to be permitted to nurse the victims, which he did for two years without a break until he himself died of the same disease in 1591. Aloysius was canonized in 1726.

Remember also your Creator in the days of your youth, before the evil days come, and the years draw nigh, when you will say, 'I have no pleasure in them,'... and the spirit returns to God who gave it. (Ecclesiastes 12.1,7b)
'You also must be ready; for the Son of man is coming at an hour you do not expect.' (Luke 12.40)

This short story of Aloysius gives us a glimpse of the selflessness of a young man in the face of almost certain death in begging permission to relieve the dying struggles of plague victims. What a task, what nobility of purpose! For some time, without proper rest or relief, Aloysius gave comfort. His own poor health had troubled him throughout his life and there was little resistance when he finally succumbed to the plague.

In our prayers: thanks for the life, example and intercession of Saint Aloysius Gonzaga; for all those who spend their lives nursing the victims

of infectious and contagious diseases; for all public health authorities; for those who suffer.

Saint Aloysius, pray for us, for youth and for the city of Rome.

❦

June 22   Saint John Fisher *(Bishop, Cardinal and Martyr)*; Saint Thomas More *(Martyr)*

John was born in 1469. He was learned and holy. As Bishop of Rochester he performed his duties with meticulous care and attention. On refusing the oath demanded by the Act of Succession, John was arrested, charged with treason and placed in the Tower of London.

Thomas was born in 1478. He was a personal friend of King Henry VIII, and rose to the high position of Lord Chancellor of England. Thomas, like John Fisher, was a learned man. He too refused the oath and was incarcerated in the Tower.

John was beheaded on June 22 and Thomas on July 5, 1535. Both declared on the scaffold that they were dying for the Holy Catholic Church. They were canonized in 1935.

The Lord is good to those who wait for him, to the soul who seeks him. It is good that one should wait quietly for the salvation of the Lord. Let him sit alone in silence when he has laid it on him; let him put his mouth in the dust – there may yet be hope; let him give his cheek to the smiter, and be filled with insults. (Lamentations 3.25,26,28,29,30)

Some would take the oath and mean nothing by it, confess their sin and return to their positions. This was not an option that John could entertain. He was a holy and honest man who did simply as his conscience dictated for the good of the Holy Church.

Likewise, Thomas, often regarded as wilfully stubborn, could not take the oath for the sake of peace and quiet. He could have done so and retired into the country with a handsome pension. But Thomas saw danger to the integrity of the Church in England if he were to agree and honoured for it. Both were martyrs for the purity of the Faith and for the integrity of the Catholic Church.

In our prayers: thanks for the lives, examples and intercession of Saint John Fisher and Saint Thomas More.

Give me the grace, good Lord, to be joyful in tribulation, to walk the narrow way that leads to life, to pray for pardon before the judge comes, to have continually in mind the Passion that thou suffered for me and unceasingly to give him thanks. Give me the grace, good Lord, to think my worst enemies my best friends. Lord Jesus, hear me. (From a prayer by Saint Thomas)
Saint John and Saint Thomas, pray for us, and for Parliament.

June 23   Saint Joseph Cafasso

Joseph was born in 1811. He was ordained at an early age and recognized quickly as a very fine preacher and teacher. In 1848, Joseph became the rector of the Institute of Saint Francis in Turin, where he was responsible for 60 young priests. He visited and counselled prisoners and walked with them to the gallows. He was a fine example and encouraged many others to charitable pursuits – not least Saint John Bosco (January 31). Joseph died in 1860 and was canonized in 1947.

Create in me a clean heart, O God, and put a new and right spirit within me. Cast me not away from thy presence and take not thy Holy Spirit from me. Restore to me the joy of salvation, and uphold me with a willing spirit. Then I will teach transgressors thy ways, and sinners will return to thee. (Psalm 51[50].10–13)

To motivate others into charitable work, to be chaplain to many young priests, to strengthen prisoners, to hear their confessions as they mounted the scaffold were all demanding tasks undertaken with gentleness and faith. The prisons of Turin were notorious – the squalid conditions, degrading treatment, and the relief of the march to their death are what awaited the prisoners. Joseph loved them and prepared them for their deaths. This little man with his grotesque gait epitomized the Christ of the woman taken in adultery and the Christ of the repentant thief.

In our prayers: thanks for the life, example and intercession of Saint Joseph Cafasso; for all prison chaplains and visitors; for those who are close to death in gaols throughout the world.

Saint Joseph, pray for us, for young priests and for Turin.

June 24   The Nativity of Saint John the Baptist

John's beheading and heavenly birthday falls upon August 29, his earthly duties done. Here his birth is celebrated, a rare honour for a saint. He was born to remind mankind of the Word of God, spoken by the Prophets and to point mankind towards the Word of God made flesh. But even before he was born, he was able to nudge his mother to greet Our Lady as 'the mother of my Lord'. John was the summary of the Prophets bound up in one man. He turned the last page of the Old Testament and opened the New. After disappearing into the wilderness (was he an Essene?) he was borne from the desert to begin his ministry of preparation. Although he was cast in the mould of the Old Testament Prophets, he was the epitome of selfless sainthood, and a veritable lighthouse and signpost of the Faith.

'What then did you go out to see? A man clothed in soft raiment? Behold, those who are gloriously apparelled live in kings' courts. What then did you go out to see? A prophet? Yes, I tell you, and more than a prophet. This is he of whom it is written, "Behold, I send my messenger before thy face who shall prepare thy way before thee."' (Luke 7.25–27)

This small boy from his very first kick in the womb was the herald of God's plan that would seem to turn God's world and its own natural law upside down. In place from the beginning of time, the gift of the Word, the Son of God, would enter humanity at an appropriate juncture. Slowly revealed through the Prophets of old, the expectation of the Messiah grew throughout the history of the Israelites until, during the Roman control of the Holy Land, Bethlehem became the setting for its realization and John, the last Prophet, entered the stage to prepare our minds to the new possibilities in Jesus.

In our prayers: thanks for the life, example and intercession of Saint John the Baptist; for all those who point us in the right direction; that we might point others in the right direction.

Saint John, pray for us, for all monks and for Florence.

June 25   Saint Maximus of Turin *(Bishop)*

Maximus was possibly the first Bishop of Turin. He was born around 380 in southern Italy. Much of his written work has come down to us. In his sermons, he stressed the need for a daily Rule for the laity, for prayers in the morning and prayers in the evening, for grace at mealtimes, and that by the personal use of the sign of the cross, a blessing may be given. Maximus died in 467.

Why did Christ desire baptism? Please note that Christ is baptized not for his own sanctification but so that in his baptism he makes holy the waters of Baptism . . . (From a sermon by Saint Maximus of Turin)

How important is the proper use of the sign of the cross. Indeed, a blessing may be given. It is a holy sign, not a talisman. It brings home to the mind and body the sign of the instrument on which Our Lord suffered and died. It is a sign of his body being hidden away in a cave and his bursting from that cave in the Mystery and Truth of the Resurrection. It emphasizes holy things as we hear and read them; it prepares us to receive the Lord in the Most Holy Sacrament of the Altar. We can meditate upon the sign of the cross; upon the Wounds of Christ, upon his Passion, upon the words from the cross. It can keep us from sin when we feel Christ within the points we have made.

In our prayers: thanks for the life, example and intercession of Saint Maximus of Turin.

+ *In the name of the Father and of the Son, and of the Holy Spirit.*
+ *Blessed be the Holy Trinity throughout the ages of ages.*
+ *Preserve me from evil thoughts and deeds.*
+ *May I not omit to do good when I have the opportunity.*
+ *Glory be to the Father and to the Son, and to the Holy Spirit.*

Saint Maximus, pray for us, and for Turin.

June 26   Saint Anthelm *(Bishop)*

Anthelm was born in 1107. He was a secular priest who became prior of Grande Chartreuse, and Bishop of Belley. He was known for his administrative skills, which were put to the test both in the rebuilding of Grande Chartreuse and in the reformation of the diocese of Belley. Anthelm was a holy and charming man. He would personally visit the lepers in the house he built for them, and would ensure the poor of the diocese were fed. Anthelm died of a fever in 1178.

He has caused his wonderful works to be remembered; the Lord is gracious and merciful. He provides food for those who fear him; he is ever mindful of his covenant. He has shown his people the power of his works in giving them the heritage of the nations. (Psalm 111[110].4–6)

Anthelm's confidence in his ability to carry out the work he was given to do enabled him to motivate those around him. His charm was born of his happy and complete faith and confidence in God; it was not a studied charm with an eye on preferment and popularity. Charm is simply a symptom of Christianity. With deep faith we enter the leper houses we have built and visit those who live there; we not only provide bread but also give it to the hungry. We do these things because our feet are Christ's feet, our hands are Christ's hands, our minds are Christ's.

In our prayers: thanks for the life, example and intercession of Saint Anthelm; for all lepers and for those who care for them.

Saint Anthelm, pray for us, and for charitable organizations specializing in the cure and prevention of disease throughout the world.

❦

June 27 Saint Cyril of Alexandria *(Bishop and Doctor of the Church)*; Saint Ladislaus of Hungary

Cyril was born in 376. He is perhaps most known for the bitter debate over the Nestorian heresy. However, much of Cyril's valuable writing has come down to us and he can be seen as a great champion of orthodoxy and the theology of the great Fathers of the Church. He died in 444 and was declared Doctor of the Church in 1882.

Ladislaus became King of Hungary in 1077. For much of his time, he was engaged in protecting Hungary against many tribes and races. He was, nevertheless, devout and generous and a fair and just king. Ladislaus was a strong guardian of the Church but permitted freedom to Jews and to Muslims as sons of Abraham. He died in 1095 and was canonized in 1110.

Blessed is the man who makes the Lord his trust, who does not turn to the proud, to those who go after false gods! (Psalm 40[39].4)
But although he assumed flesh and blood, he remained what he was, God in essence and in truth. Neither do we say that his flesh was changed into the nature of divinity, nor that the ineffable nature of the Word of God was laid aside for the nature of flesh; for he is unchanged and absolutely unchangeable, being the same always, according to the scriptures. (From the epistle to Nestorius by Saint Cyril of Alexandria)

Nestorius was the Patriarch of Constantinople, who perpetuated the heresy that confused the two natures of Christ into representing two personalities bound together in one moral person. The heresy also denied Mary, the *Theotokos* (January 1). Cyril's expositions of the theology and the Mystery of the Holy Trinity serve us well to this day and reward us in deep contemplation. Ladislaus also, 600 years later, was a great defender of the Church. In his case, he defended it from those who would attack it physically and by force, but he was generous to all the sons of Abraham within his country. Did he deem it probable that they would be receptive to the gospel, as revealed through the lives of his Christian subjects? Doubtless he was hopeful of that outcome.

In our prayers: thanks for the lives, examples and intercession of Saint Cyril of Alexandria and Saint Ladislaus of Hungary; for all who teach the orthodox Faith; for all monarchs who care for their people in the Faith of Christ.

Saint Cyril, pray for us, and for all writers of theological works. Saint Ladislaus, pray for us, and for Hungary.

June 28 Saint Irenaeus of Lyons *(Bishop)*

Irenaeus was born in about 125 and as a young man was acquainted with Saint Polycarp (February 23). Irenaeus was a brilliant scholar who had been schooled by Justin Martyr (June 1) in Rome. He became Bishop of Lyons and brought peace to the troubled region. He was a champion of the Faith and produced a work setting Gnostic heresy against apostolic teaching, which was instrumental in the demise of Gnosticism. Irenaeus died in 202 or thereabouts.

In order to show gratitude to our creator, we must make offering of thanks to God in the holiness of thought, the ingenuousness of faith, the solidity of hope, and the unquenchable fire of love. (From Against Heresies, *by Irenaeus)*

Gnosticism preached a salvation dependent upon special enlightenment and knowledge about the Deity. The trains of thought probably pre-dated Christianity, although the Gnostics gathered ideas from many sources including Christianity. They accepted the divinity but not the humanity of Jesus. Men like Irenaeus with carefully considered theological argument were responsible for maintaining the purity and clarity of the Faith. Irenaeus points us along a way that is untainted by popular misconceptions, misunderstandings, misinterpretations, and malformations of thought about the moral law.

In our prayers: thanks for the life, example and intercession of Saint Irenaeus; for strength to point to the error of the moral law of society and to remain faithful to the moral law of the Catholic Church.

Saint Irenaeus, pray for us, and for Lyons.

ᏋᏋ☘ᎧᎦ

June 29 Saint Peter and Saint Paul *(Apostles)*

Peter and Paul were both martyred in Rome within a few years of each other. They were very different men and not at all close associates; however, both were great forces in the spread of the Faith. Peter was the *Peter* (that is, the rock) upon whom Jesus declared that he would build his Church. Paul, on the other hand, was converted from an enthusiastic persecutor of Christians to the ardent apostle of the Mediterranean. They died, in all probability, in 64 and 67 respectively.

'Let all the house of Israel therefore know assuredly that God has made him both Lord and Christ, this Jesus whom you crucified.' (Saint Peter, Acts 2.36)
Therefore be imitators of God, as beloved children. And walk in love, as Christ loved us and gave himself up for us a fragrant offering and sacrifice to God. (Ephesians 5.1,2)

Peter leads the Church in its first steps, spreading the gospel and, at the same time, organizing its structure and its methods of work. It was a difficult beginning but inspired by the Holy Spirit. With tireless work, the Church spread inexorably throughout Greece and on to Rome, the stage for so many Christian martyrs who would become, quite literally, the footings of what would be built over them. Paul keeps the new pockets and cells of Christianity alive and on their toes with hand-written sermons delivered by couriers, sometimes in person. And death stalked every Christian journey. Should we have remained faithful?

In our prayers: thanks for the lives, examples and intercession of Saint Peter and Saint Paul; for those who assist in the government of the Church; for His Holiness the Pope.

Saint Peter, pray for us, for seamen and fishermen, for all places dedicated in your name, and for the Pope. Saint Paul, pray for us, for makers of tents and sails, for all places dedicated in your name, and for preachers of the gospel.

June 30 The Martyrs of Rome under Nero

In addition to the Apostles Peter and Paul (June 29), there were martyred many in Emperor Nero's reign. In blaming Christians for the great fire of Rome in 64, Nero manufactured a reason for their persecution. He devised many ingenious ways to make them suffer and die distressing deaths. His methods were to be copied and developed further in some subsequent reigns. These men and women were among the pioneers to the crowns of martyrdom and they can remind us what an easy matter it is to bear the mere inconveniences of life.

What is it thou sayest, my son? Cease to complain when thou consider-est my Passion, and the sufferings of other holy persons. Thou hast not yet made resistance unto blood. (Saint Thomas à Kempis, Of the Imitation of Christ*)*

We may not have to contend with the depravity of Nero and there may not be bears and lions, but the Church has to contend with the scorn and derision shown by society's encouragement of much that is inimical to the Church. We are called to be diligent Christians, to uphold the Faith and to allow Christ to be revealed through our very lives. If we fulfil that obligation with perseverance and fortitude, society might again be ready to hear the word and respond. In addition to the pain of his scourging and crucifixion, Our Lord suffered scorn and derision. Perhaps we can continue a little longer without despair.

In our prayers: thanks for the lives, examples and intercession of the Holy Martyrs of Rome under Nero; that the Church might again influence society and government as to the moral law.

Holy Martyrs of Rome, pray for us, and for the conversion of Europe.

July

I am very taken by the conversion of Camillus (July 14), who began his maturity as a pleasure-seeking gambler! On July 29, Jesus' friends of Bethany – Martha, Mary and Lazarus – are celebrated. They are among my favourite saints; we all know a bustling Martha and a Mary who is content to sit, oblivious of the movement around her. We can learn a lot from these two sisters.

July 1 Saint Oliver Plunkett *(Bishop and Martyr)*

Oliver became Archbishop and Primate of Ireland in 1669. For a few years he was able to restore a little order to the Church in Ireland. After 1673, however, Parliament's attitude to Catholicism became more aggressive and Oliver lived cautiously in the houses of friends and relations. He was eventually arrested in Dublin in 1679, and tried the following year in London on a charge of treason. Oliver was hanged, drawn and quartered in 1681 and canonized in 1975.

Hear my cry, O God, listen to my prayer; from the end of the earth I cry to thee, when my heart is faint. Lead thou me to the rock that is higher than I; for thou art my refuge, a strong tower against the enemy. Prolong the life of the king; may his years endure to all generations! May he be enthroned for ever before God. (Psalm 61[60].1–3,6,7)

Under the cloak of the Reformation, faithful priests and laity were caught and killed to satisfy political lusts. There was also distaste for the authority of Rome and the demands Catholicism made on the individual. During these times, clever manipulations of the law often equated Catholicism and, almost certainly, priesthood, with treason. We are not in fear of the authorities, but to prevent conflict and argument do we keep the Faith to ourselves? Even if our tongues are often silent on the subject, the way we live our lives ought to make Christ manifest.

In our prayers: thanks for the life, example and intercession of Saint Oliver Plunkett; for those discriminated against for their faith; for all political leaders.

Saint Oliver, pray for us, and for all who are enemies of the Church.

❧❀☙

July 2 Saint Swithin *(Bishop)*

Today is the heavenly birthday of Swithin. (The translation of his relics to the new cathedral in Winchester took place on July 15, 971.) Swithin was made Bishop of Winchester in 852 and was relied upon by King Aethelwulf for his sagacity. Swithin was a humble and generous man towards those in need in his diocese. He built many churches and did much for the spread of the Faith in the kingdom of Wessex. He died in 862.

Now may our Lord Jesus Christ himself, and God our Father, who loved us and gave us eternal comfort and good hope through grace, comfort your hearts and establish them in every good work and word. (2 Thessalonians 2.16,17)

Swithin is credited, among other things, with having diverted a number of streams to run through the city to keep it free from disease. Wessex at the time was ablaze with the fire of the Faith, but 1,000 or so years later the story is somewhat different. Of course, the Church survives the many phases of man's infidelity through the ages. Despite the many obstacles placed by man between himself and the Church, Our Merciful Saviour lavishes upon us the gift of his saving grace in purifying and endless streams.

In our prayers: thanks for the life, example and intercession of Saint Swithin; for all civil engineers and public health officials; for all who call themselves Christian.

Saint Swithin, pray for us, for all places dedicated in your name and for all who seek a cure for their sickness.

July 3 Saint Thomas *(Apostle)*

Thomas was one of the twelve (Mark 3.18) and it was he who elicited from Jesus after the Last Supper 'I am the Way, the Truth and the Life' (John 14.4–6) after Thomas had stated that they (the disciples) did not know where Jesus was going, and therefore could not know the way. Thomas is the one who asks the question or makes the statement that is on everyone's lips.

'Unless I see in his hands the print of the nails . . . I will not believe.' Then he said to Thomas, '. . . see my hands . . . do not be faithless, but believing.' Thomas answered him, 'My Lord and my God!' '. . . Blessed are they who have not seen and yet believe.' (John 20.25–29)

It is helpful to us that the question we feel we need to ask has already been asked by one of the disciples. Christ is the Way – the passage to God the Father. Through him we approach and know the Father because we know that the Father is in Jesus and Jesus in the Father. We know that he is the only way to the Father because he and the Father are one. Jesus is Truth, he is the way to the Father, and he is, therefore, Life in the Father. Do we still wait awkwardly in the queue to press our finger into Our Lord's wounds?

In our prayers: thanks for the life, example and intercession of Saint Thomas; for all who show others the way to the heavenly Father; for the faithless.

Saint Thomas, pray for us, for all who seek a firmer faith, and for all places dedicated in your name.

July 4 Saint Elizabeth of Portugal

Elizabeth was the daughter of King Peter III of Aragon, and great-niece of Saint Elizabeth of Hungary (November 17). She was married at twelve to King Diniz of Portugal, and brought up their two children together with his illegitimate ones. She devoted her time to charitable works for the poor, for pilgrims, for prostitutes. She died in 1336 and was canonized in 1625.

'And who is my neighbour?' Jesus replied, 'A man was going down from Jerusalem to Jericho, and he fell among robbers . . . leaving him half dead . . . But a Samaritan, as he journeyed, came to where he was; and when he saw him, he had compassion . . . and took care of him . . .' (Luke 10.29–37)

It would have been understandable had Elizabeth overlooked the children of her husband who were not her own. But it was not surprising that Elizabeth comforted the poor and gave hospitality to pilgrims; that was respectable work, after all. However, to extend the neighbourly hand to the vice-ridden victims of all sorts of circumstances and to the children of her husband's promiscuity, was it not surely beyond the call of duty? Is there anyone who is not my neighbour?

In our prayers: thanks for the life, example and intercessions of Saint Elizabeth of Portugal; for those who overlook their neighbour; for illegitimate children; for peacemakers; for Portugal and its people.

Saint Elizabeth, pray for us, for Portugal, and for the victims of circumstance.

July 5 Saint Antony Zaccaria *(Founder)*

Antony was born in northern Italy in 1502. He was ordained in 1528. With two others he established the Congregation of Priests (later to be called Order of Clerks Regular of Saint Paul Beheaded), which, inter alia, assisted victims of the plague. His Order was firmly based upon Pauline theology; and Antony's teaching revealed a deep devotion to the Blessed Sacrament and to the Crucifix. The Order acquired the Church of Saint Barnabas in Milan, towards the end of his life, thereafter becoming known as the Barnabites. Antony died in 1539 and was canonized in 1897.

But when they came to Jesus and saw that he was already dead, they did not break his legs. But one of the soldiers pierced his side with a spear, and at once there came out blood and water. (John 19.33,34)

It is difficult not to have a deep devotion to the Blessed Sacrament – to the body and Real Presence of Christ himself. But is it always comfortable to kneel worshipfully in his presence when we know that our lives are not quite what they ought to be or, indeed, how our Lord would have them be? No, it is not, but we simply cast ourselves in the role of the penitent sinner and seek forgiveness. Before the Blessed Sacrament we raise our eyes to the Crucifix above and we see in graphic detail the effects of man's sin against God. How is it that Christ is saving us as he hangs upon the cross? How is it that he forgives; that he is concerned for the soul of the thief beside; that he does not wish his mother to be unprotected; that he wishes her to be the mother of his cousin John and the mother of us all? Love on that scale expunges death, sin and the Devil.

In our prayers: thanks for the life, example and intercession of Saint Antony Zaccaria; for the victims of plague; for all Congregations of priests.

Saint Antony, pray for us, for Milan and for all priests.

July 6   Saint Maria Goretti

Maria was born in 1890 in Ancona. She was a child of happiness, of gentle piety who was murdered by an acquaintance and a close friend of the family after his attempt to rape her had failed. As she lay dying in hospital, she received the Last Rites and forgave her attacker. Maria was canonized in 1950.

Whatever is true, whatever is honourable, whatever is just, whatever is pure, whatever is lovely, whatever is gracious, if there is any excellence, if there is anything worthy of praise, think about these things. (Philippians 4.8)

Is it true that victims of rape more often than not know their attacker as a friend or family member? In this case, the attacker had been held in high esteem and looked up to as an elder brother. Maria was but 12 years old when she was attacked and stabbed several times in the frustration of her attacker. In prison her attacker was remorseful; in her death Maria was forgiving. By putting self first untold damage can be done. In this case scarcely more damage could be envisaged but is it not easy to rape, murder and destroy innocence and innocent things simply by word and thought? Maria, the epitome of innocence, is there before us in the neighbour we have slandered just for the sake of the enjoyment of gossip; she is there with Christ as we alienate another from the Church by our behaviour.

In our prayers: thanks for the life, example and intercessions of Saint Maria Goretti; for all victims of sexual violence; for those who commit acts of violence.

Saint Maria, pray for us, for the Children of Mary, and for teenage girls.

೪೫৯

July 7 Saint Felix of Nantes *(Bishop)*

Felix was born in 513 and made Bishop of Nantes around the middle of the sixth century. He was a learned man and an aristocrat, but certainly not too grand to perform many charitable works for the poor of the city. Felix was responsible for protecting the city against invasions from Brittany. He died in 582.

He has caused his wonderful works to be remembered; the Lord is gracious and merciful. He provides food for those who fear him; he is ever mindful of his covenant. He has shown his people the power of his works, in giving them the heritage of the nations. The works of his hands are faithful and just . . . (Psalm 111[110].4–7a)

It is difficult for us to imagine aggressive tribal movement from Brittany to the region around Nantes, and it is even more difficult to imagine the responsibility for the protection of Nantes falling upon the shoulders of its bishop. The sixth century was not the twenty-first century, but perhaps we can grasp a little of Felix's extraordinary holiness and humility when we realize the significance of a man with all the ecclesiastical and secular power a man could have within his city and sphere of influence humbling himself to the extent of personally handing bread to the hungry and helping them feed. Are we too important or self-important?

In our prayers: thanks for the life, example and intercessions of Saint

Felix of Nantes; for administrators and those who have the responsibility to protect others.

Saint Felix, pray for us, and for victims of war and famine.

July 8 Saint Aquila and Saint Priscilla

Aquila and Priscilla, a married couple of Corinth, were friends and disciples of Saint Paul (June 29). They are mentioned from time to time by Saint Paul, and he notes that they permit their house to be used as a church for worship. They might be said to represent all the unsung heroes and workers of the Church up to this day.

After this, he [Paul] left Athens and went to Corinth. And he found a Jew named Aquila, a native of Pontus, lately come to Italy with his wife Priscilla, because Claudius had commanded all Jews to leave Rome. And he went to see them; and because he was of the same trade he stayed with them, and they worked, for by trade they were tentmakers. (Acts 18.1–3)

There are many saints of this period about whom we know little or nothing at all – and it is much the same in our present age. Aquila and Priscilla were tentmakers, Christian and generous. They entertained Paul and those with him, and they made space in their home for worship. Their holiness emerges from their unassuming simplicity, their openness and honesty. We draw from them that in order to live our lives in Christ and fulfil our vocations we are not necessarily called to perform the spectacular or dangerous. The vast majority of the saints in heaven must be just such people. We know, however, how difficult it is to live our lives in Christ because our own self prefers centre stage.

In our prayers: thanks for the lives, examples and intercessions of Saint Aquila and Saint Priscilla; for the faithful laity; for those who assist.

Saint Aquila and Saint Priscilla, pray for us, and for all unsung heroes of the Faith.

July 9 Saint Veronica Guiliani *(Abbess)*

Veronica was born in 1660 and became a Capuchin nun in 1677. She was a visionary and mystic devoted to Our Lord's Passion. She suffered the stigmata in various forms from 1681. Veronica was pious and level-headed at all times; she was novice mistress from 1688 and elected abbess in 1717. She has left us hundreds of letters and a full description of her spiritual experiences. Veronica died in 1727 and was canonized in 1839.

Now a word was brought to me stealthily, my ear received the whisper of it. Amid thought from visions of the night . . . dread came upon me, and trembling . . . When I say, 'My bed will comfort me, my couch will ease my complaint' then thou dost scare me with dreams and terrify me with visions. (Job 4.12,13;7.13)

The gift of visions and the gifts of a mind attuned to mysticism are precious to those who come after, even if they can be a terrible trial for the mystic visionary. Veronica served Christ as a Capuchin for 50 years, and in that capacity became a holy and worthy novice mistress and abbess. And yet her vocation was much wider than that, for she was not only called to experience Christ's Passion, among other things, but she had also to bear the marks of that Passion and write about her experiences for future generations. The process of salvation was vivid before her eyes and in her mind and confirmed in her body as a mystical witness of Christ's suffering. Veronica is a reminder of the reality of that suffering in all its graphic detail. When we contemplate the Crucifix, we do well to hold Veronica in our minds for a moment or two.

In our prayers: thanks for the life, example and intercessions of Saint Veronica Guiliani; for those who guide others by their experiences.

O Lord Jesus Christ, who bore five wounds upon the cross for the forgiveness of sin, have mercy. Amen. Saint Veronica, pray for us, for all mystics and Capuchins throughout the world.

July 10   Saint Rufina and Saint Secunda *(Martyrs)*

Rufina and Secunda were sisters who were pursued for their faith during Valerian's reign. It seems that their boyfriends, who had renounced their faith, set the authorities upon these two girls. (Perhaps their release was the consideration for their treachery?) Rufina and Secunda were consequently captured, tortured and beheaded. They died around 258.

Here is a call for the endurance of the saints, those who keep the commandments of God and the faith of Jesus. And I heard a voice from heaven saying, 'Write this: Blessed are the dead who die in the Lord henceforth.' 'Blessed indeed,' says the Spirit, 'That they may rest from their labours, for their deeds follow them!' (Revelation 14.12,13a)

Is it possible for us to imagine the circumstances of these four teenagers? Two are suspected of Christianity and soon apostatize agreeing to worship the Roman gods with all due remorse immediately. In exchange for release without scourging, they give their captors information about their girlfriends. The girls are more emphatically Christian than their friends. The governor sends his soldiers to collect the girls. They do not deny the Lord; they do not renounce their faith; they will not worship a stone image even if they mean nothing by it; they will not offend the Son of God or his Father or his Holy Spirit; they will gladly die in order to be with him for ever. How much in common have we with these girls?

In our prayers: thanks for the lives, examples and intercession of Saint Rufina and Saint Secunda; for those who are weak in their faith; for those who would place others in danger; for those who torture and kill.

Saint Rufina and Saint Secunda, pray for us, and for those who remain faithful in spite of the terrors they face.

July 11   Saint Benedict *(Abbot)*

Benedict was born in 480. Fleeing the depravity of the city of Rome, at first he lived a hermit's life but as he gathered around him many disciples, he founded the great Monte Cassino monastery. His Rule became the Rule most western monasteries adopted, and so he is rightly regarded as the father of western monasticism. Saint Gregory the Great (September 3) described him simply as 'A man of God'. Benedict died in 550.

We must refresh our faith and give ourselves high standards by which to test our behaviour and use the Gospel as a guide to prepare ourselves for service in the kingdom of Christ. (From the Rule of Saint Benedict)

A reading of the Benedictine Rule can give us much for our contemplation. The Rule reveals for us a way – the monastic way – of ordering our lives so that we can readily conform ourselves to God. We can learn from it although we are not all called to the cloister. This very book may be part of our daily Rule in addition to our performing the basic requirements of the Catholic Church. Fleeing the depravities of Rome in the fifth century, Benedict and his monks were free to pray for the world, for Rome, for all who were caught in webs of vice, for those who made money from vice, for those who were caused to suffer the effects. Benedict knew that to Christ's saving power there were no barriers save those that we ourselves created.

In our prayers: thanks for the life, example and intercession of Saint Benedict; for those who suffer in the inner cities; for those who live a life of prayer.

Saint Benedict, pray for us, for all dedications in your name, for all Benedictines, and for cavers, potholers and mountaineers, whose patron you are.

July 12 Saint John Jones *(Martyr)*

John was born in 1559 in North Wales. He joined the Friars Minor in 1590 and took his final vows in 1591. In 1592 he was in London working for the English Mission. For a few years he was able to work in London and elsewhere before his arrest in 1597. He was tortured with some brutality. John was found guilty of treason by reason of his having been ordained abroad before working in England. He was hanged, drawn and quartered in 1598, and was canonized in 1970.

Come, let us return to the Lord; for he has torn, that he may heal us; he has stricken, and he will bind us up. After two days he will revive us; on the third day he will raise us up, that we may live before him. (Hosea 6.1,2)

The ever-widening definition of treason was able to capture so many priests at this time, so fearful the authorities had made themselves of Christ and his Church. This small witness to Christ affected many – those with whom he made contact, those he reconciled and absolved and those to whom he gave counsel. All were strengthened by contact with him. Those who were able to lead relatively normal lives preserved their memory of their contact with him, they shared that memory, and then sought out other priests of the English Mission for succour – and so it went on, daily, faltering steps for Christ and his Church.

In our prayers: thanks for the life, example and intercession of Saint John Jones; for those who live under threat for their beliefs in totalitarian states; for those without freedom to worship.

Saint John, pray for us, for Wales and for missionaries.

July 13 Saint Silas
(Also today, Saint Henry II.)

Silas was a faithful worker of some seniority in the early Church. He accompanied Saint Paul (June 29) to Smyrna and Cilicia and, with Paul, was imprisoned in Philippi. Silas is mentioned a number of times in the epistles.

And Judas and Silas, who were themselves prophets, exhorted the brethren with many works and strengthened them. And after they had spent some time, they were sent off in peace by the brethren to those who had sent them. (Acts 15.32–34)

The encouragement of others, the tending of the new and vulnerable flocks, was most important work in the early Church. These essential workers for the Church fanned the flames of faith by their preaching, teaching and wise counsel. They carried messages and sermons from Saint Peter and Saint Paul, and so the organs and limbs of the Church were nurtured as one body. It is now as it was then; the joy of the gospel as joyful; the glorious Resurrection as glorious; the Redemption of the world just as redeeming; Salvation as saving. The saints throughout the ages from Silas to the very latest man or woman, whose sainthood has yet to be confirmed, are nudging us awake and pointing us to Christ.

In our prayers: thanks for the life, example and intercession of Saint Silas; for faithful works in the Church; for those who teach and preach.

Saint Silas, pray for us, and for all who spread the gospel of Christ.

୧୧✣ঌঌ

July 14   Saint Camillus de Lellis *(Founder)*

Camillus was born in 1550 of Italian nobility. He was a gambler and soldier. In hospital in Rome with an ulcerated leg, he began to mend his ways and help nurse the sick. With the help of Saint Philip Neri (May 26), Camillus and others set about forming an Order dedicated to the nursing of the sick. At his death in 1614 he had established eight hospitals and a number of houses. Camillus was canonized in 1746.

Teach me, O Lord, the way of thy statutes; and I will keep it to the end. Give me understanding, that I may keep thy law and observe it with my whole heart. Lead me in the path of thy commandments, for I delight in it. Turn my eyes from looking at vanities; and give me life in thy ways. (Psalm 119[118].33–35,37)

Camillus enjoyed the worldly pleasures for their own sake: he had, perhaps, never given himself time to harbour more elevated pursuits of thought. As his painful affliction healed, his self-pity diminished and was replaced by shame as he saw those around him who were not recovering from their injuries and diseases. He began to see Christ himself peering pathetically from their soiled couches in the hospital in pain, discomfort and despair. Suddenly he realized that he had been ignoring Christ for years by placing other objects of his affection and fascination before him. His idols had obliterated his vision of the Blessed Trinity. Camillus wasted no further time and dedicated himself and those he gathered round him to a life of nursing and spiritual care for the helpless of the world. And what of our idols?

In our prayers: thanks for the life, example and intercession of Saint Camillus de Lellis; for those who cannot see beyond their idols; for the sick and dying and those who love and care for them.

Saint Camillus, pray for us, and for all who tend the sick.

July 15 Saint Bonaventure *(Bishop, Cardinal and Doctor of the Church)*

Bonaventure – the seraphic doctor, as he was later known – was born in 1221 and joined the Franciscans in 1243. He rose to become minister general. He was made Cardinal Bishop of Albano in 1273 but died in 1274. He is particularly known for his theological works, which breathe his spirit of sanctity and his love of God. Bonaventure was canonized in 1482.

Above him stood the seraphim; each had six wings: with two he covered his face, and with two he covered his feet, and with two he flew. And one called to another and said: 'Holy, Holy, Holy is the Lord of hosts; the whole earth is full of his glory.'... And I heard the voice of the Lord saying, 'Whom shall I send, and who will go for us?' Then I said, 'Here I am! Send me!' (Isaiah 6.2,3,8)

Like Isaiah, Bonaventure was sent out, sanctified, to teach and guide and caution. He did so as a preacher and writer of some note. He saw a thorough theological grounding as essential for the preparation of the preacher and teacher. Bonaventure's three-stage path that enables an individual to live in accordance with heavenly values can best be summed up in this way: first, it is necessary to achieve tranquillity of mind, a state only possible after absolution; second, with the clear conscience it is possible to begin to appreciate the full beauty of Christ the Truth; third, the perfection of love is now the only possible destination. These progressions arrive at the beauty of holiness.

In our prayers: thanks for the life, example and intercession of Saint Bonaventure; for all those sent out to minister to others; for those who have not the courage to say 'Send me!'

Saint Bonaventure, pray for us, and for the Society of Saint Francis and all its work.

July 16 Saint Mary-Magdalen Postel *(Foundress)*

Mary-Magdalen (born Julie) worked for years preparing children and adults for the sacraments. She set up a Congregation devoted to the work of teaching and relief of the disadvantaged in society. Schools were opened and the Congregation settled in a disused abbey calling itself the Sisters of the Christian Schools of Mercy (now Sisters of Saint Mary-Magdalen Postel). Mary-Magdelen died in 1846 and was canonized in 1925.

To thee I lift up my eyes, O thou who art enthroned in the heavens! Behold, as the eyes of servants look to the hand of their master, as the eyes of a maid to the hand of her mistress, so our eyes look to the Lord our God, till he have mercy on us. (Psalm 123[122].1,2)

For many years, Mary-Magdalen's preparation of catechumens was her own preparation for something larger, bolder. She had seen the need in those she had prepared for the sacraments for something more – for a wider Christian education that would enlighten and, God willing, relieve their poverty. Often, our good deeds – say, the financial contribution to a Catholic charity – give us an insight into something more that is required, perhaps a neglected area for intercession or for practical work.

In our prayers: thanks for the life, example and intercession of Saint Mary-Magdalen Postel; for the work of the Sisters of Saint Mary-Magdalen Postel; for those who are desperate to learn.

Saint Mary-Magdalen, pray for us, and for all those who give instruction to the ignorant.

July 17 Saint Marcellina; the Martyrs of Compiègne

Marcellina, who counselled her brother, Saint Ambrose (December 7), when he became Bishop of Milan, lived an austere life in a dwelling house. She had dedicated her life to God and to the service of others. Marcellina died in 400.

The Martyrs of Compiègne had also dedicated their lives to prayer and the service of others. They were 16 Carmelite nuns and a layman guillotined in 1794 during the French Revolution. These were the first (1906) of the Martyrs of the French Revolution to be beatified. Many others followed in 1920 and 1955, and they are variously commemorated on January 1, 2, 21, 27 and June 27.

All thy works shall give thanks to thee, O Lord, and all thy saints shall bless thee! They shall speak of the glory of thy kingdom, and tell of thy power. (Psalm 145[144].10,11)

Dedication of our lives to God – the giving back to the Master the enhanced deposits we have made with the talents given us – is the natural response of a loving creature. Marcellina saw her vocation as one of abstinence and of care for the unfortunate of Milan; furthermore, that her life was the platform for her contemplation and consideration of the matters with which she assisted her brother. The firm foundation of a well-performed vocation enables us to go farther and run the extra mile for Christ. And the Martyrs of the French Revolution were called to do just that and give us a perpetual reminder of dedication and sacrifice.

In our prayers: thanks for the lives, examples and intercessions of Saint Marcellina and the Martyrs of Compiègne; for those who sacrifice their time and their lives for others; for those who kill innocent men and women; for the Carmelites.

Saint Marcellina and Holy Martyrs of Compiègne, pray for us, and for all those who care for others.

July 18 Saint Pambo

Pambo was a fourth-century desert monk known for his defence of the Council of Nicaea. He was much admired by Saint Athanasius (May 2), that other great champion of orthodoxy. Pambo earned a reputation as a fine teacher of his disciples. Knowing the dangers of a loose tongue, Pambo advocated silence rather than unnecessary speech.

My soul languishes for thy salvation; I hope in thy word. For ever, O Lord, thy word is firmly fixed in the heavens. Thou art my hiding place and my shield; I hope in thy word. (Psalm 119[118]. 81,89,114)

I said, 'I will guard my tongue; I will bridle my mouth . . .' (Psalm 39[38].1)

Pambo was a fine teacher, a defender of orthodoxy, an ardent supporter of the Nicene Creed, a holy and wise theologian. But his principal claim to sanctity was his absolute control over his tongue. Unless what we are about to say is well prepared, worthy and of the highest quality, it is best to be silent. Unless what we are about to say conveys the love of Christ, we ought to hold our tongue. If what we are about to say is born of a feeling of anger, a lascivious thought or an unkind thought, we are wise to think again.

In our prayers: thanks for the life, example and intercession of Saint Pambo; for all politicians and spokesmen for others; for the Church.

Saint Pambo, pray for us, and for Egypt and its people.

July 19 Saint Macrina the Younger

Macrina remained at home to educate and look after her brothers, who included Saint Basil the Great (January 2) and Saint Gregory Nyssa (January 10). In maturity, Basil housed his sister and his mother with other companions. At some stage Macrina became prioress of a double monastery. Saint Gregory, in his lament on her death, alludes to miracles performed by his sister, including the healing of a girl's eye. Macrina died in poverty in 379.

'. . . your eye is the lamp of your body; when your eye is sound, your whole body is full of light; but when it is not sound, your body is full of darkness . . .' (Luke 11.34)

That she was so honoured by her siblings Basil and Gregory tells a story of holiness and dedication to duty. Macrina was an important part of her brothers' growing up: she instructed them in the rudiments of the Faith and learning. She helped them begin to see. Isaiah foresaw the days when the eyes of the blind were to be opened, and our Lord himself was the realization of the prediction, and he informed the imprisoned John the Baptist accordingly. Giving sight to the blind, figuratively and physically, was one of the hallmarks of Our Lord's ministry.

Following her Master, Macrina did so for her two illustrious brothers and for the little girl.

In our prayers: thanks for the life, example and intercession of Saint Macrina the Younger; for those who open the eyes of others in their teaching; for all who suffer blindness and other eye diseases and for those who care for them.

Saint Macrina, pray for us, and for those who suffer afflictions of the eye.

July 20   Saint Joseph Barsabbas

Joseph was the unsuccessful candidate in the draw between himself and Matthias (May 14) to fill the vacancy left by Judas Iscariot. Most likely, Joseph was one of the 70 disciples sent on a missionary journey by Our Lord (Luke 10.1–20). Clearly, he had been with Jesus and the other disciples from the very beginning and was, therefore, a witness to the whole ministry of Jesus.

'So one of the men who have accompanied us during all the time that the Lord Jesus went in and out among us, beginning from the baptism of John until the day when he was taken from us – one of these men must become with us a witness to his resurrection.' (Acts 1.21–23)

We know no more about this man. Later traditions have him imprisoned by Nero but released on a submission by Saint Paul. We cannot but conclude that as a faithful disciple of Our Lord from the very beginning, he was devoted to the work Christ had left in his disciples' care. We must assume that he lived his life and died for Christ. He was not destined for high office; he was a fellow worker with the Apostles and content to be so. (Was he, we wonder, a brother to Jude Barsabbas [Acts 15:22]?) Let us be content in our vocations and not seek the reward of office or honour in this world.

In our prayers: thanks for the life, example and intercession of Saint Joseph Barsabbas; for faithful workers and unsung heroes.

Saint Joseph, pray for us, and for all junior staff.

July 21   Saint Laurence of Brindisi *(Doctor of the Church)*

Laurence was born in 1559 in Naples. He was well read and learned. Laurence was ordained in 1581 having been a Capuchin friar from the age of 16. His reputation as a fine preacher was deserved. He is known to have been chaplain-general of the army and to have ridden against the Turks holding a crucifix rather than an instrument of war. His writings were published in 15 volumes and include nearly 1,000 sermons. Laurence had particular affection for the feasts that celebrate Our Lord's humanity. He died in 1619 and was canonized in 1881.

His faithfulness is a shield and buckler. You will not fear the terror by night, nor the arrow that flies by day. A thousand may fall at your side, ten thousand at your right hand; but it will not come near you. (Psalm 91[90].4b,5,7)

A picture of Laurence holding a crucifix aloft in the face of approaching hordes is one that cannot but remain with us for a long time. We can meditate on that sight and that faith to great reward. And as a prolific writer, Laurence's value remains with us today; and it is in his special devotion to the humanity of Our Lord and the feasts of the Nativity, the Blessed Sacrament and Passion that we follow his train of thought. It was through these feasts that Laurence saw the divinity of Jesus revealed. He saw the Father in the Son and the Son in the Father. Associated closely with this devotion is his especial love of Our Lady as the Mother of God, and all the other titles that are Our Lady's. Through this humanity we can approach the divine.

In our prayers: thanks for the life, example and intercession of Saint Laurence of Brindisi; for a greater devotion to Our Lord in the Blessed Sacrament; for all writers and theologians.

Nativity of Christ, swathe me; Passion of Christ, protect me. Saint Laurence, pray for us, and for the people of Italy, Austria, and Turkey.

July 22   Saint Mary Magdalene

Mary was from the west of the Sea of Galilee and one of the women who followed Jesus and cared for him and his disciples. (Our Lord may well have cured her of some psychological problem or other during the early stages of his ministry.) She is not to be identified with Mary of Bethany, or with the reformed prostitute. It was this Mary who took the news of Our Lord's resurrection to the disciples.

And also some women who had been healed of evil spirits and infirmities: Mary, called Magdalene, from whom seven demons had gone out, and Joanna, the wife of Chuza, Herod's steward, and Susanna, and many others, who provided for them out of their means. (Luke 8.2,3)
And they remembered his words, and returning from the tomb they told all this to the eleven and to all the rest. Now it was Mary Magdalene and Joanna and Mary the mother of James and the other women with them, who told this to the apostles. (Luke 24.8–10)

Mary Magdalene and the band of women who were devoted, as we are, to Our Lord, followed him from Galilee and provided food and drink for him and for the disciples. The devotion speaks volumes. They are the unsung heroines of Our Lord's ministry, but Mary's industrious life is rewarded with the duty of passing on the most significant piece of news anyone has ever conveyed: '. . . go to my brethren and say to them, I am ascending to my Father and your Father, to my God and your God'. Whatever Mary's past it matters not, it was she who was the herald of the good news of the Resurrection. When we are absolved we have a past.

In our prayers: thanks for the life, example and intercession of Saint Mary Magdalene; for those who have to live with rumour and murmur; for those who generously serve others; for preachers of the Resurrection.

Saint Mary Magdalene, pray for us, and for all places dedicated in your name.

July 23   Saint Bridget of Sweden

After raising a family of eight children, and, guided by a vision, Bridget established what became known as the Bridgettine Order dedicated to the Most Holy Saviour. The Bridgettines flourish today. She was known for her charitable works. Throughout her life she was both guided and much troubled by the visions she was granted. Bridget died in 1373 and was canonized in 1391.

And many wonders and signs were done through the apostles. And all who believed were together and had all things in common; and they sold their possessions and goods and distributed them to all, as any had need. (Acts 12.43b,44,45)

God sends his visions in many ways. To those like Bridget he enables the recipient – by means, perhaps, of a chemical imbalance or surge in the brain – to see what others cannot, and to communicate with him in a way others only dream of. Troubled though she was by these visions, she used them to guide her towards the founding of a most extraordinary and lasting Order of religious. Singled out for this duty, she responded and obeyed in the manner of Our Blessed Lady herself. Some of her visions gave her the opportunity to experience the reality of many of the great gospel events. Do we always recognize the visions we are granted?

In our prayers: thanks for the life, example and intercession of Saint Bridget of Sweden; for Sweden and its people; for the Bridgettine Order and its work.

Saint Bridget, pray for us, and for all women religious.

July 24   Saint John Boste

John was one of the Durham Martyrs of 1594. John was a Protestant cleric; became a Catholic; trained at Rheims, and was ordained at Châlons in 1581. He served as a priest in the north of England for 12 years. After his capture in 1593, he was mercilessly tortured in the Tower of London. John was returned to Durham in 1594 where he was tried, sentenced, and hanged, drawn and quartered. John was canonized in 1970.

Let us lie in wait for the righteous man, because he is inconvenient to us and opposes our actions; he reproaches us for sins against the law, and accuses us of sins against our training. (Wisdom of Solomon 2.12)

John's ministry lasted longer than that of most priests during this troubled period of our history. Life expectancy of a Second World War fighter pilot was about the same. Who can doubt the good John was able to achieve during his 12 years – the reconciliations he effected, the Masses he said, the absolutions and good counsel he gave? To seal his vocation, he was taken not to immediate trial and, under the draconian laws of England at the time, almost certain death; rather, he was taken first for torture by vindictive men, probably not simply for the purpose of gaining confessions and information but to satisfy the hungry desires of those who enjoyed his suffering. We can daily torture with our tongue.

In our prayers: thanks for the life, example and intercession of Saint John Boste; for all vindictive men and women; for gaolers and prison guards; for innocent captives.

Saint John, pray for us, for all missionaries and for the people of the city of Durham.

July 25 Saint James the Great *(Apostle)*

James was the brother of John, the beloved disciple. They were probably cousins of Our Lord, and part of Jesus' inner circle of Peter, James and John. Herod Agrippa had James 'killed with the sword' in 44 (Acts 12.1–3). (This James [James I] is usually described as 'the Great' in order to distinguish him from the other disciple named James [James II], the son of Alphaeus, and from James [James III], probably the first bishop of Jerusalem. However, some scholars believe James II and James III are one and the same!)

And after six days Jesus took with him Peter James and John his brother, and led them to a high mountain apart. And he was transfigured before them, and his face shone like the sun, and his garments became white as light. (Matthew 17.1,2)

James was the first of the Apostles to be martyred. He had witnessed the

Transfiguration of Jesus and became a messenger of the significance of this revelation, which could only explode into meaning after the Resurrection. James, like John, Peter and Andrew, was a fisherman from the seaside of Galilee. Jesus certainly knew his audience when he called them from their nets. How would they learn all that he had to teach them in, say, three years? How could mere fishermen, insular, single-minded men, be of help to Our Lord? Each one of us is singled out for special duty. If we leave our nets – those things we place before Christ – and allow ourselves to be transfigured to his purpose, that duty will become apparent.

In our prayers: thanks for the life, example and intercession of Saint James the Great; for all pilgrims to the Holy Places where Our Lord set foot, and to shrines of the saints throughout the world.

Saint James, pray for us, for those who travel to places of pilgrimage, and for all places dedicated in your name.

July 26   Saint Joachim and Saint Anne

Neither Joachim nor Anne is mentioned in the New Testament. Their names are given to us in a number of sources, including the *Protevangelium of James*, an apocryphal gospel of the second century, concerned with the Nativity and infancy of Christ. On this day we give thanks for Mary's parents – those who brought up a girl who was 'full of grace' from her very conception.

And behold, Joachim came with his flocks, and Anne stood at the gate and saw Joachim coming, and ran and hung upon his neck, saying: 'Now know I that the Lord God hath greatly blessed me' . . . *And her months were fulfilled, and in the ninth month Anne brought forth* . . . *the child and called her name, Mary.* (Protevangelium 4.4; 5.2)

We know nothing for certain about Mary's parents except this strong tradition. It was they who brought up the child who was to become the Mother of God; this child who, though 'full of grace' from the beginning of her life within Anne, was conceived and born in the natural way. God therefore denied the genetic transmission to Mary of original sin, the sin whose effect is nullified in baptism, so that Mary would enjoy the benefit of baptism from the outset. If we through the grace of baptism are disinherited from the legacy of original sin, why do we constantly and consistently repay that benevolence by doing precisely what our forefathers did? They placed themselves before God and bred that defect into the fabric of mankind. We take that old sin and make it our own despite our renovating baptism.

In our prayers: thanks for the lives, examples and intercession of Saint Joachim and Saint Anne; for all parents and those who bring up children; for homemakers.

Saint Joachim and Saint Anne, pray for us, for Brittany and northern France and for all places dedicated in your names.

July 27 Saint Aurelius, Saint Natalia and Companions *(Martyrs)*

Aurelius and Natalia were married and closet Christians in southern Spain, who became ashamed of not publicly professing their faith when they witnessed the public lashing of a Christian. They then acknowledged their faith by visiting Christians in prison, and were promptly arrested with others and condemned to death in 852 for having renounced the religion of their Moorish masters.

Jesus said to them, 'If God were your Father, you would love me, for I proceeded and came forth from God . . . Your father Abraham rejoiced that he was to see my day; he saw it and was glad.' The Jews said to him, 'You are not yet fifty years old, and have you seen Abraham?' Jesus said to them, 'Truly, truly, I say to you, before Abraham was, I am!' (John 8.42,56–58)

The Word was with God in the beginning before all worlds, and, of course, before Abraham and his seed. Aurelius's and Natalia's faith in the Word, in Christ, was too much to hide. They did not declare it publicly by the spoken word or announce it from the rooftops; the Faith they held dear was known to others by their actions, by the good work of visiting Christ himself in the imprisoned ones. Their offence was greater than some committed by Christians; in their actions they had renounced all pretence at their invaders' religion. They were done to death by those who themselves, with some irony, acknowledged descent from the Father of the Hebrews. How well concealed is our Christianity?

In our prayers: thanks for the lives, examples and intercession of Saint Aurelius and Saint Natalia; for those who have to be brave to admit their faith; for those who conceal their faith for reasons other than their safety.

Saint Aurelius and Saint Natalia, pray for us, and for all imprisoned Christians.

July 28   Saint Melchior Garcia Sampedro *(Bishop and Martyr)*

Melchior was born in 1821 in Spain. He became a Dominican novice in 1845. He was sent to Vietnam and eventually succeeded the Bishop of Tonkin. In 1858 he was captured, tortured and beheaded. Melchior was canonized in 1988.

'Go on your way; Behold, I send you out as lambs in the midst of wolves . . . He who hears you hears me, and he who rejects you rejects me, and he who rejects me rejects him who sent me.' (Luke 10.3,16)

Missionary journeys do not always end in triumph for the missionary. The journey may have sown seeds that will bear flower and fruit long after the missionary has left or died. God knows. In Vietnam, Melchior served the Church for a number of years; stepping into the shoes of his murdered predecessor in 1857 to enjoy but a short spell as bishop. Again, what ripples or waves his martyrdom caused in Vietnam only God knows. Melchior obeyed the call and worked day by day to minister to the faithful and to capture others for Christ. Each and every day was a precious gift to Melchior and his significance is just that.

In our prayers: thanks for the life, example and intercession of Saint Melchior Garcia Sampedro; for the ability to treat each day as a special gift.

Saint Melchior, pray for us, and for the Christian community in Vietnam.

July 29   Saint Martha, Saint Mary and Saint Lazarus of Bethany

The siblings of Bethany were devoted to Our Lord. Martha was a bustler and never still, always finding something to do. Mary, by contrast, was content to sit and relax in the presence of Jesus. Their brother was a close friend also but is not mentioned in the passage contained in Luke 10.38–42. We hear about the raising of Lazarus in John 11.1–44, during which account Jesus declares, in reply to Martha, 'I am the resurrection and the life.' In John 12.1–3, Jesus is again at Bethany and, on this occasion, Mary wipes Our Lord's feet with her hair.

Jesus said, 'I am the resurrection and the life; he who believes in me, though he die, yet shall he live, and whoever lives and believes in me shall never die.' (John 11.25,26)

Our Lord was clearly very close to these three. Martha elicited that profound response from him; on the other hand, he applauded Mary's seemingly idle contentment at his feet in contrast to Martha's vigorous preparations in the kitchen. The sign of Lazarus, who was brought back to life to die again, is a graphic reminder of our mortality and the passage through which we must travel to follow Our Lord, who was raised from the dead to die no more. So much teaching arises out of these three siblings; they are worth getting to know. We must allow God to use us as he wishes; we must exercise our minds to grapple with the great Mysteries in accordance with the talents we are given; and we must allow ourselves refreshment at the feet of Jesus as we kneel before the Blessed Sacrament.

In our prayers: thanks for the lives, examples and intercession of Saint Martha, Saint Mary, and Saint Lazarus of Bethany; for friends and relations; for those who wait upon others; for all contemplatives; for cooks and chefs.

Saint Martha, Saint Mary and Saint Lazarus, pray for us, and for all places dedicated in your names.

July 30 Saint Peter Chrysologus *(Bishop and Doctor of the Church)*; Saint Leopold Mandic

Peter was Archbishop of Ravenna during the first half of the fifth century. He was a reformer of the fabric of the Church and an important champion of orthodoxy. He gained a reputation for fine preaching and many of his sermons are known today. Peter died in 450.

Leopold Mandic was Croatian. He entered a Capuchin seminary and joined the novitiate after two years. He was ordained in 1890, spent 7 years in Venice, 12 in his homeland, and the rest of his life in Padua. He devoted his life to the confessional, spending a dozen or so hours each day hearing confessions. Leopold was crippled with arthritis, only four and a half feet tall, and was often the object of derision. He died in 1942 and was canonized in 1983.

Seek the Lord while he may be found, call upon him while he is near; let the wicked forsake his way, and the unrighteous man his thoughts; let him return to the Lord, that he may have mercy on him; and to our God, for he will abundantly pardon. (Isaiah 55.6,7)

These two saints seem to contrast dramatically with each other. Peter swept through his ministry building up the future of the Church and teaching the Faith with clarity and zeal. Fourteen hundred years later, Leopold's calling wrote fewer headlines. His deformed, painful body was put entirely to God's use. He suffered the mockery of men but performed his duties resolutely and reconciled thousands to Christ in the confessional where his counsel was as beautiful as his deformity was ugly.

In our prayers: thanks for the lives, examples and intercession of Saint Peter Chrysologus and Saint Leopold Mandic; for all students of theology; for all who counsel and reconcile; for those who suffer disablement of the body.

Saint Peter and Saint Leopold, pray for us and for all bishops and priests, for Capuchins and writers of theological works.

July 31 Saint Ignatius Loyola *(Founder)*

Ignatius, the founder of the Society of Jesus, was of noble Spanish birth, and a scholar. After recovering from a severe wound sustained in battle, and after experiencing a life-changing vision of Our Lady, he turned his skills to the service of the Church. Ignatius was ordained and formed a missionary society, and created colleges for the proper education of ordinands. The foundation received papal assent in 1540. Ignatius died in 1556 and was canonized in 1622.

Contend, O Lord, with those who contend with me; fight against those who fight against me! Take hold of shield and buckler, and rise for my help! (Psalm 35[34].1,2)

The discipline, the tactics, strategies and gruesome wounds of military life, together with a vision of Our Lady, moulded Ignatius into the dedicated founder of the Society of Jesus. This army of Jesus would sometimes enter into another's land boldly and publicly to comfort and relieve the downtrodden; at other times by stealth to seek out the isolated pockets of catholicity. The members of the Society of Jesus were trained meticulously in these matters and armed with the theological expertise necessary for their encounters. Our training, in whatever field, can be put to Christ's use; after all, any expertise we have is born of the talents given us.

In our prayers: thanks for the life, example and intercession of Saint Ignatius Loyola; to be equipped with the armour of Faith; for the Society of Jesus and its work.

O Christ Jesus, when all is darkness and we feel our weakness and our helplessness, give us the security and feeling of your presence, your love and your comfort. Help us to have perfect trust in your protecting love and strengthening power, so that we may fear nothing. For living close to you we shall see your hand and your purpose and your will in and through all things. (Saint Ignatius Loyola)
Saint Ignatius, pray for us, and for all places dedicated in your name.

August

I love the dedication of the Curé d'Ars (August 4). His only concern was for the salvation of the souls of his parish. And what a life was that of Teresa Benedicta (9)! After a painstaking conversion, she put her fine mind to work into many volumes of Christian apologetics, only to be gassed at Auschwitz. Monica (27), the patron of all mothers, had to deal with the youth of her wayward son, who eventually became Saint Augustine of Hippo (28).

August 1 Saint Alphonsus Liguori *(Bishop, Doctor of the Church and Founder)*

Alphonsus was born in 1696. He put aside a successful legal career to be ordained in 1726. He was the founder of the Redemptorists, whose teething difficulties dogged him for the rest of his life. He was made Bishop of Sant' Agata dei Goti, but retired on account of failing health in 1775. (He suffered the consequences of rheumatic fever.) Alphonsus published a number of editions of his *Moral Theology* and the popular *Glories of Mary*. His last years were a struggle between ecstasy and terrible depressions. He died in 1787 and was canonized in 1839.

And now my soul is poured out within me; days of affliction have taken hold of me. The night racks my bones, and the pain that gnaws me takes no rest. But when I looked for good, evil came; and when I looked for light, darkness came. (Job 30.16,17,26)

The 'success' of a life can often be seen more readily in retrospect – that is, the true legacy. Difficulties, illnesses and opposition beset Alphonsus's troubled life. However, great achievements were there along with the frustrations of everyday life. The *way* we live our lives is the way in which we use our talents, cope with difficulties and turn them to good use, for our own discipline or for the benefit of others.

In our prayers: thanks for the life, example and intercession of Saint Alphonsus Liguori; for those who struggle against opposition and poor health in their vocation; for the work of the Redemptorists.

My God I love thee above all things and in all things with my whole soul because thou art worthy of all love. (Alphonsus Liguori)
Saint Alphonsus, pray for us, and for all theologians.

❦

August 2   Saint Eusebius of Vercelli *(Bishop)*

Eusebius was probably the first Bishop of Vercelli. He is known principally for his stand against the heresy of Arianism, which denied the true divinity of Christ. He was variously under house arrest, imprisoned and violently treated. After Emperor Constantius died, Eusebius returned to Vercelli where he lived with his priests under a Rule. He died in 371.

I wait for the Lord, my soul waits for the Lord more than the watchmen for the morning, more than watchmen for the morning. (Psalm 130[129].5,6)

After the Edict of Milan, controversy raged in the succeeding years as official support was given to first one heresy then another. Those whose legacy of orthodoxy is our security fought hard for the purity of the Faith, and suffered many privations for their stance. Eventually dawn broke over the early years of the Church and future development rested with Holy Church and not with the political strength (and whim and fancy) of the Emperor. Eusebius's life epitomizes the period and a number of succeeding ones, and reveals how the Church relied upon the strength of those early courageous thinkers. But steadfastness in orthodoxy is just as much needed by priests and the faithful today.

In our prayers: thanks for the life, example and intercession of Saint Eusebius of Vercelli; for those who work to maintain the purity of the Faith; for the Pope.

Saint Eusebius, pray for us, and for those who stray from orthodoxy in the Faith.

August 3   Saint Lydia

Lydia was of Thyatira and a seller of dyed cloth. Paul baptized her, together with those of her household, whereupon she invited Paul, Luke and companions to her home. Lydia is only briefly featured in the reference below but, even so, her enthusiasm is apparent. She has an enquiring mind; she is prayerful and open to the Holy Spirit.

One who heard us was a woman named Lydia . . . who was a worshipper of God. The Lord opened her heart to give heed to what was said by Paul. And when she was baptized, with her household, she besought us saying, 'If you have judged me to be faithful to the Lord, come to my home and stay.' And she prevailed upon us. (Acts 16.14,15)

Once baptized, Lydia felt free to invite Paul, Luke and their companions to her house. The whole household now professed faith in Christ and was at one with the missionaries as they joined together for worship, sustenance and a bed for the night. Luke's easy reference to Lydia (he might have written O, *by the way, I have just remembered, one who heard us on the way was Lydia*) gives us a hint of the many saints who must have been made along the missionary way. Luke clearly did not remember them all. As he recalled and wrote, Lydia came to mind vividly. Whom did she tell about Christ after they had left her premises? What new strands of the Christian web would now be woven? Every little conversion makes its mark. And the very opposite is also true.

In our prayers: thanks for the life, example and intercession of Saint Lydia; for those who are new to the Faith; for those who are hospitable.

Saint Lydia, pray for us, and for those who hear the word and keep it.

August 4   Saint John Vianney

John (Le Curé d'Ars) was of peasant stock and grew up as a herdsman. He was secretly educated in the Faith by priests loyal to Rome – these were the early years of the French Revolution. After a lengthy and difficult training, he was ordained priest in 1815. In 1817, John was made parish priest of Ars-en-Dombes where he immediately became a popular confessor, and where he remained for the rest of his life transforming what had been a 'dead end' parish into a place of pilgrimage, and famous throughout France. He died in 1859 and was canonized in 1925.

The Lord is my shepherd, I shall not want; he makes me lie down in green pastures. He leads me beside still waters; he restores my soul. He leads me in paths of righteousness for his name's sake. (Psalm 23[22].1–3)

John was a dedicated parish priest with a special devotion to Our Lord in the Blessed Sacrament. He overcame his difficulties through prayer and devotion to duty, by living an ascetic life. This is how a saintly life is made. It is in the abnegation of self – in the denial of those whims and fancies that tend to become more important in our lives than anything else – that we become truly responsive to God's call. He has our full attention because nothing stands between.

In our prayers: thanks for the life, example and intercession of Saint John Vianney; for those who lead an ascetic life; for all priests and confessors.

Saint John, pray for us, and for all parish priests.

August 5   Saint Oswald *(Martyr)*

Oswald, converted by Ionan monks, was a devout monarch of Northumbria and much of the surrounding area. He was responsible for installing Aidan (August 31) on Lindisfarne, and therefore instrumental in the establishment of monasteries and churches in much of the north-east of England. He died in battle with Penda of Mercia in 642.

Thy hands have made me and fashioned me; give me understanding that I may learn thy commandments. Let thy steadfast love be ready to comfort me according to thy promise made to the servant. (Psalm 119[118].73,76)

The early Christian monarchs of Britain often enabled successful founding of monasteries and dioceses within their region of control by means of their support and patronage. They used their power and influence to further the work of the Church; they allowed their faith to imbue their lives. Do we allow Christ into all areas of our lives – our leisure and our work? In the alternative, do we confine our following of Christ to our attendance at Mass on Sundays and on other days of Obligation? Oswald welcomed Christ into every compartment of his life.

In our prayers: thanks for the life, example and intercession of Saint Oswald; for all monarchs and rulers; for the people of Zug in Switzerland and for the people of the north of England and of Scotland.

Saint Oswald, pray for us, and for all places dedicated in your name.

August 6 The Transfiguration of the Lord; Saint Hormisdas *(Pope)*

Hormisdas was known as a wise peacemaker, diplomat and negotiator. He used these skills to establish orthodoxy, and gain the acceptance of papal authority by the eastern bishops. Much of this he achieved in this difficult period when the Universal Church was finding its feet. Hormisdas died in 523.

The day of sanctification hath dawned upon us; come ye nations and adore the Lord: because this day a great light hath dawned upon the earth. (Alleluia for the Transfiguration, Sarum Missal)
All wisdom comes from the Lord and is with him for ever. To fear the Lord is the beginning of wisdom. A pleasant voice multiplies friends, and a gracious tongue multiplies courtesies. Let those that are at peace with you be many, but let your advisers be one in a thousand. The wise man makes himself beloved through his words, but the courtesies of fools are wasted. (Sirach 1.1,14; 6.5,6; 20.13)

It can be seen that Hormisdas's diplomacy went some way towards enabling the Church to concentrate upon the important matters of the Faith. The significance of Jesus gradually dawned upon and was confirmed in the minds of Peter, James and John in the light of the Transfiguration. Learning from significant moments in our lives is, of course, the way we gain experience, but do we make full use of the significant moments in Scripture and in the history of the Church in quite the same way to help us grow in the Faith?

In our prayers: thanks for the life, example and intercession of Saint Hormisdas; for a better understanding of the Faith; for the unorthodox and separated brethren; for our own transfiguration to the will of Christ.

Saint Hormisdas, pray for us, and for all diplomats.

August 7 Saint Sixtus II *(Pope and Martyr),* Saint Agapitus, Saint Felicissimus and Companions *(Martyrs)*

Sixtus succeeded Pope Stephen I in 257 and about the same time Emperor Valerian began his persecution of Christians. Sixtus was killed as he seated himself to deliver his sermon. The six deacons – Agapitus, Felicissimus, Januarius, Vincent, Magnus and Stephen – were probably beheaded at the same time. They did not resist in order that the congregation might disperse without molestation by the Imperial Guard. Sixtus and Companions died in 258.

Therefore you also must be ready; for the Son of man is coming at an hour you do not expect. Who then is the faithful and wise servant, whom his master has set over his household, to give them their food at the proper time? Blessed is that servant whom his master when he comes will find so doing. Truly, I say to you, he will set him over all his possessions. (Matthew 24.44–47)

Are we able to envisage the horror of this scene? The congregation in terror and panic are fleeing as their pope and his assistants are about to be slaughtered as they sit defiantly at the sedilia. 'No, I am afraid we shall not move; you must do what you have to but we shall not assist you by standing or by coming with you.' And quietly they prayed as they prepared to meet their deaths: 'God bless and comfort us and graciously permit our congregation safe passage out of this place and in peace to their own homes.' Absolute selflessness was their last concern on earth. What a passport to the blessed life!

In our prayers: thanks for the lives, examples and intercession of Saint Sixtus II, Saint Agapitus, Saint Felicissimus and their Holy Companions; for steadfastness in the Faith; for those who would kill innocent people.

Saint Sixtus, Saint Agapitus, Saint Felicissimus and Holy Companions, pray for us, and for the faithful.

August 8   Saint Dominic *(Founder)*

Dominic was born in Spain in 1170 or thereabouts. He first became an Augustinian Canon, and then founded a convent of nuns in order to create a cell of orthodoxy where earlier heresies seemed to be maintaining a foothold. Dominic created the Friars Preachers a little afterwards, and this was the core and the beginning of his Order of Preachers. He was a pious and devout preacher and teacher who spent his entire life in the service of others. Dominic died in 1221 and was canonized in 1234.

And there appeared to them tongues as of fire, distributed and resting on each one of them. And they were all filled with the Holy Spirit and began to speak in other tongues, as the Spirit gave them utterance. And they were amazed and wondered, saying, 'Are not all who are speaking Galileans? And how is it that we hear each one of us in his own language?' (Acts 2.3,4,7,8)

The essential feature of a good preacher is an ability to convey what he has to say attractively to his audience. There needs to be a little of the actor in him, perhaps. He also requires a fine wit to be successful. How does he measure success? Dominic's Order was (and is) devoted to good orthodox preaching and teaching, and conversion of souls. His aim was identical to that of the Apostles after Pentecost – to preach the gospel in the enthusiasm of the Holy Spirit, and be understood by all who heard him. Dominic's life also preached the gospel with as much clarity as the spoken word in the example he gave to those around him. Does ours?

In our prayers: thanks for the life, example and intercession of Saint Dominic; for all preachers; for the Order of Preachers.

Saint Dominic, pray for us, and for all Dominicans.

August 9 Saint Teresa Benedicta of the Cross

Teresa (Edith Stein) was born in Breslau in 1891 of a large Jewish family. In her teens she was an atheist, but at university her mind was opened to new thought, in particular, to the teaching of her professor, Husserl, a Christian of Jewish descent. After this broadening, Teresa read the autobiography of Saint Teresa of Avila (October 15) and was baptized. Ten years later, she joined the Carmelites taking the name, Teresa Benedicta of the Cross. She wrote *The Science of the Cross* in the Netherlands. In 1942 she was taken to Auschwitz and gassed. Teresa was canonized in 1998.

For it is he who gave me unerring knowledge of what exists, to know the structure of the world and the activity of the elements; the beginning and the end and middle of times, the alternations of the solstices and the changes of the seasons, the cycles of the year and the constellations of the stars, the nature of animals and the tempers of wild beasts, the powers of spirits and the reasoning of men, the varieties of plants and the virtues of roots; I learned both what is secret and what is manifest . . . (Wisdom of Solomon 7.17–21)

Like Thomas (July 3), Teresa needed to ask, to search. Everything she required was all around her, but she had to seek it, find it and study it. Thomas declared to the Lord 'we do not know the way'. He sought an answer and was given one. He needed to feel the wounds the nails had left; he was able to do so. After wrestling with her Jewishness, with new thought, with the influences and minds of others, she was receptive to the mysticism of Saint Teresa of Avila. This was her road to Damascus. She saw her duty quite clearly; she saw that she must carry the cross for her Jewish family; she saw quite suddenly how all is bound within the Mystery of the Cross.

In our prayers: thanks for the life, example and intercession of Saint Teresa Benedicta of the Cross; for all who suffered at Auschwitz; for Poland.

Saint Teresa, pray for us, and for all who search for the truth.

August 10 Saint Laurence *(Martyr)*

Laurence, a deacon, was put to death a few days after Pope Sixtus II (August 7). As a deacon he was responsible for the Church's goods and chattels under his care. He was ordered to collect together the Church's riches for the benefit of the Emperor Valerian, and was given three days in which to do so. Laurence sold the goods and gave the proceeds to the needy. After three days, Laurence presented the Emperor with the Church's valuables – the destitute, the unlovely and the disabled. Laurence was roasted on a gridiron for this grave insult and insubordination to the majesty of the emperor. Laurence died in 258.

Blessed be the Lord, who daily bears us up; God is our salvation. Our God is a God of salvation; and to God, the Lord, belongs escape from death. (Psalm 68[67].19,20)

Many onlookers were converted to Christ at the sight of Laurence's patience and faithfulness in death. What temerity in presenting to the emperor, instead of fine golden cups, plate and coin, the sick, the lame and the lazy! That these are the valuables of the Church is brought home to us only because the emperor felt insulted and Laurence died as a consequence. How are they the valuables of the Church? Christ himself squints from the eyes of the nearly blind man stumbling along the road; Christ is there in the woman racked in pain; Christ is in the tramp asking for money. Moreover, Christ is there in the generous response we make to those less fortunate than ourselves.

In our prayers: thanks for the life, example and intercession of Saint Laurence; for the destitute and for those who respond to their needs.

Saint Laurence, pray for us, and for those who suffer in death.

August 11   Saint Clare of Assisi *(Foundress)*

Clare, inspired by his preaching, became a disciple of Saint Francis of Assisi (October 4) and dedicated her life to the poor by becoming 'a servant of servants'. Under the guidance of Saint Francis, she founded the Poor Clares. Clare was abbess for nearly 40 years until she died in 1253 after an illness at the age of 60. She was canonized in 1255. She made linen corporals and cloths for the churches in Assisi and is patron of embroiderers and those who work for television companies.

Take off the garment of your sorrow and affliction, O Jerusalem, and put on for ever the beauty and the glory from God. Put on the robe of the righteousness from God; put on your head the diadem of the glory of the Everlasting. (Baruch 5.1,2)
And they went with haste, and found Mary and Joseph, and the babe lying in a manger. (Luke 2.16)

It was the sight of the crib in her cell that brought Christmas to Clare as she lay on her sick-bed. She imagined the singing of the Christmas chant in chapel and felt that she was part of the solemn celebrations. Clare's desire to serve the poor in the most humble capacity – she would even bathe the feet of the nuns and ensure that they were tucked up in bed at night – was her life's aim, for she had dedicated it entirely to Christ in the poor. How does our sense of duty to the poor compare?

In our prayers: thanks for the life, example and intercession of Saint Clare; for those who emulate Clare; for all those who work in television; for the Poor Clares.

Saint Clare, pray for us, and for all those who work with needle and thread.

August 12   Saint Porcarius and Companions *(Martyrs)*

Porcarius was abbot of Lérins, an island near Provence. On hearing that a raiding party of Moors had been sighted, he despatched the novices and boys to the mainland in the boats, but remained in the monastery to face ill use and death along with his brethren. They died in 732.

Blessed are you when men revile you and persecute you and utter all kinds of evil against you falsely in my account. Rejoice and be glad, for your reward is great in heaven, for so men persecuted the prophets who were before you. (Matthew 5.11,12)

The overriding sense of duty to those who had been placed in his care governed Porcarius's action at the predicted attack. Doing what is right at stressful moments and times of great trials is not at all easy because consideration for one's own safety naturally rises to the surface. With our souls came a responsibility to others and the ability, if we wish to do so, to repress instinctive desires – to put self last. We are not all called to make life-or-death decisions, but any selfless action, no matter how small, is evidence of our discipleship of Christ.

In our prayers: thanks for the lives, examples and intercession of Saint Porcarius and Companions; for those who put themselves last and for those who cannot.

Saint Porcarius and Holy Companions, pray for us, and for those who are in danger.

August 13   Saint John Berchmans

John, born in 1599, was a student at the Jesuit College, and later joined the novitiate. He spent a little time at the Roman College where he met Saint Henry Morse (February 1). He had a fine mind but no ambitions for himself. John was a thoroughly good-humoured, holy, young man. He died of an unknown illness in 1621 and was canonized in 1888.

How lovely is thy dwelling place O Lord of hosts! My soul longs, yea faints for the courts of the Lord; my heart and my flesh sing for joy to the living God. Even the sparrow finds a home, and the swallow a nest for herself, where she may lay her young, at thy altars, O Lord of hosts, my King and my God. (Psalm 84[83].1–3)

This young man shows us what living in the Lord truly means. His reputation as a charming young man, who was diligent in his studies, was widely known in his lifetime. He had wit, an ability to act and recite, but no ambition for greatness. His vocation to the priesthood was clear to him and he saw his future in terms of his ordination. He was content to fulfil his duties and do all that he ought to do in preparation for his priesthood. As it turned out he was never called to that office, he had simply been called to show Christ to others around him for the years of his short life. It was a vocation he fulfilled – a vocation to become a lovely dwelling place for the Son of God.

In our prayers: thanks for the life, example and intercession of Saint John Berchmans; for the simple life; for those who are called to encourage others.

Saint John, pray for us, and for the Society of Jesus.

August 14 Saint Maximilian Kolbe *(Martyr)*

Maximilian was a priest from a humble but pious home. He was enthusiastic to communicate the Catholic Faith by means of the written word while responsible for a Franciscan Friary in Grodno in Poland. The invasion of Poland in 1939 thwarted his plans to expand his ideas through radio and film. In 1941, he was taken to Auschwitz. At his own request he took the place of one of the ten men selected to be starved to death, a reprisal for an escape. They were stripped and confined in squalor to await their end. Maximiliam prayed and comforted the others during the two weeks of slow torture. He was the last to remain conscious and was then despatched by lethal injection.

Jesus said, 'If any man would come after me, let him deny himself and take up his cross daily and follow me. For whoever would save his life will lose it; and whoever loses his life for my sake, he will save it.' (Luke 9.23,24)

We read with horror at the crosses our fellows, through the ages, have carried. Maximilian's journey to Auschwitz would, in itself, be as much cross as many of us could have borne. At Auschwitz, he was generous with what little he had; he heard confessions (strictly forbidden), absolved and counselled. Countless people suffered as Maximilian suffered at the hands of their fellows, but few have made the ultimate sacrifice in quite such a generous way. The man into whose shoes Maximilian stepped had a wife and children, and it was for the family that he volunteered and died. From Nero to the present day, man's inhumanity never fails to shock but it is only against this tableau of beastly and cruel men that the martyr's crown can be gained.

In our prayers: thanks for the life, example and intercession of Saint Maximilian Kolbe; for all those who suffered in concentration camps and for those compelled to assist.

Saint Maximilian, pray for us, and for all who work for the spread of the gospel in the written and spoken word through radio and television.

August 15   The Assumption of Our Lady

The celebration of the Assumption of Our Lady allows us to concentrate fully on the example of Mary's purity and steadfastness. That she should be absorbed into the heavenly realms, body and soul, underlines for us that purity and steadfastness, that freedom from original sin, and that unsullied life. Though the location of these heavenly realms is beyond our comprehension (whether it is here and everywhere, separated from us only by the mere gossamer screen we call earthly life, or beyond knowable space and time, we cannot yet know, and it matters not), we have the certainty in faith that the wholeness of the Mother of God is there.

Gem to her worth, spouse to her love ascends,
Prince to her throne, queen to her heavenly King,
Whose court with solemn pomp on her attends,
And quires of saints with greeting notes do sing;
Earth rendereth up her undeservèd prey,
Heaven claims the right, and beams the prize away.
('The Assumption of Our Lady', Saint Robert Southwell [February 21])

In the Assumption of Our Lady, God is uniquely indicating the reward for her steadfastness from the moment of her assent to his will to her death through the trials of life and the devastating end of her Son's ministry. Mary's signpost is one of absolute trust in God. She was called in a state of grace – she did not carry the congenital disease of original sin – and she remained faithful to her promise throughout her life. Does this mean that she was not predisposed to put herself before God because she had not inherited that human tendency? No, Mary was merely placed in an ideal state, a state that prevailed before mankind realized and exercised the possibility of rebelling against the Almighty; she retained the freedom to rebel.

In our prayer: thanks for the life, example and intercession of Our Lady; for steadfastness in our faith; for the willingness to say yes to God.

Holy Mary, Mother of God, pray for us, for the people and government of France, and that we may be made worthy of the promises of Christ.

August 16   Saint Stephen of Hungary

Stephen became King of Hungary in 1001. He created bishoprics, built churches and consolidated the work his father had begun in establishing the Benedictine monastery of Saint Martin. Stephen was renowned as a good ruler, faithful to God and to his people. He died in 1038 and was canonized in 1083.

The Lord reigns; he is robed in majesty; the Lord is robed, he is girded in strength. Thy throne is established from of old; thou art from everlasting. (Psalm 93[92].1a,2)

This saintly monarch enabled the Faith to grow and expand within his country; his work built the foundations of the Church for the succeeding centuries. Stephen, in a broad sweep of gentle but firm authority encouraged and caused the Church to root itself firmly in his country, his inheritance. It is never easy when presented with an opportunity to seize that opportunity and make use of it to the glory of God. Our opportunities are unlikely to be as potentially far reaching (how do we know?), but do we recognize them when they are presented to us? Just such an opportunity for us may involve only a kind word, a good work or a friendly gesture – and so often we miss it!

In our prayers: thanks for the life, example and intercession of Saint

Stephen of Hungary; for the strength to seize opportunities to further the gospel.

Saint Stephen, pray for us, and for Hungary.

ᏫᏋ✿᎒Ꭶ

August 17   Saint Joan of the Cross *(Foundress)*

Joan was born in 1666 and became something of a money grabber when she inherited the family shop and bazaar from her mother. She lodged pilgrims who were on their way to the shrine of Notre Dame des Ardilliers. Joan was not, at that time, a very pleasant or loving person. From about 1700 she began to care for orphans, the sick and the hungry, and soon her rather ramshackle premises were unable to cope and fell down. However, by the time she died in 1736, Joan had founded many congregations and hospices under the dedication of Saint Anne of Providence. Joan was canonized in 1982.

Before I formed you in the womb I knew you, and before you were born I consecrated you. (Jeremiah 1.5)
When the poor and needy seek water, and there is none, and their tongue is parched with thirst, I the Lord will answer them, I the God of Israel will not forsake them. (Isaiah 41.17)

Joan and her family had lived for their business and, it is probably true, every penny counted. The business was not extraordinarily lucrative. When compared with her later sanctity, her early life pales. Even so, her early sentiments were not far from our own – the concern over the annual bonus; the increase in the price of fuel; the leaking roof; the increment that has failed to appear this year. Our earnest desire for financial stability is hardly new. In Joan's case, other matters rose up out of what was under her nose all the time. The poor and orphaned were all around her and she had ignored them throughout her life. Gradually the importance of the least of people began to assume a significant place in her life and they transformed her slowly but surely. The rich man had Lazarus at his doorstep but discovered him too late. Who is on our doorstep?

In our prayers: thanks for the life, example and intercession of Saint Joan of the Cross; for all those who care for those around them; for those who cannot see the Lazarus at their doorstep.

Saint Joan, pray for us, for your Foundation, and for the orphaned poor.

August 18 Saint Helen

Helen was the mother of the Emperor Constantine. She became a Christian in 312 (under the Edict of Milan promulgated in 313, it was lawful to be a Christian), and in 326 Helen enthusiastically travelled to the Holy Land anxious to locate all the sites of particular significance in our Lord's earthly life. At these locations she established (re-established in some cases) churches. She is also credited with the finding of the True Cross. Helen devoted the rest of her life to the destitute children, the poor and the imprisoned of Palestine. She died there in 330.

'. . . for every one who asks receives, and he who seeks finds, and to him who knocks it will be opened . . .' (Matthew 7.7)
Stretch forth your hand to the poor, so that your blessing may be complete. Do not shrink from visiting the sick man, because for such deeds you will be loved. In all you do, remember the end of your life, and then you will never sin. (Sirach 7.32,35,36)

We can understand the enthusiasm with which Helen undertook the location of the principal cities of the Gospels. She wanted to capture the feel of the places; she wanted to find herself thrust back in time so that she could touch the wood Our Lord touched, walk in the sand in which he walked. Helen confirmed the locations she discovered with grand ecclesiastical buildings, and much of her work or the tradition of it is still of significance and authority. We are grateful for it. Places and relics are extremely important for our contemplation and veneration. However, not only did Helen discover much of what she set out to discover, she found Christ himself still there in the sick, hungry and imprisoned.

In our prayers: thanks for the life, example and intercession of Saint Helen; for all who live in the Holy Lands and tend the Holy Places; for the sick, hungry and poor in the land.

Saint Helen, pray for us, and for all places dedicated in your name.

213

John was born in 1601. He was ordained priest and served for several years in the Oratory in Paris. He spent time with plague victims in Paris, and in Caen, where he went as spiritual director. John preached throughout Normandy, rejuvenating a tired and lax faith. He was responsible for spreading the devotion to the Sacred Hearts of Jesus and Mary in those parts. In 1643, John founded the Congregation of Jesus and Mary, a community of priests whose function was to train ordinands in the seminaries. The Congregation was strong enough to survive the worst of the French Revolution, after which it reformed and is of note to this day in the Americas. John died in 1680 and was canonized in 1925.

Let us then acknowledge the infinite grace and incomprehensible favour with which our merciful Saviour has honoured our Congregation by giving to it his most adorable Heart with the most lovable Heart of his blessed Mother. These are two priceless treasures that comprehend immense heavenly and everlasting riches of which he makes them the depository in order to pour them out into the hearts of the faithful. (From a letter to his Congregation by Saint John Eudes)

John's devotion to the adorable Heart of Jesus and the lovable Heart of Mary was a devotion which was not in the least sentimental in the superficial sense, but concerned itself with the recognition that Jesus our Lord shared a common humanity with us, shared our nature, our pain and suffering. Christ's adorable Heart was representative of these facts and enabled John to attach himself to the physical – a lightning conductor, as it were, bringing the Deity down to earth in the Word. The lovable Heart of Mary represents Our Lady's selflessness and adoration of God in her Son.

In our prayers: thanks for the life, example and intercession of Saint John Eudes; pray for a widening devotion to the Sacred Heart of Jesus and Immaculate Heart of Mary; for the work of the Congregation of Jesus and Mary.

Saint John, pray for us, and for the Americas.

August 20 Saint Bernard of Clairvaux (*Abbot and Doctor of the Church*)

Bernard was born in Dijon in 1090. He joined the Cistercians at Cîteaux and later became the abbot of the new congregation at Clairvaux. He opened over 60 Cistercian houses, and was a writer of many notable works. Bernard was renowned as a peacemaker during many theological and political disputes and upheavals. He died in 1153 and was canonized in 1174.

Jesu, the very thought of thee
With sweetness fills my breast;
But sweeter far thy face to see,
And in thy presence rest.

O my sweet Jesu! Hear the sighs
Which unto thee I send;
To thee mine inmost spirit cries,
My being's hope and end!

A renowned organizer, writer and developer of the Cistercian Order (which strove to follow the Rule of Saint Benedict in the original and most complete form) Bernard was an extraordinary and tireless worker. Among his written works are many poems and prayers, which reveal his deep devotion to Our Lord and his Mother. He was not sidetracked from this devotion by political and ecclesiastical worries and workload. His focus was truly upon the light of Christ, and it was under that light that Bernard performed his varied duties. Let us so focus.

In our prayers: thanks for the life, example and intercession of Saint Bernard of Clairvaux; for theologians and scholars; for the Cistercian Order.

Stay with us, Lord, and with thy light;
Illumine the soul's abyss;
Scatter the darkness of our night,
And fill the world with bliss. ('*Jesu dulcis memoria*', *Saint Bernard, trans. E. Caswall*)
Saint Bernard, pray for us, and for all places dedicated in your name.

August 21 Saint Pius X *(Pope)*

Pius (Giuseppe) was a gentle and humble man born of lowly stock in 1835. Nevertheless, he possessed appropriate boldness and courage in dealing with slackness in worship and knowledge of the Faith. He encouraged the faithful to receive the Blessed Sacrament more frequently than was then the custom, and urged them to be more conversant with the High Mass. He was anxious to restore the place of Gregorian chant and Renaissance polyphony in the Mass. Pius died in 1914 and was canonized in 1954.

O send out thy light and thy truth; let them lead me, let them bring me to thy holy hill and to thy dwelling! Then I will go to the altar of God, to God my exceeding joy; and I will praise thee with the lyre, O God, my God. (Psalm 43[42].3,4)

Every so often we need to be reminded that from our worship we must eliminate things that militate against seemliness and sanctity, such as the bad choice of music and instrumentation, and the perfunctory wave of the cantor's arm. Often these things are bound up in a desire to entertain, and that is not the purpose of church music in the context of the Mass and other offices. Pius desired a general return to the use of Gregorian chant and other sacred settings, a desire that has recently been expressed by the present Pope. Throughout the history of the Church we find that it has been necessary to do a little liturgical housekeeping. It is also necessary for us. How well, for example, do we prepare for Mass and offer our thanks afterwards for the gift of Christ in the Blessed Sacrament?

In our prayers: thanks for the life, example and intercession of Saint Pius X; for church musicians and liturgists; for servers and other church workers.

Saint Pius, pray for us, and for all places and organizations dedicated in your name.

August 22 Saint Symphorian *(Martyr)*

The third-century saint Symphorian was martyred in the French town of Autun on the order of the governor Heraclius. Symphorian had shown contempt and disrespect for the statue of Cybele as it had been paraded and exhibited on a carriage. After he was beaten, he firmly maintained his faith in the one true God and his contempt for stone idols. He was beheaded forthwith. A church was later erected over the place of his burial.

But thou, O Lord, be not far off! O thou my help, hasten to my aid! Deliver my soul from the sword, my life from the power of the dog! Save me from the mouth of the lion. My afflicted soul from the horns of the wild oxen! (Psalm 22[21].19–21)

Our lives are full of ceaseless parades of idols. There are those who have made themselves notorious; there are 'leisure activities'; there are food and drink; there are clothes. Have we even our own secret idol tucked away in its private shrine? Symphorian was resolute in not allowing other matters to come between him and his faith in God; nothing would distract him, even on pain of death. There are many things that can come between us and God, between us and our seeing Christ in others but our lives must be balanced, of course. Quiet contemplation before the Blessed Sacrament cannot fail to ensure that proper balance.

In our prayers: thanks for the life, example and intercession of Saint Symphorian; for the strength to avoid the worship of idols; for advertisers and promoters.

Saint Symphorian, pray for us, and for all who would follow your signpost.

ᛠᏓ

August 23 Saint Claudius; Saint Asterius; Saint Neon; Saint Domnina; Saint Theonilla *(Martyrs)* (Also today, Saint Rose of Lima.)

The three brothers Claudius, Asterius and Neon were reported Christians by their stepmother and were taken before the authorities in Aegea. The two women, Domnina and Theonilla were also tried for their beliefs alongside the three men. The men were tortured and crucified; the women tortured and thrown into the sea. They died in 303.

I will turn their mourning into joy, I will comfort them, and give them gladness for sorrow. Keep your voice from weeping, and your eyes from tears; for your work shall be rewarded, says the Lord. (Jeremiah 31.13b,16)

There is no doubt that these five faithful Christians were worthy of their martyrs' crowns. There was forgiveness on their lips. Was remorse in the informer's eyes as she saw her stepsons hanging on crosses in the steps of Our Lord? Regret at this stage would affect her for the rest of her life. Happily, most of the immoral, unkind, ungenerous, unloving, unchristian things we think and do daily do not result in the death of other parties. There is usually reparation we can make, in addition to the sacrament of penance, either by apology, or by correction of an omission. And as we anxiously make good in this way we remember that we forgive others without hesitation.

In our prayers: thanks for the lives, examples and intercession of Saint Claudius, Saint Asterius, Saint Neon, Saint Domnina and Saint Theonilla; for the grace to make good the wrongs we have done others and to forgive readily the wrongs we think others have done us.

Saint Claudius, Saint Asterius, Saint Neon, Saint Domnina and Saint Theonilla, pray for us, and for those who find it difficult to forgive.

August 24   Saint Bartholomew *(Apostle)*

Nathanael Bartholomew (that is, Nathanael, son of Tolmai) is known by his surname in the Synoptic Gospels, but by his first in John. It seems right to identify one with the other as all four Gospels associate Philip with him. After Pentecost, Bartholomew is thought to have preached in Arabia, Mesopotamia and Egypt.

Philip found Nathanael and said to him, 'We have found him about whom Moses in the law and also the prophets wrote, Jesus of Nazareth, the son of Joseph.' Nathanael said to him, 'Can anything good come out of Nazareth?' Philip said to him, 'Come and see.' Jesus saw Nathanael coming to him, and said to him, 'Behold an Israelite in whom there is no guile!' (John 1.45–47)

From the scant Gospel evidence we have, Nathanael was a witty man – a bright spark. His friend Philip knew this well enough. Can we not see this clearly painted for us between the lines? Nathanael sighed and raised his eyebrows, and his beard seemed to smile with sudden enthusiasm. 'Can any good come out of Nazareth?' Philip thought to himself. Ah, he is in one of those chirpy moods: I think I have more than his equal in banter and badinage. 'Come and see!' Jesus stretched out his arms in welcome, 'Behold an Israelite in whom there is no guile!' Jesus matched and bettered Nathanael's smile and warmly greeted the other. Do we always (or ever) display openness and warmth?

In our prayers: thanks for the life, example and intercession of Saint Bartholomew; for openness in our lives; for those who would make us smile.

Saint Bartholomew, pray for us, for places dedicated in your name, and for all tanners and leather workers.

August 25   Saint Louis IX of France

Louis, a man of his age, was a competent ruler of France. He was devoted to the Faith and anxious to improve the moral standing of his country. He cared for the destitute most generously and paid little heed to his own comfort. He engaged two crusades to the Holy Places, but was imprisoned during the first and died of typhus during the second in 1270. Louis was canonized in 1297.

When one rules justly over men, ruling in the fear of God, he dawns on them like the morning light, like the sun shining forth upon a cloudless morning, like rain that makes grass to sprout upon the earth. (2 Samuel 23.3b,4)

Louis was not in any way a successful crusader to the Holy Land, but as leader of a nation his responsibilities were correctly judged. However, to be instrumental (in the thirteenth century) in caring for the poor of the land, and in urging the country to raise its standards of morality are unusual characteristics in a leader. They speak volumes about Louis' response to the gospel. Furthermore, he was not a leader who pampered himself, and carefully tended his own desires. Let us be guided by Louis and begin in our own spheres of influences.

In our prayers: thanks for the life, example and intercession of Saint Louis IX of France; for those who care for others; for the raising of our country's moral standards.

Saint Louis, pray for us, for all places dedicated in your name and for the people of France.

August 26   Saint Teresa of Jesus *(Foundress)*

Teresa was born in Spain in 1843. She became a teacher and spent some time with the Poor Clares before founding, in 1872, the Little Sisters of the Abandoned Aged, which developed and expanded rapidly throughout Spain and abroad. Teresa was humble and devout and tender in her care for the aged. She died in 1897 and was canonized in 1974.

Do not cast me off in the time of old age; forsake me not when my strength is spent. So even to old age and grey hairs, O God, do not forsake me, till I proclaim thy might to all the generations to come. (Psalm 71[70].9,18)

Helping the aged is not a modern phenomenon. In these days of 'social awareness' we might be led to believe so, but Teresa's attention to the elderly was born of love not of statute. And it is the love of Christ that we, as Christians, must exercise in our individual ministries.

In our prayers: thanks for the life, example and intercession of Saint Teresa of Jesus; for all communities that follow the example of Teresa's Little Sisters of the Abandoned Aged.

Saint Teresa, pray for us, for the elderly, and for Spain.

August 27   Saint Monica

Monica was the loving mother of Saint Augustine of Hippo (August 28) and clearly concerned for his moral wellbeing. Monica was born of a Christian family and gave birth to three children at least. It was because of his mother that Saint Augustine ultimately embraced the Faith with enthusiasm and was then able to see her virtues and devout nature more clearly. She died in 387 at the age of about 56.

The day drew near when my mother was to die – this was known to you but not to us. We were looking through the window at the garden of the house in which we lodged. We talked happily and we speculated upon what might be the lives of the saints in your presence. We reasoned that the joy of eternal life could not compare with the finest pleasures of this world. (From The Confessions of Saint Augustine*)*

It is frustrating to see the great potential in others unrealized. Naturally enough, we always believe ourselves the best judges of these things; it may be that we are. By patience and example Monica was able to see her son as she had always hoped to see him, completely transformed from the wayward. However, Augustine, as a young man, knew that he fell short of the ideal and Monica was astute enough to focus upon the part of her son that acknowledged the fact. Monica's skill was in not only seeing the good that was there but having the patience to nurture it in the most appropriate way so that in God's good time Augustine would develop the strength to cast off the unlovely.

In our prayers: thanks for the life, example and intercession of Saint Monica; for all mothers; for the wisdom and skill to know when and how to encourage others and to correct errors.

O God, nothing is like your Word, our Lord, which is always with you, never ageing but breathing new life into all. When shall we enter into the joy of the Lord? When we rise again . . . (Extracted from The Confessions of Saint Augustine*)*
Saint Monica, pray for us, and for all places dedicated in your name.

August 28   Saint Augustine of Hippo *(Bishop and Doctor of the Church)*

Augustine, born in 354, was one of the children of Saint Monica (August 27) who misspent his youth much to the distress of his mother. He was well educated but he only fully embraced the Faith later in life by the intercession of his mother and the influence of Saint Ambrose (December 7). He became the Bishop of Hippo in 396, and was a prolific writer and defender of orthodoxy in the Church. He died in 430.

A wise son makes a glad father, but a foolish son is a sorrow to his mother. Treasures gained by wickedness do not profit, but righteousness delivers from death. (Proverbs 10.1,2)

Augustine, as we all know, appealed to God to make him good, 'but not yet'. He was enjoying life so much but deep down knew that carnal enjoyments and the delights of the world were transitory. He knew he could do better but was reluctant to relinquish certain pleasures. He wanted God to give him a little extra time in which to enjoy them. How patient is our God? We know not when the Bridegroom will come; we are always reluctant to believe that it will be soon and that we do not have plenty of time in which to become good. However, once we acknowledge our sin and ask for strength to be as we ought to be, we are clearly on the path to which Augustine's life points.

In our prayers: thanks for the life, example and intercession of Saint Augustine of Hippo; for all wayward youth and those who help and counsel them.

My God, I cry to you and invite you into my soul, which you are making ready to receive you by means of the desire you cause me to have. You expunged my sins, O Lord, because you would not punish me as I deserved for that I did, which kept me far from you. (Extracted from The Confessions of Saint Augustine)
Saint Augustine, pray for us, and for all places dedicated in your name.

August 29 The Beheading of Saint John the Baptist; Saint Sebbi

John (also June 24) emerges from the desert and points others to Jesus as the Lamb of God. (In the Gospel the same word is used for lamb and kid. So John predicts that Jesus would himself be both the scapegoat bearing the sin of mankind and the sacrificial lamb. We know this was the case.) John was beheaded by Herod Antipas through the agency of the manipulative Herodias. John's work was done – he had prepared the way and had turned the last page of the Old Testament and the last page of the Age of the Prophets and, at the same time, he had opened the beginning of the New.

Sebbi was co-ruler of the East Saxons. He assisted Bishop Jaruman in his mission to convert and baptize. Sebbi may have founded the first Westminster monastery. After a 30-year reign, he gave his wealth to the poor and entered a monastery for his remaining time. He died in 694.

'I baptize you with water for repentance, but he who is coming after me is mightier than I, whose sandals I am not worthy to carry; he will baptize you with the Holy Spirit and with fire.' (Matthew 3.11)

Pointing the way to Christ throughout his life, John was killed, a victim of lust and embarrassment. He had done what was asked of him. He was sealed as the last of the Prophets and the first of the martyrs who died for Christ after the Holy Innocents. John continues to point the way and shows us precisely what our lives should be – signposts to others pointing the way to Christ. Sebbi paid heed to the example and made the way simpler and easier for the conversion of East Saxon pagans by the missionaries sent out by Bishop Jaruman. He sealed his period as ruler with a magnificent gesture towards the poor of the region.

In our prayers: thanks for the lives, examples and intercession of Saint John the Baptist and Saint Sebbi; for all those in retirement and about to retire; for the ability to show the love of Christ.

Saint John and Saint Sebbi, pray for us, and for all places dedicated in your names.

August 30   Saint Margaret Ward *(Martyr)*

Margaret was a Catholic companion to a London woman of good standing – one Mrs Whittle. Margaret became involved in the escape of a rather colourful priest, who was imprisoned in Bridewell; she was captured and suffered brutal torture in irons, was beaten, and eventually hanged in 1588.

So Peter was kept in prison; but earnest prayer for him was made to God by the Church. The very night when Herod was about to bring him out, Peter was sleeping between two soldiers, bound with two chains; and sentries before the door were guarding the prison; and behold, an angel of the Lord appeared, and a light shone in the cell; and he struck Peter on the side and woke him, saying, 'Get up quickly!' And the chains fell off his hands. (Acts 12.5–7)

As a part of the team responsible for the deliverance of a priest from prison, Margaret was bravely playing a very dangerous game. Being instrumental in securing the release of a priest was a crime that would saddle you with the charge laid against the priest in addition to the charge you would face. The authorities had to encourage informants and discourage those who were sympathetic towards the religious prisoner. The point for us of Margaret's self-sacrifice is to show that the principal work need not be ours to perform. We may well fulfil what is required of us simply by enabling others to do what is required of them.

In our prayers: thanks for the life, example and intercession of Saint Margaret Ward; for the wisdom to see when we can assist others to carry out their calling.

Saint Margaret, pray for us, and for all worthy assistants.

August 31   Saint Joseph of Arimathea and Saint Nicodemus
(Also today, Saint Aidan [*Bishop*].)

Joseph and Nicodemus were probably both members of the Sanhedrin, and secret disciples. Of them one might say, in modern parlance, that they 'kept a low profile' but were both instrumental in giving Jesus' body a respectable burial. Joseph features after the Crucifixion; Nicodemus is recorded as 'coming to Jesus by night' in John 3.1–20, and speaking up for him in John 7.50ff.

After this, Joseph of Arimathea, who was a disciple of Jesus, but secretly, for fear of the Jews, asked Pilate that he might take away the body of Jesus . . . Nicodemus also . . . came bringing a mixture of myrrh and aloes, about a hundred pounds' weight. (John 19.38,39)

How difficult it is to say or do the 'right thing' when we are in an awkward position of authority, say, or when friendship complicates or compromises the situation. We try to steer the middle course and hope for the best. However, showing Christ to others by the way we work, by the way we treat our friends and those we dislike, without noising it abroad like the Pharisees, is the way in which we are all called as Christians. When a difficult decision has to be made, we pray earnestly for guidance and wisdom. Our heavenly Father knows what is in our hearts. But there are times when the more obvious practical gesture must be made and we can do nothing but provide the tomb and the spices.

In our prayers: thanks for the lives, examples and intercession of Saint Joseph of Arimathea and Saint Nicodemus; for wisdom in our actions and words; for courage in our commitment to Christ; for those who take care of the dead.

Saint Joseph and Saint Nicodemus, pray for us, and for all places dedicated in your names.

September

Peter Claver (September 9) was deeply concerned for the welfare of black slaves long before it was usual to show such compassion for their plight. Phocas of Sinope (22), the patron of gardeners and horticulturalists, is a special delight for me as I share his interest. And no calendar of saints would, for me, be complete without Vincent de Paul (27) whose tireless work in the steps of Christ, to this very day, is changing attitudes to the poor and downtrodden through the agency of the Saint Vincent de Paul Society.

September 1   Saint Giles *(Abbot)*

Giles was born around 640. Nothing is known of his early life, but in 670 he was given land (now Saint-Gilles in Provence) on which to build a monastery. He became abbot and, in life, was regarded as a saint. When he died in the early part of the eighth century his monastery became a shrine and Giles was acclaimed patron of those who were the frequent visitors to the shrine.

Do two walk together unless they have made an appointment? Does the lion roar in the forest, when he has no prey? Does a bird fall in a snare on the earth when there is no trap for it? (Amos 3.3,4a,5)

When a man is hailed a saint in his lifetime, it is usually because he leads a saintly life, in other words, living his life by heavenly values as though he were in heaven. The evidence for Giles's saintly life is simply that people flocked to him for counsel and guidance and, after his death, acclaimed him saint. How likely is it that our sanctity in life will have been so obvious? How will the good we did balance with the good we did not; and the bad we did not with the bad we did? Are we attractive enough to those who seek help?

In our prayers: thanks for the life, example and intercession of Saint Giles; for the patience and will to examine our lives; for the disabled and nursing mothers and those who care for them; for beggars; for blacksmiths, and shepherds.

Saint Giles, pray for us, and for all places dedicated in your name.

September 2 The Martyrs of September

The martyrs commemorated today are the 191 individuals, in custody, shot or hacked to death by rampaging lynch mobs fired with enthusiasm for the French Revolution in 1792, with the connivance, encouragement and help of the Executive Council of the Revolution. Most of the martyrs were priests, but many were unnamed; many were children.

For he has not despised or abhorred the affliction of the afflicted; and he has not hid his face from him, but has heard when he cried to him. The afflicted shall eat and be satisfied; those who seek him shall praise the Lord! May your hearts live for ever. (Psalm 22[21].24,26)

Few things are as frightening as a crowd out of control – a witless mob bent on destruction, violation and violence. Today's martyrs – priests and children among them – were guilty of holding the Faith and serving the Catholic Church. A mob does not like authority; it is envious of others' possessions, whether they be faith and trust or jewels and money. Our dislikes and envies probably will not end in our participation in mob violence but they often cause us to participate in rumour, the consequences of which we never know, by listening, adding spice and perpetuating. Do we see Christ in the malicious gossiper any more than in the murderer?

In our prayers: thanks for the lives, examples and intercession of the Holy Martyrs of September; for those entangled in the habits of rumour and of violence, and their victims.

Holy Martyrs of September, pray for us, and for all innocent victims.

September 3 Saint Gregory the Great *(Pope and Doctor of the Church)*

Gregory, born in 539, was elected pope in 590. He was the first monk to be raised to the papacy. Gregory was responsible for Saint Augustine's (May 27) mission to England. Gregory wrote much that has come to us – letters, prayers and homilies – and it is also true that he interested himself in the purification of the chant and its uses in the Mass and the daily Offices. Gregory died in 604.

Let us consider carefully how we, who have received more than others on this earth may well be examined more closely by the Creator of the earth. The more we have of his gifts, the greater the final reckoning. We must be humbler and more anxious to serve in acknowledgement of these gifts and benefits. (Extracted from Homily 18, *Saint Gregory the Great)*

There is no doubt whatsoever that Gregory used to the full his talents and gifts; they were employed in every area of his jurisdiction and responsibility. This was a matter close to Gregory's heart. He is the first saint within these covers to put the matter so succinctly. Our strengths are appropriate to our vocations and commensurate with them and assist us to fulfil them. Clearly, if we do not use our gifts we are like the employee who buried his single talent to await the return of his master.

In our prayers: thanks for the life, example and intercession of Saint Gregory the Great; for the Pope, the Vatican, all cardinals and bishops; for theologians.

Saint Gregory, pray for us, and for all church musicians.

September 4   Saint Boniface I *(Pope)*

Boniface was elected pope and consecrated in 418, when he was already an old man, amid a good deal of controversy. However, the disputes and arguments were largely resolved in the following year and, by most, his papacy was recognized. Boniface was meticulous and, though firm, revealed throughout his papacy his humility and his kind and gentle nature. He died in 422.

Therefore lift your drooping hands and strengthen your weak knees, and make straight paths for your feet, so that what is lame may not be put out of joint but rather be healed. Strive for peace with all men, and for the holiness without which no one will see the Lord. (Hebrews 12.12–14)

Not unusually the papal throne is achieved late in life. The elderly Boniface had to contend with dispute and acrimony due to the circumstances of his election. And yet he overcame these difficulties and enabled the papacy to emerge stronger and more effective from his tenure. And is this not the test of whatever we do, however small the task? Boniface teaches us that if we leave someone in a better state because we have revealed even the smallest glimpse of Christ, we have succeeded in our work. And this principle never ends.

In our prayers: thanks for the life, example and intercession of Saint Boniface I; for all who leave a situation in a better state; for the elderly in retirement and for the elderly who remain active in work.

Saint Boniface, pray for us, and for all whose position in life is controversial.

September 5   Saint Bertinus *(Abbot)*

The monk, Bertinus, accompanied Saint Omer (September 9) when the latter was consecrated Bishop of Thérouanne, to assist with the foundation of two monasteries and the evangelization of the country around what would become Saint-Omer. Bertinus became abbot of the second monastery and founded an annexe and a church, which was the forerunner of the cathedral church of Saint-Omer. Bertinus was a hard working and holy abbot and died in 700, or thereabouts.

Welcome one another, therefore, as Christ has welcomed you for the glory of God . . . Isaiah says, 'The root of Jesse shall come, he who rises to rule the Gentiles; in him shall the Gentiles hope.' May the God of hope fill you with all joy and peace in believing, so that by the power of the Holy Spirit you may abound in hope. (Romans 15.7,12,13)

It was Bertinus's untiring welcome of people into the Christian fold that eventually gave this area of northern France the enthusiastic and sizeable body of laity and religious upon which the future diocese of Saint-Omer would be built. The painstaking preparation of the country was as necessary for the future as any long-term projects whether commercial, industrial or ecclesiastical. Bertinus did not see the result of what he was preparing for, but his hope in the power of the Holy Spirit gave him and his fellow monks strength and confidence in their tilling of the soil. Every step in the right direction is an achievement. Indeed, our whole vocation may well require of us only a few steps in the God-ward pilgrimage of mankind.

In our prayers: thanks for the life, example and intercession of Saint Bertinus; for patience and freedom from despair.

Saint Bertinus, pray for us, and for all who welcome others in the name of Christ.

September 6   Saint Magnus of Füssen

Magnus was asked by the Bishop of Augsburg to leave his monastery in Saint Gall to evangelize Allgäu in Bavaria. He founded a centre for his mission in Füssen, and there a church was built. Magnus was not only diligent for the souls of his converts but also for the circumstances of their day-to-day lives. He was skilled in the art of cultivation and in generally making the most of the land for habitation. Magnus died in 772.

Thou visitest the earth and waterest it, thou greatly enrichest it; the river of God is full of water; thou providest their grain, for so thou hast prepared it. The meadows clothe themselves with flocks, the valleys deck themselves with grain, they shout and sing together for joy. (Psalm 65[64].9,13)

Like Bertinus (September 5) Magnus formed a large congregation of faithful upon which he built for the future. However, Magnus's particular strength was in responding to Christ's call to care for his flock by caring for each individual. After all, if one in a hundred sheep requires special attention, you give it special attention. Each individual is an important component of the flock. Magnus personally attended the families in his care and worried about their lives and circumstances. He helped them exploit the land for their benefit and that of their neighbours. Where we can we help others by donating clothing, food and money; often, though, we overlook a situation that calls for our assistance in some other way so that self-help is possible.

In our prayers: thanks for the life, example and intercession of Saint Magnus of Füssen; for all those who volunteer and help others in practical ways and for those who organize them.

Saint Magnus, pray for us, and for those who cultivate land for the feeding of others.

September 7   Saint Mark, Saint Stephen and Saint Melchior *(Martyrs)*

Mark, Stephen and Melchior were engaged in pastoral work in Kosice, in Slovakia, when it came under the influence of Prince Gabor. The three men were instructed to renounce their Catholic Faith and were shamefully treated and killed for their refusal to do so. They died in 1619 and were canonized in 1995.

Heaven and earth are full of the majesty of thy glory. The glorious company of the apostles, praise thee; the goodly fellowship of the prophets, praise thee; the noble army of martyrs, praise thee. (Te Deum 6–9)

To die as a martyr bravely and unswervingly has always counted highly in the Church. These three men were carrying out their ministry quietly and faithfully little knowing what was in store for them; they did not foresee that they would die at the hands of an opponent of their work. They knew not the hour of the Bridegroom but by the way they lived their lives, they were ready.

In our prayers: thanks for the lives, examples and intercession of Saint Mark, Saint Stephen and Saint Melchior; for the people of the Czech Republic, Slovakia, Slovenia and Hungary; for bullies and cruel men.

Saint Mark, Saint Stephen and Saint Melchior, pray for us, and for all those who submit to the bully.

September 8   The Nativity of Our Lady

Traditions have it that Mary was born of Joachim and Anne (July 26) in either Jerusalem or Nazareth; but whatever the circumstances of her birth, this day celebrates the prelude to the realization of the heavenly Father's promise to make his Word, flesh.

After having promised the Lord, they returned home, and lived in a cheerful and assured expectation of the promise of God. So Anne conceived, and brought forth a daughter, and, according to the angel's command, the parents did call her name, Mary. (The Gospel of the Birth of Mary 3.10,11, *generally a picturesque fourth-century work*)

The parents of Mary gave birth to their daughter in pride and happiness, uncontrollable smiles breaking out on their faces as they looked at their newborn child swaddled in the custom of the age. They had desired a child and had petitioned the heavenly Father: Anne conceived. This is a story heard daily throughout the world – it is the story of the Creator's continuing work in his world. The conception and birth of each and every child is the precious gift of life, no matter the circumstance. What is in store for *any* new birth? God knows. In the case of this child, no one knew what lay in the future. But she was God's choice for the fulfilment of his promise.

In our prayers: thanks for the life, example and intercession of Holy Mary; for all midwives, nurses and those who care for babies and small children; for all societies that protect the unborn child.

Holy Mary, pray for us, now and at the hour of our death.

September 9   Saint Peter Claver
(Also today, Saint Omer [*Bishop*].)

Peter was born in 1580 in Palma. He joined the Society of Jesus and in 1610 began to evangelize and minister to the West African slaves who were transported to Colombia in South America. He cared for them, baptized them and did all he could for their welfare before they were sold for work in the fields and mines. He concerned himself also with the welfare of sailors, traders and criminals – whether Catholic or Protestant. For the last few years of his fairly long life, Peter continued his work as a sick man. He died in 1654 and was canonized in 1888.

And the Egyptians were in dread of the people of Israel. So they made the people of Israel serve with rigour, and made their lives bitter with hard service, in mortar and brick, and in all their work they made them serve with rigour. (Exodus 1.12b–14)

Peter was most anxious to do what he could for the slaves transported from one end of the earth to the other. He was a man rather in advance of his time; the plight of slaves did not often attract lasting attention, although there were a number of saints who acted in their defence. Around us there are still those who are overlooked – those neglected individuals whose problems are not the subject of a charitable organization or who do not attract public attention. Peter's ministry embraced many others he encountered in his principal mission – sailors, general traders and criminals – all in need of spiritual sustenance and love. We are called to be observant and to seek out the neglected among whom we shall meet others who do not necessarily fit into any particular category.

In our prayers: thanks for the life, example and intercession of Saint Peter Claver; for all those whom we all readily pass by; for those for whom Peter cared.

Saint Peter, pray for us, and for all children and adults who are used as slaves.

September 10   Saint Nicholas of Tolentino

As a boy, Nicholas studied in an Augustinian friary and became a popular member of the community by the time he was 18 in 1263. He was ordained in 1269 and, after a few years, was sent to Tolentino where he began to preach regularly in the streets. His pastoral work and healing touch were renowned. Nicholas was a humble, holy and simple priest who carried out his duties tirelessly. He died in 1305 and was canonized in 1446.

Jesus said to them again, 'Peace be with you. As the Father has sent me, even so I send you.' And when he had said this, he breathed on them and said to them, 'Receive the Holy Spirit. If you forgive the sins of any, they are forgiven; if you retain the sins of any, they are retained.' (John 20.21–23)

With no extravagance, with no flamboyance, Nicholas, a gentle Augustinian priest, set out to serve the people of Tolentino. His touch – the comforting clasp of the upper arm; the gentle support of the elbow; the sympathetic pat on the shoulder; the tender clasp of the arthritic hand; the cooling hand on the aching forehead – was a healing touch, just a touch of Christ. There was Nicholas in the homes of his sick and troubled flock. There he was showing Christ to others and receiving the blessing of his Saviour as he did so.

In our prayers: thanks for the life, example and intercession of Saint Nicholas of Tolentino; for all those who serve others in the steps of Saint Nicholas.

Saint Nicholas, pray for us, and for all mariners.

September 11   Saint Deiniol *(Bishop)*

Deiniol founded a monastery at Bangor, in Wales. It became a large establishment of many hundreds of monks. At some stage, he was consecrated bishop – possibly by Saint David (March 1) himself – and founded what was later to become the diocese of Bangor. Deiniol died in 584. He became a popular saint not only in Wales but also in Brittany.

Every one, then, who hears these words of mine and does them will be like a wise man who built his house upon a rock . . . And when Jesus finished these sayings, the crowds were astonished at his teaching, for he taught them as one with authority, and not as their scribes. (Matthew 7.14,28,29)

We are concerned once again with foundations and beginnings. Deiniol's reputation was widespread and we can have no doubt that it was justified. (With the constant traffic of faithful priests, the Christian fellowship of Wales, Cornwall and Brittany grew and blossomed in a shared devotion to many local saints, including Deiniol.) He was known as a healer and a fine preacher, but primarily for his simple holiness. People can see through a cloak of affectation and pretence at piety; his was a holiness upon which the faithful of north Wales built and prepared for their future.

In our prayers: thanks for the life, example and intercession of Saint Deiniol; for those who lay foundations; for those who strive to be holy.

Saint Deiniol, pray for us, and for Wales, Cornwall and Brittany.

September 12   The Six Martyrs of Omura

On February 6 there is a general feast day for the Martyrs of Japan, but today is specifically celebrated the martyrdom in 1622 of six Japanese converts slowly burned to death for their faith, in Omura – Mancio Shibato, Dominic Mogoshichi, and four companions. They were beatified in 1867.

But thou, O Lord, art a shield about me, my glory and the lifter of my head. I cry aloud to the Lord, and he answers me from his holy hill. I lie down and sleep; I wake again, for the Lord sustains me. (Psalm 3.3–6)

In so many cases we read about the crowns of martyrdom being set upon the heads of the newly converted. There were a few hundred thousand Christians in Japan by the end of the sixteenth century, but by the beginning of the seventeenth century the Japanese faithful were liable to be killed by the particularly heartless method of slow burning. We find it difficult to understand this cruelty, but the slow burning hatred we nurture for some is not too far removed. We can easily destroy Christ's home within us if we, for example, convince ourselves that we are perfectly justified in maintaining our hatred on account of the terrible wrongs committed against us. In his Passion, Our Lord had upon his lips: 'Father, forgive them.'

In our prayers: thanks for the lives, examples and intercession of the Six Holy Martyrs of Omura; for those who cannot forgive others; for the generosity to forgive.

O Holy Martyrs, pray for us, and for Japan.

৻৽৽৳

September 13   Saint John Chrysostom *(Bishop and Doctor of the Church)*

John was born in Antioch in 350 or thereabouts. He became Archbishop of Constantinople in 398. In this capacity he founded benevolent institutions, sent out missionaries, and corrected the errors of the Church in Ephesus and elsewhere. Due to his forthright tongue against the prevailing heresies, he was twice banished from his see by Empress Eudoxia. He was a gifted preacher and many of his sermons survive to this day. John died in exile in 407.

There is not a thing icier than a professing Christian who has no thought for the salvation of other people. You cannot argue poverty: the poor widow will be against you. You cannot suggest a lack of knowledge: the apostles were largely uneducated men. You cannot plead sickness: Timothy was of poor health. Every one of us can be of assistance to his neighbour, if only he will respond to his individual vocation. (Extracted from a sermon by Saint John Chrysostom)

We often look for excuses for our failure to perform a Christian duty. John might have allowed the tide of heresy to flow around him in the hope that the fashion would eventually die out. He did not; his duty was clear and obvious to him. John submitted that if the Faith were distorted in any way, our vocation was to correct error. We cannot propose any feeble excuse for failing to act, because there is always precedent in Scripture against that excuse.

236

In our prayers: thanks for the life, example and intercession of Saint John Chrysostom; for those who correct error and instruct others in the purity of the Faith.

Saint John, pray for us, and for all who preach.

September 14   The Triumph of the Cross; Saint Albert of Jerusalem *(Bishop and Martyr)*

In 1205, the pope sent Albert to perform the duties of a peacemaker to Palestine, in the capacity of the Patriarch of·Jerusalem. Even though much of Palestine and Jerusalem was in Saladin's hands after the third crusade, Albert was skilful enough to bring at least an understanding among the various western interests and gain the confidence of both Christians and Muslims. He is recognized as the founder of the Carmelites for the simple Rule he devised for the prior of the hermits on Mount Carmel. Albert was stabbed to death during a procession, in Akka, to celebrate the Feast of the Triumph of the Cross. Albert died in 1214.

But as for me, it behoveth us to glory in the cross of our Lord Jesus Christ: in whom is our salvation, our life, and resurrection: by whom we were saved and obtained our freedom. (From the Introit: Nos autem, for the Feast of the Triumph of the Cross)

Albert's diplomatic skills brought about a mutual respect between Christian and Muslim; what a marvellous base for further work! The Cross would triumph over a divided people; the love that emanates from the Cross would enclose the people in its embrace. Albert's painstaking work would have its reward. No, his life would end at the hands of a dishonest steward of the Holy Spirit Hospice in Jerusalem, to whom Albert had earlier given notice. We live in a web of relationships and conflicting interests, and occasionally they cross paths. If daily we offer each day to God and commend our enemies to his safe keeping, we shall follow the path indicated by Albert.

In our prayers: thanks for the life, example and intercession of Saint Albert of Jerusalem; for the Carmelites and their work; for the discipline to keep a simple daily Rule; for the standard of the Cross to be ever before us.

Saint Albert, pray for us, and for our enemies.

ᘒ❈ᕽ

September 15   Our Lady of Sorrows; Saint Valerian *(Martyr)*

Valerian was a friend of the Bishop of Lyons and others who were martyred by torture and mauling by wild beasts in the arena (June 2). Under Emperor Marcus Aurelius, the significant Christian community in this part of Gaul was subject to unspeakable brutality. Valerian suffered a year after his bishop in similar circumstances. All these martyrs were known for their forgiveness of their captors and of those who had informed the authorities about them. Valerian died in 178.

At the Cross her station keeping
Stood the mournful Mother weeping
Close to Jesus at the last.
Through her heart, his sorrow sharing,
All his bitter anguish bearing,
Now at length the sword has passed. (From the Stabat Mater*)*

When a martyr suffers a passion in the footsteps of Christ and can put aside his terror, agony and plight to cry out to God to pity and forgive the masters of the arena, does something seal itself into the soul of the martyr making it even dearer to God? One can scarcely think otherwise as one contemplates the death of martyrs. The command 'love your enemies' is a challenge to us because it is a heavenly value, not an earthly one. It is difficult enough to forgive let alone love. But Valerian's example is extreme. We have to begin with the petty hates and dislikes and master those by petition and intercession. As Our Lady watched her Son hanging from the cross, she had already heard him forgive by asking his Father to do so. Our Lady, though a sword was piercing her heart, did not cry in hatred and for revenge.

In our prayers: thanks for the lives, examples and intercession of Our Lady and Saint Valerian; for the courage to forgive and follow Christ's command.

Holy Mary and Saint Valerian, pray for us, and for all those who suffer at the hands of others.

September 16 Saint Edith of Wilton

Edith was born in 961 and seems to have been the illegitimate child of King Edgar. She entered the abbey at Wilton, where she was an accomplished artist, especially in illumination and embroidery. She was responsible for building a lavishly decorated church in Wilton, dedicated to Saint Denis (October 9). She died in 984 at the age of 23. Her taste for and use of colour indicate that she saw it as her duty to use her talents in order to praise and glorify God.

[Solomon] overlaid it on the inside with pure gold. The nave he lined with cypress, and covered it with fine gold, and made palms and chains on it. He adorned the house with settings of precious stones. The gold was gold of Parvaim. So he lined the house with gold – its beams, its thresholds, its walls, and its doors; and he carved cherubim on the walls. (2 Chronicles 3.4b–7)

Our Lord did not reject the gift of expensive perfume poured over his head; on the contrary, he used it to illustrate the continuing and desperate need of the poor who surround us, whom we consistently ignore. Like the woman who anointed Jesus' head and Mary of Bethany who anointed his feet, we can do nothing other than beautify our places of worship: it is an appropriate way to express our love and honour. We beautify the tabernacle because Christ is there; we care for the poor because Christ is there also. Religious art is a product of a precious talent to be used for the honour of the Creator, who gave the talent, and for the edification of those who see it.

In our prayers: thanks for the life, example and intercession of Saint Edith; for all who spread the gospel in their art; for all interior decorators.

Saint Edith, pray for us, and for all who use their talents to the glory of God.

September 17   Saint Robert Bellarmine *(Bishop, Cardinal and Doctor of the Church)*

Robert was born in Tuscany in 1542, and entered the Society of Jesus. He was ordained in 1570 and spent many years preaching, teaching and writing. He was made the pope's theologian and given the cardinal's hat. Robert became Archbishop of Capua in which capacity his great pastoral skills were revealed. He returned to Rome as prefect of the Vatican Library. His written output was enormous and is still of great value. Robert died in 1621 and was canonized in 1930. He was meticulous in interceding for those who opposed him in theological matters.

Now there are varieties of gifts, but the same spirit; and there are varieties of service, but the same Lord; and there are varieties of working, but it is the same God who inspires them all in every one. (1 Corinthians 12.4–6)

The God-inspired varieties of working were well known to Robert. He was a learned man and knew the force and merit of theological argument and encounter; he knew that testing our views against opposing thought was the best way to be sure of our conclusions or to modify them. The gift of advanced reasoning power is given for our use, to enable us to explore more deeply the works of Scripture and of learned men. Those who oppose us are, therefore, those who can set us on the right path if we have strayed, or who can confirm the path on which we are travelling. The interaction is important and good. It applies in all our endeavours, for we are not all called to academic and theological dispute.

In our prayers: thanks for the life, example and intercession of Saint Robert Bellarmine; for all academics and thinkers.

Saint Robert, pray for us, for those who write, and for violinists and all string players.

September 18 Saint Joseph Copertino

Joseph was born in 1603, possibly an epileptic, and certainly not considered a very clever boy. Despite these difficulties, he was ordained
and spent his life in various friaries. He was not well treated by his
superiors largely because they did not understand his condition and
were impatient with him. All this Joseph bore with fortitude.
Nevertheless, he was visited by the high and the low, and remarkable
phenomena were reported. Joseph died in 1663 and was canonized in
1767.

And when they came to the crowd, a man came up to him and kneeling
before him said, 'Lord have mercy on my son, for he is an epileptic and
he suffers terribly; for often he falls into the fire, and often into the water
. . .' (Matthew 17.14–17)

What remarkable courage had Joseph. He worked hard throughout his
life and placed his handicaps behind him so that they did not inhibit his
duty to God. To bear a physical difficulty stoically is one thing, but to
bear it along with the lack of understanding of one's superiors and
brethren is quite another. It was Joseph's infinite patience and genuine
sanctity that raised him above his fellows, most of whom found in him
nothing more than an embarrassment. He gave wise and gentle counsel
when he was permitted to receive visitors. What a shameful thing is the
disgust at another's disability. And yet, are we ever free from guilt? Do
we avoid those who have conditions we do not understand?

**In our prayers: thanks for the life, example and intercession of Saint
Joseph Copertino; for those who are misunderstood by others through
ignorance; for those who care for epileptics and slow learners.**

Saint Joseph, pray for us, and for all who suffer as you did.

September 19 Saint Emily de Rodat *(Foundress)*
(Also today, Saint Januarius [*Bishop and Martyr*].)

Emily, at 18, began assisting nuns in Villefranche in the teaching of
children. She later began a free school for children and, in 1819, she

bought a disused monastery in order to found a teaching and visiting order, which eventually became the Congregation of the Holy Family of Villefranche. After initial difficulties, the work of teaching children, visiting the sick and imprisoned flourished. Emily succumbed to cancer in 1852 and was canonized in 1952.

'. . . Then all the maidens rose and trimmed their lamps. And the foolish said to the wise, "Give us some of your oil, for our lamps are going out." But the wise replied, "Perhaps there will not be enough for us and for you; go rather to the dealers and buy for yourselves." And while they went to buy, the bridegroom came, and those who were ready went in with him to the marriage feast; and the door was shut . . .' (Matthew 25.7–10)

Emily dedicated her short life to the spreading of knowledge among the children of Villefranche. They were given a good basic education in the light of the Faith. For the last months of her life her health deteriorated rapidly; she resigned as superior-general of the Congregation and bore her suffering with prayerful patience. Like Joseph (September 18), Emily was concerned with activities outside and beyond herself, focusing on God who had given her the skill and will to carry out his work. Why was her life so short? Clearly her Foundation and the example given by her fortitude were her vocations. Do we ask for the strength and ability to work beyond our health and pride – beyond ourselves?

In our prayers: thanks for the life, example and intercession of Saint Emily de Rodat; for those who work diligently through their sufferings; for those who care for cancer sufferers.

Saint Emily, pray for us, and for all who suffer from cancer.

September 20   Saint Andrew Kim, Saint Paul Chong and Companions *(Martyrs)*

On this day are commemorated 103 Korean martyrs who died between 1839 and 1867, and who were canonized in 1984. In 1839 this long period of persecution began, during which these saints were imprisoned, starved, stripped, tied to crosses, and finally beheaded.

Do not remember against us the iniquities of our forefathers; let thy compassion come speedily to meet us, for we are brought very low. Why should the nations say, 'Where is their God?' Let groans of the prisoners come before thee; according to thy great power preserve those doomed to die. (Psalm 79[78].8,10a,11)

These pages brim with the evil acts perpetrated by those who did not know Christ; those who feared the unknown and feared for their own authority and place in society. The missionaries and, in particular, the native converts were often hideously done to death. No one knows the extent of the value of their witness at the time – the repercussions and ripples in the pond. Their value to us is clear – their joy at finding Christ and at the privilege of suffering in his name. They did not even mind being tied to a cross because that is what they had committed themselves to in baptism. Of course, we always feel just the same, do we not?

In our prayers: thanks for the lives, examples and intercession of Saint Andrew Kim, Saint Paul Chong and their Holy Companions; for Christians in the Eastern countries.

Saint Andrew Kim, Saint Paul Chong and Holy Companions, pray for us, and for the people of North and South Korea.

༼༽

September 21   Saint Matthew (Apostle and Evangelist)

Matthew was the son of Alphaeus – we can reasonably suppose that Levi and Matthew are one and the same – according to Mark's Gospel, which perhaps suggests he was the brother of James II (May 3), who is also referred to as the son of Alphaeus. Of course, the name Alphaeus was not uncommon. Matthew, however, was a tax collector at Capernaum and was called away from his duties by Jesus. As far as the Jews were concerned, he was a collaborator and, therefore, most undesirable company, in the category that contained prostitutes and other sinners. The Gospel bearing Matthew's name, it is reasonable to suppose, comprises material from a collection of Matthew's written reminiscences (now lost), Saint Mark's Gospel and material from another source, used also by Saint Luke.

As he was walking along, he saw Levi, son of Alphaeus, sitting at the tax booth, and said to him, 'Follow me.' And he got up and followed him. (Mark 2.14)

Acting as a tax gatherer for the Romans was a good job, and the financial rewards were worthwhile. However, the Jewish tax gatherer paid the heavy price of isolation from his fellow Jew. He was a traitor and consequently an unclean sinner. But collaboration with an occupying power at the expense of the indigenous population is always difficult to accept. However, Matthew possessed the character Jesus was looking for. 'Follow me!', and there is no hesitation admitted in the Gospel. Jesus picks us all for special duties and calls us all from our disreputable activities or indolence. Do we respond in Matthew's decisive way or do we keep one hand on the tax booth?

In our prayers: thanks for the life, example and intercession of Saint Matthew; for alertness; for the strength to leave our petty sins.

Saint Matthew, pray for us, for all who work with figures, and for all places dedicated in your name.

September 22   Saint Phocas *(Martyr)*

Phocas (often called Phocas the Gardener) lived at Sinope in Pontus, and was renowned for his piety and benevolent hospitality. With his horticultural skills and interests, he was able to provide food for his many visitors, and pilgrims to the city. During a period of persecution he was beheaded early in the fourth century.

Thou makest springs gush forth in the valleys; they flow between the hills. Thou dost cause the grass to grow for the cattle, and plants for man to cultivate, that he may bring forth food from the earth. (Psalm 104[103].10,14)

Phocas lived for others: he found great pleasure in serving others, in entertaining them, in caring for them on their journeys. He saw how God responded with such generosity to his request for daily bread that he could do no other than share. Phocas's hospitality soon attracted the attention of the authorities; his service was overtly Christian, after all.

What an accolade! He was seen to be a Christian just by the way he lived his life. Can the same be said of us?

In our prayers: thanks for the life, example and intercession of Saint Phocas; for all who produce food for others; for the ability to be hospitable; for all who care for pilgrims and travellers.

Saint Phocas, pray for us, and for garden designers and landscape gardeners.

ᏨᏨᏒᎵᎵ

September 23   Saint Linus *(Pope)*

Linus followed Saint Peter (June 29) as Bishop of Rome and, therefore, Pope. He may be identified with the Linus noted in 2 Timothy 4.21. He has the honour of being one of the saints listed in the Roman Canon of the Mass. Linus died in about 80. Life in those early days of the Church was a difficult and dangerous business. All the faithful of the time were responsible for placing their small foundation stones around the rock that was Peter.

Unless the Lord builds the house, those who build it labour in vain. Unless the Lord watches over the city, the watchman stays awake in vain. (Psalm 127[126].1,2)

Linus was one of those trained by the Apostles who carried the baton to the next stage. Little by little the Church grew and flourished, spreading throughout the Roman Empire. Linus was there to speak for continuity, consolidation and expansion. Our good works are the batons for those we have served to take and carry to others. This is the way our lives bear fruit; this is the way we carry the gospel to others. Can we be even more effective in the team?

In our prayers: thanks for the life, example and intercession of Saint Linus; for the work of missionaries and pathfinders.

Saint Linus, pray for us, and for those who carry the baton to others.

ᏨᏨᏒᎵᎵ

September 24   Saint Gerard of Csanad *(Bishop and Martyr)*

Gerard was born in Venice around 1000. He spent a number of years in the Benedictine monastery of San Giorgio Maggiore. Intent upon a pilgrimage to Jerusalem, he found himself in Hungary where he became tutor to the king's (Saint Stephen [August 16]) son, Emeric (Blessed Emeric [November 4]) and, ultimately, Bishop of Csanad. After Saint Stephen's death in 1038, there followed a period of conflict over succession and a concurrent anti-Christian fanaticism fired by one of the claimants to the throne. Eight years after the death of Saint Stephen, Gerard was attacked by soldiers, lanced and thrown into the River Danube. He died in 1046.

Even though princes sit plotting against me, thy servant will meditate on thy statutes. Princes persecute me without cause but my heart stands in awe of thy words. Let my cry come before thee, O Lord; give me understanding according to thy word! (Psalm 119[118].23,161,169)

Gerard's story is an extraordinary one, is it not? His journey to Jerusalem was profoundly interrupted; God had already earmarked the place in which he was to serve. Gerard created a pocket of faithful Christians, which would thrive and flourish. As if this were not enough, Gerard had the privilege of a martyrdom inflicted by the soldier's lance, one of the instruments of Our Lord's Passion. He was not destined to tread the earthly Jerusalem, but he reaps his reward in the heavenly one.

In our prayers: thanks for the life, example and intercession of Saint Gerard of Csanad; for those who are bitter in their rivalry; for the people of Venice, Hungary and Jerusalem.

Saint Gerard, pray for us, and for all private tutors.

September 25   Saint Annacharius *(Bishop)*

Annacharius was made Bishop of Auxerre in 561. He was highly respected in his day and noted for the improvement of clergy discipline and order in his diocese that he achieved, and, as a consequence, the greater care of the faithful. He encouraged among the faithful a more seemly demeanour in church. Annacharius died in 605.

The Passover of the Jews was at hand, and Jesus went up to Jerusalem. In the Temple he found those who were selling oxen and sheep and pigeons, and the moneychangers at their business. And making a whip of cords, he drove them all, with the sheep and oxen, out of the Temple; and he poured out the coins of the moneychangers and overturned their tables. And he told those who sold the pigeons, 'Take these things away; you shall not make my Father's house a house of trade.' (John 2.13–16)

We receive timely reminders from a number of the saints about our behaviour and lack of discipline; about falling into bad habits; about growing accustomed to slack ways and sloppiness. We can fall into these traps very easily in our prayer life and in our church worship. If this framework should fall into ruin, everything built upon it will fail. We need to maintain a discipline that is appropriate to us. We are not all called to asceticism, of course, but we must aim for a suitable balance in all our doings. We must guard against our ever being the cause of the Church's falling into disrepute by the way we live our lives.

In our prayers: thanks for the life, example and intercession of Saint Annacharius; for the strength and discipline to follow our Rule of Life diligently.

Saint Annacharius, pray for us, and for those that give the Church a bad name.

September 26 Saint Cosmos and Saint Damian *(Martyrs)*

Cosmos and Damian are believed to have been Arabian twins who practised medicine after study in Syria. They were Christian and preached as they cured, always refusing payment of any kind. Cosmos and Damian were arrested – probably in Cyrrhus (where recognition of their sanctity began) – during an anti-Christian purge in Diocletian's reign, tortured and beheaded in about 285.

The Lord created medicines from the earth, and a sensible man will not despise them. Was not water made sweet with a tree in order that his power might be known? And he gave skill to man that he might be glorified in his works. By them he heals and takes away pain; the pharmacist makes of them a compound. (Sirach 38.4–8a)

Here two men were so brimming with faith that they could not hide it. They were so full of joy that they felt compelled to share it with all those with whom they came into contact. Can a Christian ever lose this joy? It is the joy of Creation, of the Nativity, of the Resurrection, of the heavenly realms, and so on. Can we keep it from those among whom we live and work? Simply the joy of knowing the Lord will suffuse what we do, and preach a thousand words. But do our worldly cares and our very selves often blot out our joy in case it gets in the way?

In our prayers: thanks for the lives, examples and intercession of Saint Cosmos and Saint Damian; for the selflessness to show our joy; for those who do not know the joy of the Lord.

Saint Cosmos and Saint Damian, pray for us, for all herbalists and confectioners, and those who cure.

September 27   Saint Vincent de Paul *(Founder)*

Vincent was born in Pouy in 1581, and received a good and thorough education. He was ordained in 1600; in 1612 he was parish priest in a suburb of Paris; in 1617 he was at Châtillon-les-Dombes where his vocation to the poor and destitute fully manifested itself. With untiring effort he formed charities for the relief of the needy; he created an infectious desire in others to help. He was instrumental in obtaining better training for ordinands and, ultimately, changed the face and attitude of the Catholic parish for ever. Vincent died in 1660 and was canonized in 1737.

If there is among you a poor man, one of your brethren, in any of your towns within your land which the Lord God gives you, you shall not harden your heart or shut your hand against your poor brother, but you shall open your hand to him, and lend him sufficient for his need, whatever it may be . . . You shall give to him freely, and your heart shall not be grudging when you give to him . . . For the poor will never cease out of your land; therefore I command you, you shall open wide your hand to your brother, to the needy and to the poor in the land. (Deuteronomy 15.7,8,10a,11)

Vincent was a splendid saintly organizer: he knew what had to be done; he did it and encouraged and enthused others into sharing his vision. That he was entirely successful no one can doubt; the evidence is all around us in every society, cell and area. Indeed, many other societies have copied the style of the Vincent de Paul structures and have produced good work. It is a fine thing if we devote our lives to the less fortunate, but it is the crowning touch if we have the ability to influence others to do likewise. Sometimes it takes only a humble example.

In our prayers: thanks for the life, example and intercession of Saint Vincent de Paul; for all charities and those who engage themselves in charitable work.

Saint Vincent, pray for us, and for all charitable societies and places dedicated in your name.

ⱥⱥⱥ

September 28 Saint Laurence Ruiz and Fifteen Companions *(Martyrs)*

Laurence is the first Filipino saint. He left the Philippines for Japan, but there, in 1603, Christianity was banned and Christians were obliged to renounce their faith and stamp on images of Our Lady and Child or face death by slow burning and beheading. Laurence and the 15 others were killed in this way between 1633 and 1637. They were canonized in 1987.

Do not lay up for yourselves treasures on earth, where moth and rust consume and where thieves break in and steal, but lay up for yourselves treasure in heaven where neither moth nor rust consumes and where thieves do not break in and steal. For where your treasure is, there will your heart be also. (Matthew 6.19–21)

A choice is given: renounce Christianity, abuse a picture you regard as holy, and you will receive the approval of the authorities. In the alternative, you will be cooked until almost dead when you will be shown mercy and beheaded, because the emperor is benevolent and generous.

The choice is yours. Peter renounced his faith in Jesus and in that terrible moment he caught Our Lord's eye and the dawn cockerel gave his alarm. Even with no threat we are all capable of denying Jesus and renouncing our faith, or, at least, putting it in abeyance, if scarcely more than an urgent desire intrudes. Christ raises us up time and again when we repent and shamefacedly ask for forgiveness. Laurence and his companions show us that we can all find the strength, with the help of Christ, to withstand the demand of self or even a pagan emperor.

In our prayers: thanks for the lives, examples and intercession of Saint Laurence Ruiz and his Holy Companions; for a strengthening of our faith in Christ.

Saint Laurence and Holy Companions, pray for us, and for the Philippines and Japan.

September 29   Saint Michael, Saint Gabriel and Saint Raphael *(Archangels)*

Angels and Archangels in all their choirs and categories were created to assist at God's throne. They are all in one way or another messengers of God, transmitters of his will, and, more often than not, communicate with mankind in human form whether in physical reality or in dreams or in conscience. (Wings are rather the fruits of the imagination of the artist, although the figurative use of wings does indicate speed, directness and immediacy.) Michael (the Strength of God) emboldens us to resist evil; Gabriel is the principal messenger of the word of God, who reveals God's will; Raphael carries the healing power of God, the Almighty. Perhaps these three created spirits *angelify* God's strength, message and healing power, and are called to convey and distribute these things from God to humanity.

'And I tell you, every one who acknowledges me before men, the Son of man also will acknowledge before the angels of God . . .' (Luke 12.8)

Let us not be confused by the visions of others. Visions are, usually, specific to the recipient, who uses them for his own edification and instruction. The appearance of angels will differ from circumstance to circumstance, from person to person. These Holy Archangels are revealed to us in Scripture, and help convey the meaning of the narrative in which they appear. In these beings we recognize the strength that is God's, the message that comes from God, and the healing power of God. When we ask for their intercession, we ask in the light of these revealed truths about them and in confident hope.

In our prayers: thanks for the guidance and intercession of the Holy Archangels; for strength against the forces of evil; for understanding of God's word; for the healing of the wounds of our bodies and souls.

O Holy Archangels, pray for us, and reveal and convey to us the attributes of the Most High God.

᭤

September 30 Saint Jerome *(Doctor of the Church)*

Jerome was born in about 342 in Aquileia. He was a learned, scholarly and austere man and an outspoken one for the sake of orthodoxy. He spent four years in the desert living a hermitic life. Later, in Rome, he directed a group of women in their Christian studies. He retired to the Holy Land with Paula (January 26) and her daughter, and, in particular, to Bethlehem where he founded a community of monks and three for women. He began writing scriptural commentaries and translating most of the Old Testament from the original Hebrew into Latin. He had earlier produced a revised version of the New Testament in Latin. The combination of this work became the *Biblia Vulgata*. Jerome died in 420.

And he stood up to read; and there was given to him the book of the prophet Isaiah. He opened the book and found the place where it was written, 'The Spirit of the Lord is upon me, because he has anointed me to preach good news to the poor . . . to proclaim release to the captives and recovery of sight to the blind . . .' And he closed the book, and gave it back to the attendant, and sat down . . . And he began to say to them, 'Today, this Scripture has been fulfilled in your hearing.' (Luke 4.16b–21)

We have Jerome's learning and writing with us today. Most of what we have read in Scripture is based upon Jerome's work. And upon his work others were able to develop their theological strengths and exegetical skills. The worth of his work is incalculable. His female companions, having studied with him in Rome, travelled with him to the Holy Land where they assisted in the foundation of the communities in Bethlehem. Jerome's outspokenness won him a few enemies, who attempted to cast doubt upon the innocence of his relationship with Paula – but the attempt was simply malicious. How easy it is to create fictions about those who have corrected us or who are clearly our superiors. We pass them on to a receptive audience and eventually believe them ourselves.

In our prayers: thanks for the life, example and intercession of Saint Jerome; for all scholars of the Holy Bible; for the innocents who suffer slander, libel and false witness.

Saint Jerome, pray for us, and for all writers on theology and Scripture.

October

Thérèse of Lisieux (October 1) must always be of help to us in this brash and throwaway age – her simplicity, her dedication to prayer, and her insistence on the need to carry out the smallest task well, are of special note. The life and death of Philip Howard (19) is inevitably of huge importance to us; his was a conversion brought about in part by his wife and in part by the martyrdom of Saint Edmund Campion (December 1).

October 1 Saint Thérèse of Lisieux

Thérèse was born in 1873. When only 15, she was permitted to enter the Carmelite convent in Lisieux and there she remained for the rest of her short life. The duty of an individual, she believed and practised, was to aim for perfection in the small things of life – in whatever duty one was given to carry out, and no matter how seemingly trivial. She also saw it as her personal mission to pray for all priests. She left a significant body of work, not least her autobiography *The Story of a Soul*. Thérèse died in 1897 and was canonized in 1925.

Illustrious deeds are contrary to my vocation. I can neither preach the gospel nor give my blood. My brothers and sisters work in my stead, and I, but a little child, remain beside the royal throne

Because she was unable to be a missionary and perform practical work in the field, Thérèse devoted her life to writing, to intercession and to performing her duties perfectly. If we perform well the duties God gives us we are fulfilling our vocations, which is, of course, our goal in life. There are indeed many other equally and more important duties undertaken in God's name around the world, for which we are not equipped and to which we are simply not called. We can assist those who are equipped and who are called, through intercession and by responding to the answers God gives us.

In our prayers: thanks for the life, example and intercession of Saint Thérèse of Lisieux; for all priests at home and abroad; for diligence in our intercessions.

I love thee, O heavenly Father, through the vocations of those who are serving you. (Extracted from The Story of a Soul, *Saint Thérèse of Lisieux)*
Saint Thérèse, pray for us, and for France.

October 2   The Guardian Angels;
Saint Leger *(Bishop)*

Leger was born in 616 and educated in Poitiers. He was consecrated Bishop of Autun in 663 and was concerned immediately with the reformation of the diocese, and with charity to orphans, the needy and the destitute. He urged the monks of the monasteries he reformed to obey and to be faithful to their Rule and the principles of their foundations. He instructed them that only then would they be able to set about what they were called to do – to live lives of prayer and to intercede ceaselessly for all mankind. Involved in the dangerous politics of the day, Leger was first tortured in 668, and then murdered in 670.

'See that you do not despise one of these little ones; for I tell you that in heaven their angels always behold the face of my Father who is in heaven.' (Matthew 18.10)
Remember, O Lord, how thy servant is scorned; how I bear in my bosom the insults of the peoples. (Psalm 89[88].50)

The pure spirits that are the angels are at all times making the connection between ourselves and the heavenly realms, so that lines of communication we cannot begin to imagine are ever open. We pray that knowledge of their presence reminds us at all times of our duty. Leger's duty to the 'little ones', about whom the angels are particularly concerned, was clear in his mind and was the guiding principle in his diocesan reformation. His monks, he maintained, could not fulfil their obligation to God and intercede daily with an uncluttered mind until they were able to make a faithful response to the Rule under which they had vowed to work. Getting our own spiritual house in order is, therefore, necessarily an important part of our calling.

In our prayers: thanks for the Holy Guardian Angels and for the life, example and intercession of Saint Leger; for the needy; for self-discipline.

Saint Leger, pray for us, for all who are blind and suffer from diseases of the eye, and for those who work with flour and grain.

October 3   Saint Thomas of Hereford *(Bishop)*

Thomas became Chancellor of Oxford University in 1261 and became Chancellor of England during the struggle between the barons and King Henry III until Henry defeated the barons. Although Thomas had taken the side of the barons, Henry invited him to resume his chancellorship in 1273. In 1275, he was consecrated Bishop of Hereford. His reforms were thorough and, inevitably, made him some enemies. Thomas died in Rome in 1320. His shrine in Hereford became an important attraction for pilgrims.

A wooden beam firmly bonded into a building will not be torn loose by an earthquake; so the mind firmly fixed on a reasonable counsel will not be afraid in a crisis. (Sirach 22.16)

Diocesan reforms again feature in another saintly bishop's life. Reforms were never concerned with innovation; they were attempts to return to the piety of former times, to remove the accretions of the modern world where, perhaps, the demeanour of the marketplace had intruded. In our private prayer we aim to concentrate upon the subject without distraction whether we are interceding formally, contemplating an image or meditating on the words of Scripture. If there is distraction, we return to the crucifix and begin again.

In our prayers: thanks for the life, example and intercession of Saint Thomas of Hereford; for those in public office, locally and nationally.

Saint Thomas, pray for us, and for the Queen and her ministers.

October 4   Saint Francis of Assisi *(Founder)*

This son of a merchant was born in 1182. Francis fostered military ambitions in his youth, which came to naught and, although he was always considerate of the poor, he was himself, if not an habitual reveller, someone who enjoyed much merry-making. After a disagreement with his father, he relinquished his claim to his inheritance and began a life of poverty. Inspired by Matthew 10.4–19, he preached in the highways of Assisi. Soon, disciples collected around Francis and he was ordained deacon. The Order of Friars Minor grew from this cell, and by 1220 there were many thousands in the Order. In 1224, Francis supernaturally received the marks of the Passion of Christ (the stigmata). Francis died in 1224 and was canonized in 1228.

Therefore I prayed, and understanding was given me; I called upon God, and the spirit of wisdom came to me. I preferred her to sceptres and thrones, and I accounted wealth as nothing in comparison with her. (Wisdom of Solomon 7.7,8)

Often a vocation is embarked upon after a complete break with the past, a sudden conversion, when the individual realizes he is on the wrong path. Perhaps the life of a saint has had influence or perhaps there is a sudden distaste for the life to date. In Francis's case his early life was unsettled, confused – he simply had not found the path he yearned to find. On the way to yet another military expedition he began to see more clearly what he should do and, after an encounter with a leper, began to visit colonies and hospices. In only a short time others were attracted to his life and work. The foundation of his preaching was, quite simply, the gospel of repentance and knowledge of Christ.

In our prayers: thanks for the life, example and intercession of Saint Francis of Assisi; for openness to Christ and his perfect love.

Most High and glorious God, enlighten the darkness of our minds. Give us a pure faith, a firm hope and perfect love, so that we may ever and in all things act in accordance with your Holy Will. Amen. (Prayer of Saint Francis of Assisi)
Saint Francis, pray for us, and for all Franciscans and their work.

October 5   Saint Galla

Galla was a Roman widow, and daughter of a prominent Roman citizen put to death by the Goth, Theodoric. With other like-minded women, Galla dedicated herself to prayer and to the service of the poor. Shortly before she died – she suffered from breast cancer – she experienced a comforting vision of Saint Peter (June 29). She died halfway through the sixth century.

He told them another parable. 'The kingdom of heaven is like leaven which a woman took and hid in three measures of meal, till it was leavened.' (Matthew 13.33)

Galla's cell was a little leaven working in Rome near Saint Peter's. The day's routine of this group was firmly based upon heavenly values – the self was ignored and the only thoughts were for others, in practical help and prayer. These days we believe most of the works of mercy are nicely sewn up by the State, with a few charities filling in the gaps. How far from the truth this is. Our prayers need to be informed – and the many Catholic charities are an excellent source of information and startling facts. As Galla found, our service to the poor may be required closer to home than we ever expect. Her example is clear and she also brings before us the plight and terror of those affected by breast cancer and the specialists now working with their gifts to find satisfactory cures and treatments.

In our prayers: thanks for the life, example and intercession of Saint Galla; for all charitable organizations; for all who suffer from breast cancer, their families, friends and medical specialists.

Saint Galla, pray for us, and for all who work in your steps.

October 6   Saint Bruno (Founder)

Bruno was born in 1035 or thereabouts, and was involved in ecclesiastical politics for most of his life, despite his efforts to maintain a solitary existence at La Chartreuse. There a chapel and a number of small monastic cells were built. This settlement became the motherhouse of the Carthusian Order. The monks lived their lives in poverty with meagre rations and threadbare habits. They met for two Offices each day. Bruno died in 1101. Some of his written work is extant.

How lovely is thy dwelling place, O Lord of hosts! My soul longs, yea, faints for the courts of the Lord; my heart and my flesh sing for joy to the living God. Blessed are those who dwell in thy house, ever singing thy praise! (Psalm 84[83].1,2,4)

Bruno was in demand for his sagacity and diplomacy, gifts he was obliged to use for the benefit of others. He longed, however, to be left alone to lead an ascetic life in prayer. Sometimes our vocations seem to be in conflict, and sometimes our own desires are in conflict with our vocations. Bruno, however, clearly was called to found the Carthusian Order and to play his part on the larger stage. In the first he earnestly prayed about the second.

In our prayers: thanks for the life, example and intercession of Saint Bruno; for all members of the Carthusian Order.

Saint Bruno, pray for us, and for all who lead the ascetic life.

October 7 Saint Mark *(Pope)*

Mark was the successor to Pope Saint Sylvester (December 31). He was pope for a few months only, but was responsible for devising a list of the burial sites of the popes and martyrs of Rome. This was an important first step in the documentation of these things, ultimately leading to the production of the Roman Martyrology and to the Calendar of Saints. It is thought that Mark began the building of what would become Saint Mark's Church in Rome. He died in 336.

The sons of Ham: Cush, Egypt, Put and Canaan. Canaan became the father of . . . the Amorites, the Girgashites, the Hivites . . . the families of the Canaanites spread abroad. To Shem also, the father of all the children of Eber, children were born. Eber became the father of Peleg, the father of Reu, the father of Serug, the father of Nabor, the father of Terah, the father of Abraham. (Extracted from Genesis 10 and 11)

The study of the lives of the saints is rewarding and edifying. How else can they be signposts for our journey through life? Mark's work was the first stop towards the calendars devised through the centuries for the ordering of feasts and festivals. The tombs of the martyrs had played an important part in constantly connecting the Church with her saints and martyrs during the periods of persecution when Christians met in the catacombs. The tombs became the altars of the early Church, and to this day relics are sealed into our altars or altar stones. Mark saw the need to associate ourselves daily with those who had gone before in a vast communion of saints living in this world and the next.

In our prayers: thanks for the life, example and intercession of Saint Mark; for a better knowledge of the lives of the saints.

Saint Mark, pray for us, and for all archivists, and cataloguers.

October 8   Saint Pelagia *(Martyr)*

Pelagia was a young virgin who lived in Antioch and who was martyred for her Christian Faith late in the third century, or very early in the fourth. She was venerated in Antioch as a saint, and acknowledged by Saint Ambrose (December 7) and Saint John Chrysostom (September 13).

'Behold I am coming soon, bringing my recompense, to repay every one for what he has done. I am the Alpha and the Omega, the first and the last, the beginning and the end.' (Revelation 22.12,13)

Pelagia is known only for her martyrdom during the persecutions of Diocletian. The fabulous stories constructed around her can safely be ignored. We have a number of young saints in the calendar who were killed in their virginity, pregnancy or early motherhood. The powers did not discriminate where defiant Christian women were concerned. Perhaps less is known about Pelagia but the form of her martyrdom can be guessed without difficulty. What more do we need to know? Pelagia clearly refused to deny Christ, and with faithful utterances on her lips died for the entertainment of others. That she had lived and died a saintly life is clear from the fact that Pelagia was immediately acclaimed a saint. We know how to live a saintly life with Christ at our centre; it is so easy, yet we keep getting in the way! We pray that we learn the lesson of the cross – 'I' expunged, 'I' crossed out.

In our prayers: thanks for the life, example and intercession of Saint Pelagia; that we might be moulded to the will of God.

Saint Pelagia, pray for us, and for all young women who are ill used.

ᏨᏌᎥᎤᏦ

October 9   Saint John Leonardi *(Founder)*
(Also today, Saint Denis [*Bishop*].)

John was ordained in 1572 and with the help of others was a missionary to the poor and sick of Lucca, and a preacher of note. His view was that in order to preach Christian morality successfully, the priest must be morally beyond reproach. He was adamant that it was with the youth that any campaign for moral reformation in the Church must begin. His followers became a community of secular priests taking religious vows in 1621. John died of disease after visiting victims of the plague in 1609. He was canonized in 1938.

My son . . . the gift of the Lord endures for those who are Godly, and what he approves will have lasting success. Do not wonder at the works of a sinner, but trust in the Lord and keep at your toil . . . The blessing of the Lord is a reward of the Godly, and quickly God causes his blessing to flourish. (Sirach 11.10a,17,21a,22)

John's views on morality were not, of course, unique to him. He did not stray from the teaching of the Church. His assertion was that unless the moral standards expected of every Christian were taught and well known to the faithful, there were no 'bench marks' against which to set the imperfections in our lives. It is one thing to fall short of the ideal and receive absolution, but quite another to be ignorant of the standards expected and, perhaps, indifferent as to whether or not we meet those standards. Today, the acceptable moral standards of society are far removed from those of the Church's teaching.

In our prayers: thanks for the life, example and intercession of Saint John Leonardi; for all those who fall short of the ideal in the Church; for disgraced priests and laymen.

Saint John, pray for us, and for all youth.

October 10   Saint Francis Borgia

Francis was born in Spain of that noble family in 1510, and spent most of his life performing duties associated with his position in society, which he was anxious to leave. He only partly achieved this when he entered the recently formed Jesuit Order and was ordained. He was tireless in his work for the spread of the Society and was diligent when asked to perform other duties for the sake of international concord. In 1565 he became the Society's general. Francis died in 1572 and was canonized in 1671. Much of his written work is extant.

The righteous flourish like a palm tree, and grow like a cedar in Lebanon. They are planted in the house of the Lord, they flourish in the courts of our God. They still bring forth fruit in old age, they are ever full of sap and green, to show that the Lord is upright; he is my rock, and there is no unrighteousness in him. (Psalm 92[91].12–15)

Rather like Bruno (October 6), Francis was often called upon to perform diplomatic missions. Unlike Bruno, however, Francis did not seek the solitude of the cell. Spreading concord rather than discord is much less easy. The inappropriate comment, the remark that raises a question in people's minds, and the miscalculated casual piece of slander couched in jest are all capable of causing discord, doubt, and, sometimes, everlasting harm. The careful tongue is a great blessing: Francis employed silence as often as skilful negotiation. Do we enjoy the sound of our voice so much that often we know not what we are saying?

In our prayers: thanks for the life, example and intercession of Saint Francis Borgia; for those in public life; for the wisdom to guard the tongue at all times.

Saint Francis, pray for us, and for the work of the Society of Jesus.

October 11 · Saint Mary Soledad

Mary was born in Madrid in 1826, and at an early age became part of a group formed by the parish priest for the purpose of tending the sick of the parish. Later, the infant community was divided between Madrid and a new site in Africa. Mary was responsible for the Madrid community, which, ultimately, became the 'Handmaids of Mary serving the Sick'. Many hospitals were established in Spain by this foundation. Mary ensured that her sisters received both spiritual training and training for the cure of the sick. She died in 1887 and was canonized in 1970.

The compassion of man is for his neighbour, but the compassion of the Lord is for all living beings. He rebukes and trains and teaches them and turns them back, as a shepherd his flock. He has compassion on those who accept his discipline and who are eager for his judgements. (Sirach 18.13,14)

Mary's story speaks for itself – a holy life serving the sick, and more than that. She established a tradition out of which grew so much. Those she trained were drawn to the community because they were responding to the command to visit and tend the sick, in whom Christ himself is honoured.

In our prayers: thanks for the life, example and intercession of Saint Mary Soledad; for doctors and nurses and all who train them.

Saint Mary, pray for us, and for the work of all communities specializing in the care of the sick.

October 12 · Saint Edwin *(Martyr)*
(Also today, Saint Wilfrid [*Bishop*].)

Edwin was born in 584 and became King of Northumbria in 616. He was then a pagan. Edwin weighed the pros and cons of the Christian religion with his council very carefully, and perhaps he was also nudged in the right direction by a generous letter from Saint Gregory the Great (September 3). However, he was finally convinced and converted. Edwin worked hard at evangelizing his kingdom without the aggression often associated with the zeal of the convert. He died in battle with King Penda of Mercia in 635.

Inspired decisions are on the lips of a king; his mouth does not sin in judgement. In the light of a king's face there is life, and his favour is like the clouds that bring the spring rain. (Proverbs 16.10,15)

Edwin's conversion was solid and founded upon his careful reasoning. He looked at the written word; he heard the words of the missionaries; he studied the lives of those who professed Christianity, and arrived at an informed decision. Were lives actually changed as was claimed by the preachers and teachers? Did they then behave differently? Did they display the joy of the Resurrection? All these questions were answered positively and to Edwin's complete satisfaction. Would an association with us convince him so surely? If we live in the joy of the gospel, we cannot be seen as anything other than as a follower of Christ.

In our prayers: thanks for the life, example and intercession of Saint Edwin; for the joy of the gospel to be revealed in our lives.

Saint Edwin, pray for us, and for all those who are converting to Christ.

October 13 Saint Edward the Confessor

Edward was born in 1005 and succeeded Ethelred the Unready as King of England in 1042. His reign was certainly peaceful and exercised an ability to compromise and accommodate. Edward was wise in his ecclesiastical appointments and was meticulous about the men he chose. He established the present abbey's predecessor at Westminster. Edward died in 1066 and was canonized in 1161. In his lifetime he was known for his holiness and concern for the poor. Edward became the patron saint of England until Saint George (March 23) was adopted.

It is better to be of a lowly spirit with the poor than to divide the spoil with the proud. He who gives heed to the word will prosper, and happy is he who trusts in the Lord. The wise of heart is called a man of discernment, and pleasant speech increases persuasiveness. (Proverbs 16.19–21)

King Edward was first and foremost a man who confessed the Faith and allowed that Faith to permeate his life and work. He was born to kingship, his job and his vocation. Everything he did he tried to do in the light of the Faith, in both matters of the state and of the Church. Many stories abound concerning his sanctity in office and some may be fanciful, but such stories are usually only constructed to emphasize what is already an apparent truth. Do we allow Christ into every compartment of our lives?

In our prayers: thanks for the life, example and intercession of Saint Edward the Confessor; for all responsible for making senior political appointments; for those who suffer from epilepsy and skin disorders.

Saint Edward, pray for us, and for England.

October 14   Saint Angadrisma
(Also today, Saint Callistus I [*Pope and Martyr*].)

Angadrisma was an abbess near Beauvais. She had lived in a convent for most of her life when she died in 695 at the age of about 80. There is nothing remarkable about her life except that many were inspired by it as a holy and selfless life – in itself a fine legacy.

'Shower, O Heavens from above, and let the skies rain down righteousness; let the earth open, that salvation may sprout forth, and let it cause righteousness to spring up also; I the Lord have created it.' (Isaiah 45.8)

The uncomplicated life of selflessness and sanctity was the abiding memory of those who knew the abbess from within and from outside her convent. It was remembered that in her early life she had suffered from leprosy, and in later life she had performed a number of miraculous works. If we blot out self from most of our days, miracles will undoubtedly occur.

In our prayers: thanks for the life, example and intercession of Saint Angadrisma; for those caught in natural calamities of fire, flood and famine.

Saint Angadrisma, pray for us, and for Beauvais.

October 15 Saint Teresa of Avila *(Foundress and Doctor of the Church)*

Teresa was born in 1515 and joined the Carmelites at an early age. She left to recover her health, developing during that time a deeply considered approach to and practice of mental prayer and meditation. She founded a new Carmelite convent in 1562 in Avila under a reformed Rule of poverty, prayer and penance. Teresa founded as many as 16 such convents throughout Spain. A large body of important written work has come down to us – an autobiography, many letters, mystical works, and general essays. Teresa died in 1582 and was canonized in 1622.

O Cross, the majesty you bring
So precious I 'pon you reflect,
You, e'en though so few accept,
Were bonded to the Lord Most High,
To you, so full of Joy, I fly
In love deserving not a thing. (From a poem by Saint Teresa of Avila)

Teresa's deeply mystical approach to prayer and contemplation of the great Mysteries is revealed in much of her writing. To enter fully into these Mysteries – these windows into the Creator's plan – let us consider the Holy Incarnation in the light of our understanding of the Immaculate Conception of Our Lady and of the Annunciation. Let us consider the Visitation and then see the child swaddled and wriggling in the hay. Let us consider how God poured himself into Mary's womb so that he would know birth, childhood, maturity and pain and suffering on a tree. Through his Son, mankind would be reconciled to the Father and the way to eternal life clearly shown.

In our prayers: thanks for the life, example and intercession of Saint Teresa of Avila; for all retreat conductors and theological writers.

Saint Teresa, pray for us, and for the Carmelites and for Spain.

October 16   Saint Margaret-Mary Alacoque

Margaret-Mary was born in Burgundy in 1647 and entered a convent of the Visitation Order in 1671. She reported visions encouraging her to promote the devotion to Our Lord's Sacred Heart. At first she was condemned by many of those in authority, in the convent and outside, as delusional. Later, she was able to spread the devotion to her novices and in 1688 a chapel was built in honour of the Sacred Heart of Jesus. Margaret died in 1690 and was canonized in 1920. Much of her written work survives (see Saint John Eudes [August 19]).

Included in the promises made to Margaret in her visions in respect of those who practised and propagated devotion to the Sacred Heart were the following:
1 *Peace would come to their families;*
2 *Comfort would be given in their trials;*
3 *Sinners would find in the Sacred Heart an 'Ocean of Mercy';*
4 *A blessing would be given on every habitation in which an image of the Sacred Heart was shown and honoured.*

Margaret-Mary made many feel uncomfortable, but her gentle insistence and beautiful logic of the devotion she proposed ultimately convinced even her sternest critics and detractors. We know that so much in our lives wounds Christ to the very heart as much as and more than the well-directed lance; we know that our sins of omission are as painful as our sins of commission. We know Christ is there in those we ignore and in those we harm in thought, word and deed. If we simply immerse ourselves in that 'Ocean of Mercy' we need not despair of ourselves. Christ does not.

In our prayers: thanks for the life, example and intercession of Saint Margaret-Mary Alacoque; for a greater devotion to the Sacred Heart in our homes.

O Sacred Heart of Jesus, have mercy. Saint Margaret-Mary, pray for us, and for all who promote this important devotion.

October 17 Saint Ignatius of Antioch *(Bishop and Martyr)*

Ignatius was Bishop of Antioch in 69 at the age of 32. He was arrested during the reign of Emperor Trajan in about 110, and transported to Rome. There he was condemned and taken to the arena for the pleasure of the lions. His writings addressed to the early Church reveal to us the depth of his spirituality and learning. He had a profound understanding of the Eucharist.

But consider those who hold false doctrine touching the grace of Jesus Christ which came to us, how that they are contrary to the mind of God. They have no care for love, none for the widow, none for the orphan, none for the afflicted, none for the prisoner, none for the hungry and thirsty. They . . . allow not that the Eucharist is the flesh of our Saviour Jesus Christ, which flesh suffered for our sins, and which the Father of his goodness raised up. (From an address by Saint Ignatius of Antioch)

The long life Ignatius enjoyed was cruelly terminated in the most sadistic way. His flesh, like Our Lord's, suffered deeply at his end and sealed his holy life with the martyr's crown. He knew and taught the great gift of the sacred Body of Our Lord in the Holy Eucharist. This Holy Sacrament is the very Body of the Saviour, his presence in the consecrated Host, true and real. To practise the presence of Christ when we kneel at the altar or before the tabernacle or the monstrance, is to open ourselves to him who came, was destroyed with our sin, and who was raised up on the third day conquering that sin and its effects.

In our prayers: thanks for the life, example and intercession of Saint Ignatius of Antioch; for a greater devotion to Christ in the Blessed Sacrament.

O Jesu in the Most Holy Sacrament, have mercy. Saint Ignatius, pray for us, and for all societies devoted to the Blessed Sacrament.

October 18 Saint Luke *(Evangelist)*

Luke was a Greek Gentile and a physician, a companion of Saint Paul (June 29) and the writer of the Gospel of Saint Luke and of the Acts of the Apostles. He addresses his Gospel to the non-Jewish world and to the well heeled. One of the principal sources of much of the Gospel unique to Luke is likely to have been Our Lady herself. Luke shows that Jesus in fulfilling the promises made to Israel opened his arms to mankind; to Jew and non-Jew; and to those from all strata of society.

Jesus said, 'Go and tell John what you have seen and heard; the blind receive their sight, the lame walk, lepers are cleansed, and the deaf hear, the dead are raised up, the poor have good news preached to them . . .' (Luke 7.22)

By tradition, Luke was also a painter of note. Whether or not it is true that he painted with brush and pigment, he certainly painted most beautifully in word. The first draft of his Gospel – perhaps his research and interviews – was carefully moulded into the Gospel we know today, along with most of Mark's Gospel and another source often called 'Q'. He was, perhaps, influenced by other techniques in his Nativity narratives, and there used his poetic tongue to guide us towards an understanding of the Holy Incarnation. And if, in our meditations, we wish to enter into this great Mystery, then this is where we begin – in the crowded inn and manger bed.

In our prayers: thanks for the life, example and intercession of Saint Luke the Evangelist; for those who spread the gospel; for those who teach in paint and the written word.

Saint Luke, pray for us, and for all doctors and nurses.

October 19   Saint Philip Howard *(Martyr)* (Also today, Saints John Brébeuf and Companions [*Martyrs*]; Saint Paul of the Cross)

Philip was born in 1557 and was a popular man, a partygoer and reveller in Elizabeth's court. His child bride, Anne, influenced his decision to become a Catholic (or, perhaps, resume and rekindle his Catholicism) along with the experience of watching the Jesuit martyr Saint Edmund Campion (December 1) during his contests with the theologians of officialdom. Anne and Philip decided to leave for the continent, and Philip wrote to Queen Elizabeth accordingly. He was arrested and imprisoned in the Tower of London, and later condemned to death for treason. He devoted his time there to penance and prayer, He died in 1595 in prison before the sentence could be carried out. Philip was canonized in 1970.

The greater the affliction we endure for Christ in this world, the greater the glory we shall obtain with Christ in the next. (The inscription on the fireplace in Philip's quarters in the Tower, carved by Saint Philip Howard)

The return to the fold of a lost sheep is, we are assured, the cause of much rejoicing in heaven. Philip was, as Earl of Arundel, both of high rank at court and well liked by Queen Elizabeth. She was affronted by his attempt to leave the country without her specific approval. Philip's value to us is enormous. He turned away from that which argued against his Faith; he embraced again that Faith under several influences; he accepted his incarceration in the spirit revealed in his graffito. Let us not be too proud to learn from the experiences of others. We do not live our lives in isolation, even if we happen to be contemplatives.

In our prayers: thanks for the life, example and intercession of Saint Philip Howard; for the humility to allow others to guide us where their experience and knowledge is greater.

Saint Philip, pray for us, and for all those who suffer for their Faith.

October 20 Saint Acca of Hexham *(Bishop)*

Acca was a companion of Saint Wilfrid (October 12) and succeeded him as Bishop of Hexham in 709. Acca was a friend of Saint Bede (May 25) who wrote warmly about Acca's learning and orthodoxy. Among other significant works, Acca adorned Hexham Abbey with colourful decoration and encouraged a much purer and more perfect singing of the chant. Acca enlarged the library there. He died in retirement in 740.

For Bishop Acca himself was a very cunning musician, well learned in Holy Scripture, sound and perfect in the Catholic Faith, expert and skilful in all orders, rules and disciplines of the Church. (From History of the Church of England, *by Saint Bede)*

How can a creature of God show his respect to the Creator? Our places of worship ought to be as beautiful as we can make them for the honour of God and our own edification and uplift. Our singing should be pure and our music appropriate. So felt Acca; and he cannot be faulted. The discipline of orderliness and perfection in the execution of all elements of worship reflects the orderliness and symmetry of nature, God's own tool of Creation.

In our prayers: thanks for the life, example and intercession of Saint Acca; for all church musicians; for artists and painters; for sculptors and architects.

Saint Acca, pray for us, and for all those in retirement.

October 21   Saint John of Bridlington

John was a member of the Austin Canons in Bridlington. A portion of his priory still stands. He was a quiet and pious religious, and in 1360 became prior. His life was dominated by prayer, and by constant meditation on Saint John's Gospel. John died in 1379 and was canonized in 1401.

He was in the world, and the world was made through him, yet the world knew him not. He came to his own home, and his own people received him not. But to all who received him, who believed in his name, he gave the power to become children of God; who were born, not of blood, nor of the will of the flesh, nor of the will of man, but of God. And the Word became flesh and dwelt among us ... (John 1.10–14a)

John was renowned for his orderly life as a monk. His was a life of prayer, of intercession for the world; for the poor, the neglected and the sick; for those in authority; for enemies of the realm and of the person; for friends, family and acquaintances. For his personal development he chose to delve deeply into the Gospel of Saint John. In so doing he exercised his theological mind and informed his prayers. Several of the October saints point us, in their different ways, to a better, fuller prayer life. Most of us cannot spend the time available to John on our knees in chapel, but we can hold all that we do in thanksgiving to Almighty God and dwell on the beauty of holiness throughout each day.

In our prayers: thanks for the life, example and intercession of Saint John of Bridlington; for all contemplatives and those who pray for others.

Saint John, pray for us, and for all those who have forgotten how to pray.

October 22 Saint Donatus of Fiesole *(Bishop)*

The Irish monk, Donatus, became Bishop of Fiesole, close beside Florence, in 829 or thereabouts. Donatus was known as a poet and teacher, and was highly thought of in Rome as a confidant of the Pope. He died in 876.

Blessed art thou, O Lord, God of our Fathers, and to be praised and highly exalted for ever; And blessed is thy glorious, holy name and to be highly praised and highly exalted for ever; Blessed art thou, who sittest upon the Cherubim and lookest upon the deeps, and to be praised and highly exalted for ever. Blessed art thou in the firmament of heaven and to be sung and glorified for ever. ('The Song of the Young Men', Daniel 3.29,32,34)

The ability to convey, in heightened form, truths and Mysteries of the Faith is an artistic gift so many have used for the benefit of mankind and to the praise of the heavenly Father. That we ought to respond to God in the best way we are able by using the gifts he has given us is only right and proper. In the gifts of music and the word, man comes as close as he can to the Creator's art, and it is fitting that they should be exercised in his honour.

In our prayers: thanks for the life, example and intercession of Saint Donatus of Fiesole; for all who use their gifts to the glory of God; for all charities concerned with the welfare of actors, musicians and artists.

Saint Donatus, pray for us, and for all poets and teachers.

October 23   Saint John of Capistrano

John entered the Order of Friars Minor in 1416 and was ordained in 1420. His was an ascetic life in the extreme, travelling and preaching barefoot. His concern was for the moral standing of the clergy who, he believed, ought to be shining examples for the rest of society. Duties abroad, imposed by the pope, took John from his friary for the remaining five years of his life. He died from cholera in 1456 and was canonized in 1724.

Sing aloud to God our strength; shout for joy to the God of Jacob! Raise a song, sound the timbrel, the sweet lyre with the harp. Blow the trumpet in the new moon, at the full moon, on our feast day. For it is a statute of Israel, an ordinance of the God of Jacob. He made it a decree in Joseph, when he went out over the land of Egypt. (Psalm 81[80].1–5)

Here is another priest, another saint who was insistent about the example to be set by the clergy. He wrote on the subject most passionately, asserting that the very life of a good and faithful priest would cast a bright ray of sanctity on all who came into contact with him. John's arduous missions to the faithful and the lapsed and, more than anything, his ardent and enthusiastic preaching was most persuasive. John was extremely severe with himself and his is a graphic reminder to us of what we lavish upon ourselves, how much we waste because it is in excess of our needs. We pamper ourselves with much care and attention and consider carefully how much we can afford to place in the charity box.

In our prayers: thanks for the life, example and intercession of Saint John of Capistrano; for ascetics and those who are harsh with themselves in order that we might learn something about extravagance; for those who are dying from disease and malnutrition.

Saint John, pray for us, and for all military chaplains.

October 24   Saint Antony Mary Claret *(Founder and Bishop)*

Antony was born in 1807 and became priest in 1835. Until 1850, when he was consecrated Archbishop of Santiago in Cuba, he was a great motivator and many parish cells were created to enable women to encourage devotion to the Heart of Mary, and to teach the Faith. He established the Congregation of Missionary Sons of the Immaculate Heart of Mary, for priests. He wrote, edited and published hundreds of booklets and tracts to aid the spread of the Faith. In Cuba, he showed the same zeal for work and created new parishes, and formed the Confraternity of Christian Doctrine. Antony returned to Spain in 1857 where he founded the Congregation of Catholic Mothers, and the Academy of Saint Michael. He died in 1870 and was canonized in 1950. Many of his tracts remain in print.

So I exhort the elders among you, as a fellow elder and a witness of the sufferings of Christ as well as a partaker in the glory that is to be revealed. Tend the flock of God that is your charge . . . being examples to the flock. (1 Peter 5.1–3)

With extraordinary energy Antony worked hard to spread and encourage the Faith through the agencies of others. He trained them and nurtured them and set them to their tasks. Antony saw much merit in the teaching booklet and tract for the faithful to hold as a reference. If we have the ability to enthuse others in the spread of the gospel, we are obliged to make use of it. Indeed, there are few abilities that cannot be used to this end. How do we fare?

In our prayers: thanks for the life, example and intercession of Saint Antony Mary Claret; for writers, motivators and organizers.

Saint Antony, pray for us, and for Cuba.

October 25   The Forty Martyrs of England and Wales

These martyrs were canonized in 1970, and five of the saints are featured within this book on their appropriate days. Martyrdom has featured in the history of the Church from the very beginning. It is important to value and to be guided by their examples of steadfastness in the Faith.

They have given the bodies of thy servants to the birds of the air for food,

273

the flesh of thy saints to the beasts of the earth. They have poured out their blood like water. (Psalm 79[78].2,3)

So many on these shores were killed in the name of Christianity. Most were innocent of any real crime and were simple, honest folk. It is well to dwell a little on man's inclination to harm and kill those who oppose him in thought and word. The public morality and judicial system of the Renaissance and Reformation were very much of their own time, of course, and we cannot but judge by the standards of the time. However, how do we react to those who disagree with us? Are our reactions always honourable? On the other hand, are we so liberal, unsure and agnostic in our Faith that we no longer feel strongly on any point? Our Faith ought to permeate the very fabric of our lives, as it did the Forty Martyrs. Are we strong enough to stand firm in orthodoxy even without the threat of trial and death?

In our prayers: thanks for the lives, examples and intercession of the Forty Martyrs; for those who stand firm in the Faith of Christ; for those Christians who are persecuted.

O Holy Martyrs, pray for us, and for England and Wales.

October 26   **Saint Rusticus of Narbonne** *(Bishop)*

In 427, Rusticus was consecrated Bishop of Narbonne in Gaul, and became depressed by the fact that there were so many factions at loggerheads. Saint Leo the Great (November 10) gave him encouragement, and Rusticus, fired by fresh enthusiasm, set about building a new cathedral and a basilica. It is known that he was highly thought of by his peers. He died in 461.

O come let us worship and bow down, let us kneel before the Lord, our Maker; for he is our God, and we are the people of his pasture, and the sheep of his hand! O that today you would hearken to his voice! (Psalm 95.6,7)

Factions arise. We find them mentioned in the Acts of the Apostles and in the Epistles; we find them somewhere in every age. It is probably simplistic to argue that factions arise from selfishness and are an almost inevitable consequence of too feeble a leadership. There are probably many other causes. However, the advice given by Saint Leo to Rusticus was simply that if we fail to focus upon Christ himself, other matters will take our attention and distract us. Leo's advice was heeded and Rusticus shepherded his united flock to the glory of God and the confusion of the devil. Rusticus's ministry is our worthy signpost.

In our prayers: thanks for the life, example and intercession of Saint Rusticus of Narbonne; for strength and encouragement for the diffident and those who lack confidence.

Saint Rusticus, pray for us, and for all who lead.

October 27 Saint Frumentius *(Bishop)* and Saint Aedesius

Frumentius and Aedesius, originally from Tyre, were Christian members of the court of the king of Ethiopia. Aedesius returned to his native Palestine, became a priest and served his countrymen faithfully. Frumentius left in order to visit Athanasius (May 2); he was consecrated bishop and returned to Ethiopia to continue the work of spreading the Faith. He died in 380. This is a simple story of two men going their separate ways in faith – one to the land of his birth, the other remaining where he was a foreigner. Wherever the gospel takes us, we take the gospel.

'You are my witness,' says the Lord. 'And my servant whom I have chosen, that you may know and believe me and understand that I am he. I, I am the Lord and besides me there is no saviour. I am God, and also henceforth I am he.' (Isaiah 43.10,11,13)

Their stories have come down to us over the many centuries because they were significant stories to those who knew and trusted the ministries of Saint Frumentius and Saint Aedesius. It did not matter where they ministered or to whom because God remained the same, and the needs of the faithful and the pagan were the same in Ethiopia and in Palestine. Our good counsel and our propagation of the Faith (whether by word of mouth or by the way we live) is as valid in our homes as it is in our place of work or recreation. If we live the gospel of Christ it is impossible to leave the Faith at home hanging in a wardrobe only to be worn on Sundays and other Holy Days of Obligation.

In our prayers: thanks for the lives, examples and intercession of Saint Frumentius and Saint Aedesius; for missionaries at home and abroad.

Saint Frumentius and Saint Aedesius, pray for us, and for all who take the gospel with them.

〆❦〇

October 28   Saint Simon; Saint Jude *(Apostles)*

Simon, the Canaanite, or the Zealot, was probably in favour of armed insurrection before called to be one of the twelve. In the Gospels, Jude is variously named Judas, not Iscariot; Judas, son of James; and Thaddeus. (The Epistle of Jude is likely to have been written by another – possibly the brother of James, Joseph and Simeon, cousins of our Lord, but not disciples during his earthly life.) Simon the Canaanite was clearly converted from his inclination to violence; Jude, also a fairly obscure character, is usually known only as the Patron of lost causes.

And when they had entered, they went to the upper room where they were staying; Peter and John and James and Andrew, Philip and Thomas, Bartholomew and Matthew, James the son of Alphaeus and Simon the Zealot and Judas, son of James. All these with one accord devoted themselves to prayer . . . (Acts 1:13,14)

That these two saints walked with Our Lord in his ministry on earth and talked with him, listened to him and witnessed his loving care of others, is surely of sufficient interest to us to desire to hold them in our minds and place our feet in their sandals. We can now follow Our Lord on his journey, we can sit on the hillside with him, and we can be sent out with others to carry the gospel afar. Simon and Jude remained faithful during the testing time of the Passion and Death of Jesus, and devoted themselves to prayer in the upper room along with the other nine. They would all have their important duties to perform before their deaths: the Church, the Bride at one with Christ the Bridegroom, was now vested in their courage, evangelization, their hearts and souls.

In our prayers: thanks for the lives, examples and intercession of Saint Simon and Saint Jude; for all those who endeavour to stay close to Our Lord.

Saint Simon and Saint Jude, pray for us, for those who are depressed, and for all places dedicated in your names.

≈✧≈

October 29 Saint Theuderius *(Abbot)*

In his early life as a monk and a priest, Theuderius was responsible for a number of foundations. For the last years of his life, however, he lived in a cell beside Saint Laurence's church in Vienne, in south-eastern France. There he heard confessions and gave absolution, and spent his life in prayer and penance on behalf of the people of the area. Theuderius died at the end of the sixth century.

O God of my fathers and Lord of mercy, who has made all things by thy word, and by thy wisdom hast formed men, to have dominion over the creatures thou hast made, and rule the world in holiness and right-eousness, and pronounce judgement in uprightness of soul, give me the wisdom that sits by thy throne . . . (Wisdom of Solomon 9.1–4)

Theuderius's teaching contained in the example of his last years under-lines the importance of intercession. It matters that we pray for others in their various circumstances throughout the world, and that we pray for the souls of the departed who need our prayers. Theuderius dedicated his last years to others and had no concern for himself. He absolved and blessed and bade his penitents to return to their homes in joy and in the service of others through prayer and deeds. That done, Theuderius would return to his prie-dieu and in earnest intercession pray for the for-giveness of those who did not seek forgiveness and absolution. For them he would deprive himself of another comfort and do penance.

In our prayers: thanks for the life, example and intercession of Saint Theuderius; for those we know are in need of our prayers.

Saint Theuderius, pray for us, and for those who need to cultivate better self-discipline.

October 30   Saint Alphonsus Rodriguez

Alphonsus, a largely uneducated man in his youth, late in life educated himself and became a Jesuit lay brother in Majorca. There he spent his life in prayer and spiritual exercises. He was sought after as a spiritual adviser to both priest and layman. Alphonsus was born in 1533, died in 1617 and was canonized in 1888.

May God grant that I speak with judgement and have thoughts worthy of what I have received, for he is the guide even of wisdom and the corrector of the wise. For both we and our words are in his hand . . . (Wisdom of Solomon 7.15,16a)

As with Theuderius (October 29), Alphonsus was a man who would spend his time in meditation, contemplation and prayer. Through his spiritual exercises, he became renowned as a wise counsellor for both priest and layman. Alphonsus had a genuine concern for those who sought him. How pure and unblemished this counsel must have been. Alphonsus placed abnegation of self high on the scale of virtues he practised; after all, as a wise counsellor he was the servant not the master.

In our prayers: thanks for the life, example and intercession of Saint Alphonsus Rodriguez; for all counsellors; for the will to prepare properly in prayer for whatever we do.

Saint Alphonsus, pray for us, and for Majorca.

October 31   Saint Wolfgang of Regensburg (Bishop)

Wolfgang was born in 924 and became a renowned teacher in the Catholic school at Trier. He became a Benedictine monk, was made priest and, in 972, Bishop of Regensburg. Wolfgang was an enthusiastic reformer of the clergy and monasteries in his diocese, and a fine preacher and teacher. However, for most of his life he yearned for the monastic life. He died in 994 and was canonized in 1052.

Wait for the Lord; be strong, and let your heart take courage; yea, wait for the Lord. (Psalm 27[26].14)

The duties we are given are not always those we would have chosen for ourselves. A vocation to the priesthood and to the religious life did not mean, for Wolfgang, a contemplative life. Nevertheless, Wolfgang responded effectively and appropriately, and fulfilled the demands made of him. God would not have expected more. However, a parallel yearning for another aspect of one's calling can be of enormous benefit: it will colour the work done with the attributes of the other and will be an influence and guide. Wolfgang was able to encourage his clergy with the benefits of monastic discipline in prayer, chastity and obedience and mould them accordingly. His teaching would carry references to poverty of living and generosity to the needy.

In our prayers: thanks for the life, example and intercession of Saint Wolfgang of Regensburg; for the wisdom to apply our skills in whatever we do.

Saint Wolfgang, pray for us, and for greater consideration of the merits of monastic discipline.

November

It is important to pray for the souls (November 2) of those who have not yet reached the heavenly realms. Of course, we cannot know who is not in heaven but it is a small thing for us to do. On the first of the month, how-ever, we have the opportunity to give thanks for the lives of all the saints who have been forgotten and lost from the calendars over the centuries, or who have fulfilled their earthly vocations quietly, unnoticed by anyone who might have recognized sanctity for what it was. But we all recognize the example and emphatic message of the story of Martin of Tours (11).

November 1   All Saints

These are the saints of all time – those who, by virtue of their lives, are now in heaven; those men and women, both ordinary and extraordi-nary, who fulfilled their God-given vocations, whatever they were, using their talents and skills and, at the same time, overcoming or controlling, where possible, their handicaps, their inclinations and tendencies, their excesses, their physical and mental disadvantages. These are they who lived and died in Christ.

Peter began to say to him, 'Lo, we have left everything and followed you!' Jesus said, 'Truly, I say to you, there is no one who has left home or brothers or sisters or mother or father or children or lands for my sake and for the Gospel, who will not receive a hundredfold now in this time . . . and in the age to come, eternal life.' (Mark 10.28–30)

When we join our prayers with the saints in communion and fellowship, the very foundations of creation reverberate with praise for God. Let us not confine the saints to the pages of history, to the periods in which they lived on earth.

In our prayers: thanks for the lives, examples and intercession of all the saints; for the desire to live a saintly life.

All Saints of God, pray for us, and for all places dedicated in your honour.

November 2 All Souls

These are the departed souls of men and women who wait to see the glory of God; those who have left this life but who have not yet been received into the heavenly realms and into the company of the saints. It is a simple and undemanding duty to pray for the souls of those who wait: they are in God's hands.

Behold, the eye of the Lord is on those who fear him, on those who hope in his steadfast love. Our soul waits for the Lord; he is our help and shield. Yea, our heart is glad in him, because we trust in his holy name. Let thy steadfast love, O Lord, be upon us, even as we hope in thee. (Psalm 33[32].18,20–22)

In the place of patience, the place of penitence, the place of purification, the place, maybe, of perfectionment, is the dwelling of the departed souls where the faithful departed wait at the threshold of God's presence and the Beatific Vision. Not yet in a state to achieve sainthood, these souls are the subject of our daily prayers.

In our prayers: thanks for the prayers of the Holy Souls in purgatory and for the lives of all men and women now departed; for the discipline to say a daily prayer for the souls of the departed.

Eternal rest grant to them, O Lord, and let perpetual light shine upon them. May they rest in peace until called to the heavenly realms. Grant, O heavenly Father, remission of all their sins, that through our pious supplications joining with those of the saints, they may obtain that pardon they have earnestly desired. Though Our Lord and Saviour, Jesus Christ. Amen.

November 3   Saint Martin de Porres

Martin became a Dominican lay brother in Lima in 1603 at the age of 24. He had received some rudimentary medical training when he was apprenticed to a surgeon-barber from the age of 12. As a lay brother, Martin became a trusted Infirmarium, and was renowned for similar work he undertook in the city among the sick and the slaves who had arrived from Africa. An orphanage and a hospital were founded on his example and work. He was well known and loved among the rich and the poor alike. Martin died in 1639 and was canonized in 1962.

But a Samaritan, as he journeyed, came to where he was; and when he saw him, he had compassion, and went to him and bound up his wound, pouring on oil and wine; then he set him on his own beast and brought him to an inn, and took care of him. (Luke 10.33,34)

Martin's pity for the sick and the slaves translated into a ministry among them. We are often ready to shed a tear and feel sorry for the plight of those considerably less fortunate than ourselves, but does that feeling of sorrow ever translate into a ministry? It could do so. Of course, those for whom we are particularly sorry on reading the news may well be geographically inaccessible to us. Our ministry can be effective at arm's length through the appropriate Catholic charity, whose envelope we pick up and fill, and through our intercession. If we are listening, God may ask something more of us in respect of those for whom we pray.

In our prayers: thanks for the life, example and intercession of Saint Martin de Porres; for good race relations in this country and throughout the world; for social justice.

Saint Martin, pray for us, and for all who are enslaved.

November 4   Saint Charles Borromeo *(Bishop)*

Charles was born in 1538 of a noble family. He was known for his untiring hard work in reforming the diocese of Milan, which was, at the time, in a parlous condition. Charles was consecrated bishop in 1563. He founded the Confraternity of Christian Doctrine for the purposes of giving children proper instruction. He was particularly anxious that the Liturgy should be seemly and as perfectly said or sung as possible. During a famine year, Charles got himself into debt feeding the hungry. He died in 1584 and was canonized in 1610.

Blessed are the men whose strength is in thee, in whose heart are the highways to Zion. Blessed are those who dwell in thy love ever singing thy praise. (Psalm 84[83].5,4)

The instruction of children in the Faith is an essential part of our duty. Again, there are many ways in which we can help, beginning with assisting in the purchase of suitable instructional material, for schools, churches and for families. Charles saw his calling as a Catholic Christian and as a shepherd, to feed the hungry in mind and body, and he was at pains to go to great lengths to fulfil this calling.

In our prayers: thanks for the life, example and intercession of Saint Charles Borromeo; for the good instruction of children in the Faith; for the poor and hungry; for good shepherds.

Saint Charles, pray for us, and for the diocese of Milan.

November 5   Saint Zechariah and Saint Elizabeth

Zechariah and Elizabeth were Saint John the Baptist's (June 24) parents. They were a God-fearing couple, both of priestly ancestry, who carried out God's will by producing and naming their son, John. However, Zechariah is incredulous at the announcement and is admonished for his unbelief.

And Zechariah said to the angel, 'How shall I know this? For I am an old man, and my wife is advanced in years.' And the angel answered him, 'I am Gabriel, who stands in the presence of God; and I was sent to speak to you, and to bring you this good news. And behold, you will be silent and unable to speak until the day that these things come to pass, because you did not believe my words, which will be fulfilled in their time.' (Luke 1.18–20)

Struck dumb by the unliklihood of Elizabeth's pregnancy, Zechariah meekly accepts the word of God without further ado. It fell to this couple, distantly related to Mary, to raise the child who would smooth the pathway to the Messiah so that his ministry could begin as John's preparation of the people neared completion. Was there significance in the priestly descent of this couple? Why did God choose this elderly couple? We do not know, but God does underline with some vigour that all things are possible with him – including turning the world inside out and upside down at the Incarnation and Resurrection of Jesus.

In our prayers: thanks for the lives, examples and intercessions of Saint Zechariah and Saint Elizabeth; for the faith to say yes to the demands God makes of us, no matter how curious or unexpected.

Saint Zechariah and Saint Elizabeth, pray for us, and for all elderly parents.

❧❀☙

November 6   Saint Illtyd *(Abbot)*

It is likely that this sixth-century Welsh saint, Illtyd, was ordained by Saint Germanus of Auxerre (August 7) and that he became, in effect, headmaster of a school attached to the monastery in what is now Llantwit Major, in South Glamorgan. Later, he established a monastery on Caldey Island. Illtyd's parents were probably of Brittany, and Illtyd may well have returned to his homeland towards the end of his life.

Now when they heard this they were cut to the heart, and said to Peter and the rest of the apostles, 'Brethren, what shall we do?' And Peter said to them, 'Repent and be baptized every one of you in the name of Jesus Christ for the forgiveness of your sins; and you shall receive the gift of the Holy Spirit. For the promise is to you and to your children and to all that are far off, every one whom the Lord our God calls to him.' (Acts 2.37–39)

With the training of children in Illtyd's hands, the boys arrived to further their education in the monastery, well prepared. On the other hand, those who were destined for agriculture and commerce were schooled enough for their tasks in life. Those on the doorstep of either the religious life or the secular, were ready to take their grounding in the Faith to their next stage.

In our prayers: thanks for the life, example and intercession of Saint Illtyd; for the better education of children in the Faith; for pathfinders and those who break new ground.

Saint Illtyd, pray for us, and for all schools.

November 7 Saint Willibrord *(Bishop)*

The Northumbrian Willibrord was born in 658 and educated at Ripon. In 690, now a priest, he and 11 fellow monks set out to evangelize Friesland (the Netherlands) and, in 696, Willibrord was consecrated Bishop of Utrecht. He is venerated as the Apostle to Friesland. He died in 739.

When that godly man Egbert . . . did send to [Friesland] for the setting forth of God's word certain holy and virtuous men, able and willing to take pains, among whom that notable and excellent learned man Willibrord, priest, was chief, who, after their arrival . . . went straight to the governor of France . . . who sent them to Friesland to preach, aiding and assisting them with his princely authority . . . Whereby it came to pass by the assistance of God's grace that in a short time they converted very many from idolatry to the faith of Christ. (From The History of the Church of England, *by Saint Bede)*

Bede ably drew the thumbnail sketch of Willibrord's ministry to Friesland. The journey from Northumberland to France and Friesland was not an easy excursion during the first millennium. That this rather hazardous undertaking was made at all is surprising, and yet with confidence and trust in the Faith of Christ, it was achieved and was successful. Many who knew nothing of Christ were converted and gathered into the Christian fold, and they themselves made Christ known to their fellows and brethren in their lives and in their preaching – the happy consequences of conversion.

In our prayers: thanks for the life, example and intercession of Saint Willibrord; for those who make special effort to fulfil their vocations; for all preaching friars.

Saint Willibrord, pray for us, and for the Netherlands and for Germany.

November 8 Saint Deusdedit *(Pope)*
(Also today, Blessed Duns Scotus [*Doctor of the Church*].)

Deusdedit was pope from 615 until 618. During the difficult years of his pontificate, he was concerned largely for the welfare of his priests and for those in need. He was a devout man with simple concerns. Deusdedit died in 618.

The Lord is the strength of his people, he is the saving refuge of his anointed. O save thy people, and bless thy heritage, be thou their shepherd, and carry them for ever. (Psalm 28[27].8,9)

With the prospect of an early death, Deusdedit concentrated on the welfare of the poor for in them he found Christ. Furthermore, in raising them from starvation, he was also instructing his own clergy in his example so that the work would continue apace. Deusdedit was a wise and holy man. Perhaps he saw in this activity the natural progression towards a bond between the clergy and the poor. At his death he left each of his priests a substantial sum for their welfare and wellbeing. The direct consequences of our actions are also to our credit (and discredit).

In our prayers: thanks for the life, example and intercession of Saint Deusdedit; for the poor who are ever with us.

Saint Deusdedit, pray for us, and for all poor clergy.

November 9 Saint Vitonus *(Bishop)*

Vitonus was Bishop of Verdun for 25 years. Much of his diocese was still pagan at his consecration. But he is credited with having converted most of his diocese by the time he died in 525. It was Vitonus who established, near Verdun, a seminary and Congregation of priests. The establishment later became a Benedictine priory dedicated to Saint Vitonus (Saint Vanne, in the French form).

Commit your work to the Lord, and your plans will be established. The Lord has made everything for its purpose. When a man's ways please the Lord, he makes even his enemies to be at peace with him. A man's mind plans his way but the Lord directs his steps. (Proverbs 16.3,4a,7,9)

The fruit of the devoted work of this good diocesan shepherd was the crop of faithful souls he gathered into his fold during his 25 years' stewardship of the See. To win souls for Christ was the task he had been set, and it was a labour of love – of the love of Christ, through the love of Christ, for the love of Christ. Vitonus's message to us is that to his fellow bishops – our vocations include a call to be 'other Christs' and to carry the gospel to others in whatever way our talents allow.

In our prayers: thanks for the life, example and intercession of Saint Vitonus; for all seminaries.

Saint Vitonus, pray for us, and for Verdun.

November 10   Saint Leo the Great *(Pope and Doctor of the Church)*

Leo became pope in 440 and, although renowned for his peacemaking and compromise – particularly with regard to Attila the Hun – his great strength was his crystallization of the Truth of the Incarnation and the Nativity of Our Lord, which crystallization was accepted at the Council of Chalcedon in 451. Leo's written legacy includes some 100 sermons. He died in 461.

For although in the Lord Jesus Christ there is one Person of God and man, yet . . . from what belongs to us he has that manhood, which is inferior to the Father . . . and from the Father he has equal Godhead with the Father. (From the writings of Saint Leo the Great)

Christ's person is the Person of God and the Person of man – there are not two persons but one. Therefore Christ has both a divine nature and a human. The Athanasian Creed and the writings of Leo allow us to come close to an understanding of the Mystery of the Incarnation as we steep ourselves in the texts and consider the Divine condescension of the Creator, with whom was the Word and the Intention in the beginning. If we are patient with ourselves we find in our meditations that the Holy Spirit will guide us into all Truth slowly and surely as the limits of our humanity allow.

In our prayers: thanks for the life, example and intercession of Saint Leo the Great; for a desire to delve more deeply into the theological truths; for the Pope.

Saint Leo, pray for us, and for all who strive to understand the great Mysteries of the Faith.

November 11 Saint Martin of Tours *(Bishop)*

Martin was an unwilling soldier in the Imperial Guard who famously used his sword to cut his cloak in two. He gave one half to the naked beggar who had inspired this action. In a dream, Martin saw Our Lord clothed in that very piece of cloth. When he was discharged from the army he spent ten years living a semi-hermitic life. In 371, he was made Bishop of Tours and he founded a monastery there. He was a holy and gentle man, and died in 397.

Then the King will say to those at his right hand, 'Come, O blessed of my Father, inherit the Kingdom prepared for you . . . for . . . I was naked and you clothed me . . .' 'When did we see thee . . . naked and clothe thee?' 'Truly, I say to you, as you did it to one of the least of these my brethren, you did it to me.' (Matthew 25.34ff.)

Martin's vision is one of the most telling visions ever recorded. In association with Our Lord's words, we have the clearest of directives as to what should feature in our good works. So far in the year we have read of many saints who were devoted to this work and were passionate in their zeal for clothing the naked. Our attention to those who are otherwise neglected is so important, through charities or personal donations of food and clothing, for there we see Christ and there, in that action, he sees us face to face. The rich man overlooked Lazarus at his gate.

In our prayers: thanks for the life, example and intercession of Saint Martin of Tours; for those who do not respond to Our Lord's teaching; for all those who died in the First World War.

Saint Martin, pray for us, and for all beggars.

November 12   Saint Josaphat *(Abbot, Bishop and Martyr)*

Josaphat was born in 1580 in the Ukraine. The Orthodox dioceses in Kiev had recently been united with Rome during the time Josaphat was abbot at Vilna. He was consecrated and made Bishop of Polotsk and spent his life working for the spread of the new unity. He was noted for his thorough goodness but was murdered in 1623. He was canonized in 1867.

'Or is God the God of Jews only? Is he not the God of Gentiles also? Yes, of Gentiles also, since God is one; and he will justify the circumcised on the ground of their faith and the uncircumcised through their faith.' (Romans 3.29,30)

Josaphat saw Christ's benevolent but sorrowful gaze upon the fractures in his Church and worked enthusiastically for the acceptance of the new unity with the Holy See. He now saw the whole Church in his jurisdiction under the care of the successor of Peter, and rejoiced. Many grave differences and barely concealed hatreds are still apparent between and among those who call themselves Christians.

In our prayers: thanks for the life, example and intercession of Saint Josaphat; for the unity of the Church; for the Orthodox Churches; for our own parish church.

Saint Josaphat, pray for us, and for all who are at enmity with their neighbours.

November 13 Saint Abbo of Fleury *(Abbot)*

Abbo was born around 950. He was, inter alia, a musician, theologian, a monk at Fleury, a schoolmaster at Ramsey Abbey and, in 988, Abbot of Fleury. Abbo became a negotiator in the temporal world and in the monastic. Ironically, in 1004, he was stabbed by a servant when he was attempting to bring some order to a monastery in Gascony. He left a biography of Saint Edmund, King and Martyr (November 20) and much else.

For the Lord gives wisdom; from his mouth come knowledge and understanding; he stores up sound wisdom for the upright; he is a shield to those who walk in integrity, guarding the paths of justice and preserving the way of the saints. (Proverbs 2.6–8)

That a renowned peacemaker and mediator on the world's stage should end his days a victim of a knife wielded in anger in a place of prayer and thanksgiving, is astonishing. Abbo must have been present in many more potentially dangerous situations. However, the servants of the monastery he was visiting quarrelled violently with Abbo's team of monks. Perhaps Abbo, ever the peacemaker, intervened physically and was stabbed unintentionally or because he thrust himself between the knife and the intended victim. We know how anger can rise up within us when we feel slighted and when our pride has been dented. Righteous anger is rare; self-righteous anger is commonplace.

In our prayers: thanks for the life, example and intercession of Saint Abbo of Fleury; for all peacemakers and mediators; for all teachers and theologians.

Saint Abbo, pray for us, and for all those who employ their learning in the service of others.

November 14 Saint Dyfrig *(Bishop)*
(Also today, Saint Laurence O'Toole [*Bishop*].)

Dyfrig was a founder of many monasteries and churches in South Wales and the west of England late in the fifth century and into the sixth. He was acquainted with Saint Illtyd (November 6) and Saint Deiniol (September 11).

So the Church throughout all Judea and Galilee and Samaria had peace and was built up; and walking in the fear of the Lord and in the comfort of the Holy Spirit it was multiplied. (Acts 9.31)

The industriousness of Dyfrig and the other Welsh and Celtic saints is noteworthy. Although the many monasteries and churches were likely to have been small groups of cells and small wooden structures, the establishment of them was of great significance. There they were in the town and countryside declaring to the world around them that the Christian Faith was there to stay. From these cells and churches monks and priests evangelized and gathered more souls. The monasteries developed; the churches were rebuilt in stone; soon there was a long tradition of their presence for the future to build upon yet further. We need to prepare ourselves for whatever we do, and whatever we do is in preparation for what is to come.

In our prayers: thanks for the life, example and intercession of Saint Dyfrig; for all pathfinders; for missionaries.

Saint Dyfrig, pray for us, and for South Wales.

November 15   Saint Albert the Great *(Bishop and Doctor of the Church)*

Albert was born in 1206 near Augsburg, and in 1222 entered the Dominican Order. He became director of studies at Cologne when Thomas Aquinas (January 28),whom Albert deeply respected, was a student. Albert was consecrated Bishop of Regensburg in 1260. He died in senility in 1280, his powerful and important intellect already at rest. He was canonized in 1931.

There is one who is wise, greatly to be feared, sitting upon his throne. The Lord himself created wisdom; he saw her and apportioned her out upon all his works. She dwells with all flesh according to his gift, and he supplied her to those who love him. (Sirach 1.8–10)

Albert's work was of great importance. He was a bishop and theologian, a scientist, botanist, and a biologist of note. The prospect of discovering more about the Creator by examining his handiwork excited Albert enormously. He much admired his student, Thomas Aquinas, and supported his writings against opposition by other theologians. Albert points us clearly along the path of knowledge in order to appreciate more of the Creator.

In our prayer: thanks for the life, example and intercession of Saint Albert the Great; for all who teach the natural sciences; for those who suffer from senility and for those who care for them.

Saint Albert, pray for us, and for all students of the natural sciences.

November 16   Saint Margaret of Scotland (Also today, Saint Gertrude the Great; Saint Mechtildis of Helfta; Saint Edmund of Abingdon.)

Margaret was brought up in Hungary. She was the granddaughter of King Edmund Ironside of Wessex. She sought safety in Scotland after the death of Saint Edward the Confessor (October 13), where she married King Malcolm III and produced eight children. She was the mother of Saint David of Scotland (May 24) and of Matilda, the wife of Henry I. She dedicated her life to raising her large family and to feeding the poor. She reformed the Scottish Church and endowed a number of monasteries, and re-founded Iona Abbey. She died in 1092 and was canonized in 1250.

Make a joyful noise to the Lord, all the lands! Serve the Lord with gladness! Come into his presence with singing! Know that the Lord is God! It is he that made us, and we are his; we are his people, and the sheep of his pasture. (Psalm 100[99].1–3)

Margaret's life was one of generosity of self. Simply to raise a large family within the eleventh-century court of Scotland was a vocation well satisfied. Family demands are such that, for a successful mother, there is no room for self-regard; constantly the children require fuller attention. In a devoted mother's care do we see a little of the relationship the Creator has with his creatures? As the children grew and matured under this devoted care, Margaret looked beyond the court to the poor around her and ministered to them. There she knew was her Christ, hungry and rejected.

In our prayers: thanks for the life, example and intercession of Saint Margaret of Scotland; for all those who care for others; for all Scots.

Saint Margaret, pray for us, and for Scotland.

November 17   Saint Elizabeth of Hungary
(Also today, Saint Hugh of Lincoln [*Bishop*].)

Elizabeth was born in 1207 in Hungary. She was married to Lugwig IV, by whom she had three children. She devoted much of her time to the poor and sick, and even built an infirmary into the basement of the royal castle. After her husband's death in the Crusades, Elizabeth became an ascetic and devoted the whole of her life to prayer and to the unfortunate. She died in 1231 and was canonized in 1235.

But as for me, I walk in my integrity; redeem me, and be gracious to me. My foot stands on level ground; in the great congregation I will bless the Lord. (Psalm 26[25].11,12)

And Elizabeth completes the picture for us. From the eyes of the sick, Our Lord stared hopefully at Elizabeth in the shack and hovel, and in the precincts of the castle. Elizabeth's response was sure and courageous and, like Margaret (November 16), she had little consideration for herself. Her practical help and her life of prayer combined to give the unfortunate the care and attention they needed. The clamour for recognition of her sanctity was loud and immediate upon her death.

In our prayers: thanks for the life, example and intercession of Saint Elizabeth of Hungary; for all who devote their lives to prayer and good works; for the people of Hungary.

Saint Elizabeth, pray for us, and for Hungary.

November 18   Saint Philippine Duchesne

Philippine attempted to found again the Order of the Visitation after the worst period of the French Revolution was over, but failed. She, with a few other nuns, travelled to St Louis at the invitation of the Bishop of Louisiana. There she established a school for poor children immediately and, eventually, a number of houses of the Society of the Sacred Heart. She was devoted to her work but suffered many disappointments and disillusionments, though she achieved much in her long life in her work with the poor and in the propagation of the Faith. Philippine died in 1852 and was canonized in 1988.

The apostles returned to Jesus, and told him all that they had done and taught. And he said to them, 'Come away by yourselves to a lonely place, and rest awhile.' For many were coming and going, and they had no leisure even to eat. And they went away in the boat to a lonely place by themselves. (Mark 6.30–32)

Disappointment with her failure in France led to her successes in Louisiana. But Philippine was often dissatisfied with her achievements; she felt always that she was capable of more. In truth, her work produced marvellous results and her vision of what might be done was inspiring. It is necessary for us to test ourselves against the real possibilities lest we fall into the trap of self-satisfaction. I have filled my mission box: there is nothing more for me to do until it is emptied!

In our prayers: thanks for the life, example and intercession of Saint Philippine Duchesne; for all aspects of children's education; for religious Orders specializing in education.

Saint Philippine, pray for us, and for the United States of America, in particular Louisiana.

November 19   Saint Nerses *(Bishop and Martyr)*, Saint Joseph, and Companions *(Martyrs)*

Nerses was Bishop of Sahgerd in Persia and in old age when he, and his assistant, Joseph, were arrested during King Sapor II's persecution of Christians. The king offered to commute the inevitable sentence if only they would make proper obeisance to the sun. They refused the king's offer and were beheaded along with many others. Nerses, Joseph and Companions died in the fourth century.

But they cried out with a loud voice and stopped their ears and rushed together upon him. Then they cast him out of the city and stoned him ... (Acts 7.57,58)

Nerses had been a Christian throughout his life. Now a bishop and 80 years old, he could hardly obey the king and fall down upon his knees in sincere (or even mock) obeisance, and worship the sun as though it were the all-powerful God, and not simply a part of his handiwork. The honesty and integrity of the bishop – apart from his absolute faith in and knowledge of the Blessed Trinity – forbade it. He could not even pretend and mean nothing by it for the sake of his life. Why? Because he would bring the Faith into disrepute; he would fail his flock; his example could extinguish the embryonic faith in some of the newly converted, perhaps; his action would have repercussions throughout Middle Eastern Christendom. But Nerses, Joseph and their companions chose to die instead, and receive the martyrs' crowns.

In our prayers: thanks for the lives, examples and intercession of Saint Nerses, Saint Joseph, and their Holy Companions; for those who give others the example of full assurance of faith.

Saint Nerses, Saint Joseph and Holy Companions, pray for us, and for those who need courage.

November 20 Saint Edmund *(Martyr)*

Edmund, born in 841, became the young king of the East Angles in 855. He was a Christian and was renowned as a sagacious ruler for one so young. Edmund died in 869 at the hand of Inguar, an invading Viking, who had offered him his life in exchange for a denial of the Christian Faith. Edmund was a holy young man who was resolute in his faith.

Lord, thou hast been our dwelling place in all generations. Before the mountains were brought forth, or ever thou hadst formed the earth and the world, from everlasting to everlasting, thou art God. (Psalm 90[89].1,2)

From an elderly bishop (November 19) to a young king we find the stubborn refusal to renounce the Faith. Why is it so important to die when you might keep your life with a simple denial? Quite simply, apart from the effect of the ruler's apostasy upon his subjects, it was easier to die in the Truth than to deny that Truth. How could Edmund have renounced something he knew to be true? Could he have denied the wind and the rain? No, neither could he have denied the Christ, in whom he lived.

In our prayers: thanks for the life, example and intercession of Saint Edmund; for steadfastness in the Faith; for those who bully others and seek to dominate them by threats.

Saint Edmund, pray for us, and for the people of East Anglia.

November 21 The Presentation of the Blessed Virgin Mary; Saint Albert of Louvain *(Bishop and Martyr)*

The formal dedication of Our Lady's life to God probably took place at the age of three, when Joachim and Anne would have taken Mary to the Temple at Jerusalem for the Presentation.

Albert was born of an aristocratic house in 1166 and was elected Bishop of Liège when only a non-priestly archdeacon. There was argument over the vacancy and a rival candidate. Albert's claim was upheld by the Pope, but the Emperor was adamant that Albert would not take up the post. The Archbishop of Rheims ordained Albert priest and then consecrated him Bishop of Liège. Albert remained in Rheims where he was murdered after only a few weeks.

'Therefore I tell you, do not be anxious about your life . . . but seek first [the heavenly Father's] kingdom and his righteousness . . . Therefore do not be anxious about tomorrow, for tomorrow will be anxious for itself. Let the day's own trouble be sufficient for the day.' (Matthew 6.25,33,34) And when three years were expired, and the time of her weaning complete, they brought the Virgin to the temple of the Lord with offerings. (The Gospel of the Birth of Mary 4.1)

When Mary was presented to God she had no knowledge of what was in store for her in later life. She was, as far as anyone knew, an ordinary child of a faithful and God-fearing home. Albert's consecration was different. It occurred so late in his short life that a God-given vocation to the episcopacy seems unlikely. What was the purpose? What is his signpost? The effort, the determination and resolution with which we approach the task given us is itself the cause of the outburst of joy in the heavenly realms. We may be called to do nothing other than show ourselves as willing.

In our prayers: thanks for the lives, examples and intercession of Our Lady and Saint Albert of Louvain; for resolution and steadfastness; for those of a violent nature, and murderers.

Saint Albert, pray for us, and for Rheims.

November 22   Saint Cecilia *(Martyr)*

Cecilia was a martyr of the first half of the third century, and named in the Roman Canon. Her martyrdom clearly had made a tremendous impact on the early Church. She became patron of musicians and, therefore, it is reasonable to suppose that she was known to include musicians in her intercession during her life, or that she herself was a musician of note. She was one of many martyrs of the period about whom little or nothing is known. Their witness at the time of their martyrdom was their vocation, and the value of that cannot be measured or understated.

Praise him with trumpet sound; praise him with lute and harp! Praise him with timbrel and dance; praise him with strings and pipe! Praise him with sounding cymbals; praise him with loud clashing cymbals! Let everything that breathes praise the Lord! Praise the Lord! (Psalm 150.2–6)

The sanctity of the faithful Cecilia was acclaimed at her martyrdom, and immediately the saint's following was assured. Cecilia was among many young women butchered by man or torn to pieces by beasts. Who among the eyewitnesses might have been moved to wonder why God gathered such a large harvest of immature fruit? The ways of God are not our ways; they are beyond us. However, the value of a young, steadfast witness to the Faith, whom we continue to honour 1800 years later, is not in the least insignificant to God. Cecilia's dying affirmation may well be equal to a lifetime of dedication and devotion. All those hired in the marketplace were paid an equal sum at the end of the day.

In our prayers: thanks for the life, example and intercession of Saint Cecilia; for all musicians and composers, organists and singers.

Saint Cecilia, pray for us, and for all places dedicated in your name.

November 23 Saint Clement of Rome *(Pope)*

Clement was the fourth pope following Saints Peter, Linus and Cletus, during the last few years of the first century. He was the writer of a letter to the Corinthians and may well have been the Clement noted in Saint Paul's epistle to the Philippians: 'for they have laboured with me in the gospel together with Clement and the rest of my fellow workers . . .' *(Philippians 4.3)*. Clement's letter reveals something of his gentle nature and desire for conformity and diplomacy.

These things, beloved, we write unto you, not only for your instruction, but also for our own remembrance. For we are all in the same lists, and the same combat is prepared for us all. Wherefore let us lay aside all vain and empty cares; and let us come up to the venerable and glorious rule of our holy calling. Let us look steadfastly to the blood of Christ, and see how precious his blood is in the sight of God: which being shed for our salvation, has obtained the grace of repentance for the whole world. (Letter of Saint Clement 4.1–3.5)

In writing his letter, Clement revealed the humility that marked his life. By reminding the recipients of his letter, he tells them, he is reminding himself. We are all called to the same destination. Let us lay aside the things that inhibit our journey, the things we make into idols, place in front of God, and fall down to worship. Clement knew that he was susceptible to his own idols when his focus on God was allowed to slip.

In our prayers: thanks for the life, example and intercession of Saint Clement of Rome; for the ability to recognize our idols for what they are.

Saint Clement, pray for us, and for all preachers and letter-writers.

November 24   Saint Colman of Cloyne *(Bishop)*;
Saint Chrysogonos (Martyr)

As with Saint Cecilia (November 22), Chrysogonos is known for his martyrdom and his inclusion in the Roman Canon. He was clearly a well-loved martyr of the late third century or early fourth century. His story is lost to us, but these early martyrs and witnesses were a powerful inspiration to the saints of Ireland and of these shores. Colman was born early in the sixth century in Munster and was converted late in life after a career as poet and bard. He was made bishop and established churches in Cloyne and Kilmaclenine.

Let us now praise famous men, and our fathers in their generations . . .
those who composed musical tunes and set forth verses in writing.
(Sirach 44.1,5)
'Call the labourers and give them their wages, beginning with the last
up to the first.' So the last will be first and the first last. (Matthew
20.8b,16)

The inspiration given by the early martyrs is incalculable. Colman was anxious to use his talents to propagate the Faith that he had newly embraced. His skill with the recited word helped him convey the Faith to those who did not yet know Christ. The skills and talents we use in secular employment can also be used specifically for and dedicated to the purposes of the gospel of Christ.

In our prayers: thanks for the lives, examples and intercession of Saint Colman of Cloyne and Saint Chrysogonos; for all who dedicate their lives and skills to God.

Saint Colman and Saint Chrysogonos, pray for us, and for all poets.

November 25 Saint Moses of Rome *(Martyr)*

Moses, a priest, was first among equals in a band of faithful prisoners who died in the middle of the third century during the persecution of Christians begun by Emperor Decius. Moses died in prison in 251.

About that time Herod the king laid violent hands upon some who belonged to the Church. He killed James, the brother of John, with the sword. And when he saw that it pleased the Jews, he proceeded to arrest Peter also. And when he had seized him, he put him in prison and delivered him to four squads of soldiers to guard him, intending, after the Passover, to bring him out to the people. So Peter was kept in prison, but earnest prayer for him was made to God by the Church. (Acts 12.1–5)

Not only had Moses to cope with facing charges of being a Christian and refusing to worship the gods of Rome, but he was also caught up in an internal dispute within the Church brought about by Novatian's schism. Moses died, probably under torture. (Moses opposed Novatian's stance that apostasy should not be forgiven, even if committed in extreme circumstances.) This faithful priest served his fellows in prison and became a beacon of sainthood to faithful Christians and to those who would again be reconciled with the Church. Peter's denial led to penitence and on to a strong leadership of the Church.

In our prayers: thanks for the life, example and intercession of Saint Moses of Rome; for those whose faith is tested to extremes; for all prisoners and captives.

Saint Moses, pray for us, and for those persuaded by heresy.

November 26 Saint Sylvester Gozzolini *(Abbot)*

Sylvester was born in 1177 or thereabouts. He began his ministry enthusiastically in a parish in Osimo. At the age of 50 he began an ascetic life moving to Fabriano to build a monastery in 1231, and gathering disciples around him. The Sylvestrian Benedictines exist to this day and are renowned for their simplicity of life.

You must renounce your preferences and wishes and so follow Christ unencumbered; you must spurn pride and vainglory; your goals for achievement ought to be founded only on God. No one ought to aim for a reputation for sanctity – first, we should have to achieve sanctity. (From the Rule of Saint Benedict)

Until the age of 90 Sylvester governed his monastery at Monte Fano, and 11 subsidiary houses, in austerity and holiness. Retreat and, perhaps, more rigorous self-discipline is necessary for us from time to time. It can concentrate the mind upon the essentials of life and upon the direction that life is taking. Sylvester's example is extreme and, of course, an example to which we are not all called. Sylvester's second vocation meant a new life of almost constant prayer for the world. Only when we cast a critical eye over our life can we see where we fall short in our prayer life and in other areas.

In our prayers: thanks for the life, example and intercession of Saint Sylvester Gozzolini; for all contemplatives, friars and monks.

Saint Sylvester, pray for us, and for all Sylvestrian Benedictines.

☙✤❧

November 27   Saint Maximus of Riez (Bishop) (Also today, Our Lady of the Miraculous Medal.)

Maximus was born in Provence and became Abbot of Lérins, where his reputation for holiness drew pilgrims from a wide area. Eventually, he became Bishop of Riez in which capacity he continued to live as he had lived as abbot. Maximus died in about 460.

'Beware of practising your piety before men in order to be seen by them . . . And when you pray, you must not be like the hypocrites; for they love to stand and pray in the synagogues and at the street corners, that they may be seen by men . . . But when you pray, go into your room and shut the door and pray to your Father who is in secret; and your Father who sees in secret will reward you.' (Matthew 6.1,5)

As bishop, Maximus did not reject his monastic and disciplined life. Only with reluctance had he accepted the elevation to the episcopacy, but he realized God had sought him for this important role. However, as Bishop of Riez, he was determined that he would retain the Rule to which he had submitted in the monastery of Lérins. How keen are we to remain committed to our Rule of Life? Do we avoid meditation and contemplation in case God asks us to do something that we are reluctant to do?

In our prayers: thanks for the life, example and intercession of Saint Maximus of Riez; for openness to God's call.

Saint Maximus, pray for us, and for all pilgrims.

November 28 Saint Joseph Pignatelli

Joseph was born in 1737 in Zaragoza. He joined the Society of Jesus at an early age. During many political upheavals in France, Italy and Spain, the Society, except in Russia, was almost entirely annihilated. Joseph spent much of his time tending the needs of many Jesuits who found themselves without a home. Joseph strove for the restoration of the Society, which was eventually achieved only three years after his death in 1811. Joseph was canonized in 1954.

'The bricks have fallen, but we will build with dressed stones; the sycamores have been cut down, but we will put cedars in their place.' (Isaiah 9.10)

Joseph shouldered many of the consequences of beginning again on behalf of the Society of Jesus, and was instrumental in the restoration of the society's presence throughout Europe. Often, failures in our Christian life are not so obvious to us without regular scrutiny and self-examination. Errors and bad habits will insinuate themselves so easily. Care and attention of the temple of the Holy Spirit is undoubtedly a duty of utmost importance.

In our prayers: thanks for the life, example and intercession of Saint Joseph Pignatelli; for the determination to restore and rebuild where and when necessary.

Saint Joseph, pray for us, and for the Society of Jesus.

November 29 Saint Francis of Lucera

Francis was born in 1681 and received his education in Lucera with the Friars Minor. In 1705, he was ordained, and in 1707 became lecturer at Lucera. There he remained until he died in 1742. Francis had a particular devotion to Our Lady of the Immaculate Conception. He was a noted preacher and teacher and one who was much involved in the care of prisoners. Francis was canonized in 1986.

My son; if you come forward to serve the Lord, prepare yourself for temptation. Set your heart right and be steadfast, and do not be hasty in time of calamity. Cleave to him and do not depart, that you may be honoured at the end of your life. (Sirach 2.1–3)

It is a rather different task these days to 'care for prisoners'! The visiting of prisoners is a much more formal affair. In the atrocious conditions that prevailed in many Italian prisons of the eighteenth century, it was possible to bring a little relief with a crust and a cup of water; these days, in the west at least, that sort of attention is no longer needed. Francis was passionate about prison reform and care for the poor. He knew that cruelty to the poor and imprisoned was another lash across the back of Christ. In the Immaculate Conception of Our Lady, Francis saw the beauty of the freedom from Original sin – the freedom that comes with baptism – and how Mary in her sinless life shows the baptized the state they can readily resume when absolved from the lapses that inevitably occur throughout their lives. Paying the cost of disobedience to the law of the land is another matter, of course, and unavoidable, but the Christian duty towards the imprisoned is clear.

In our prayers; thanks for the life, example, and intercession of Saint Francis of Lucera; for all who languish in gaol without visitors or contact with their families.

Saint Francis, pray for us, and for the poor and imprisoned of Italy.

November 30   Saint Andrew *(Apostle)*
(Also today, Saint Cuthbert Mayne [*Martyr*].)

Andrew was Simon Peter's (June 29) brother. They lived in Bethsaida and were fishermen in partnership with Zebedee, the father of James I (July 25) and John (December 27), Jesus' cousins. Andrew is believed to have been crucified in Achaia.

One of the two who heard John speak, and followed Jesus, was Andrew, Simon Peter's brother. He first found his brother Simon, and said to him, 'We have found the Messiah.' He brought him to Jesus. Jesus looked at him and said, 'So you are Simon, the son of John? You shall be called Cephas.' The next day Jesus decided to go to Galilee. (John 1.40–43a)
And passing along by the Sea of Galilee he saw Simon and Andrew the brother of Simon casting a net in the sea; for they were fishermen. And Jesus said to them, 'Follow me and I will make you fishers of men.' (Mark 1.16,17)

Andrew was introduced to Jesus by John the Baptist. Jesus called Andrew and Simon Peter to discipleship later (after they had spent the day with him), when he found them fishing in the Sea of Galilee. Of course, he was probably already well acquainted with them through his cousins, but in the capacity of Jesus the Carpenter rather than Jesus the Messiah. Andrew introduced Jesus to his brother as the Messiah – 'We have found the Messiah!' He might have said, 'We have found that the Messiah is, in fact, Jesus the Carpenter!' Peter, perhaps, had not expected to see the Messiah, the Christ, in Jesus. It was obvious to him once it had been pointed out, of course. Andrew gives us pause for thought. Let us see the Saviour in those unexpected places and in the people in whom we least expect to see him.

In our prayers: thanks for the life, example and intercession of Saint Andrew; for the temperament to see Christ in others; for Russia, Greece and Scotland.

Saint Andrew, pray for us, for all fishermen, sailors and spinsters, and for places dedicated in your name.

December

This is the month of Christmas, of family gatherings around the manger of Jesus. But it is also a month during which loneliness is brought home to those recently bereaved and those without families. It is, perhaps, significant that on this day of the Nativity we also celebrate the life of a champion of tramps and down-and-outs who was also a painter of note – Albert Chmielkowski. December begins with a celebration of the life of the priestly martyr Edmund Campion whose death changed many lives.

December 1   Saint Edmund Campion *(Martyr)*

Edmund was born in 1540. After a splendid period at Oxford and enjoying the patronage of many notable and influential people, he left England for the English college at Douai. After admission to the Society of Jesus and subsequent ordination, he eventually joined the English Mission in 1580. He preached, reconciled and said Mass from Berkshire to Lancashire; he wrote and circulated *Campion's Brag* – in effect his mission statement – and *Decem Rationes* – the reasons for requiring debate with theologians of the establishment. In the end he was arrested in Lyford. He was tortured, publicly examined at the 'conferences', tried, and condemned. Edmund was hanged, drawn and quartered in 1581 and canonized in 1970.

There will never want in England men that will have care for their own salvation, nor such as shall advance other men's; neither shall this Church here ever fail so long as priests and pastors shall be found for their sheep, rage man or devil never so much. (Edmund Campion)

Edmund's mission to England was simply for the care of souls. His vocation, however, was to the people of England as a defender of the

Catholic Faith at the disputes with the authorities, and as a martyr for that Faith. Edmund constantly tested his thinking and his calling in fervent prayer. Once all was clear to him he followed the path set for him, with devotion and dignity. Edmund shows us that through prayer we can discover precisely what is required of us. Once revealed to us, we fulfil it with all the talents and skills at our disposal.

In our prayers: thanks for the life, example and intercession of Saint Edmund Campion; for clear indication of the path we are required to take; for strength and resolve.

Saint Edmund, pray for us, and for all imprisoned priests.

December 2 Saint Chromatius *(Bishop)*

Chromatius lived in Aquileia, and in 388 was consecrated its bishop. Something of his writing is extant but he is primarily remembered for his anxiety quickly to make peace on matters of religion to prevent exacerbation. He was a supporter and encourager of many of the great writers of the time, notably, Saint Jerome (September 30). Chromatius died in 407 or thereabouts.

Jesus calls his disciples the salt of the earth, because they will restore the savour armed with heavenly wisdom. Then he calls them the light of the world because they have been enlightened by the one who is the true and everlasting light, and in consequence, have become a light in the darkness. (From a sermon by Saint Chromatius)

The gift of ability to interpret signs of conflict and dispute and to perceive potential areas of disagreement is one that Chromatius used to good effect. It is a gift many may have but never exercise. It takes great diplomacy to resolve a difficulty almost before it has manifested itself. But we are all called to be peacemakers in our sphere of influence. We pray for peace at large and for the wisdom to make peace when we are in a position to do so.

In our prayers: thanks for the life, example and intercession of Saint Chromatius; for the confidence and diplomacy to make peace; for those who preach and teach orthodoxy in the Faith.

Saint Chromatius, pray for us, and for all who work in the diplomatic corps.

December 3 · Saint Francis Xavier

Francis was born in 1506 and educated in Paris. He was an early companion of Saint Ignatius (July 31) with whom he was ordained priest in 1534. He set out on a missionary journey to the East Indies in 1541, and spent the rest of his life visiting, evangelizing and preparing the ground from India and Ceylon (Sri Lanka) to Malaya and Japan. He was about to enter China when he died in 1552. He was canonized in 1622.

All the ends of the earth shall remember and turn to the Lord; and all the families of nations shall worship before him. For dominion belongs to the Lord: and he rules over the nations. (Psalm 22[21].27,28)

Francis's call to those who did not know Christ was absolute and clear; and he did not shy away. We all share in this call to take Christ to others, but our duties are usually less arduous, less physical, less dangerous. Even if we are not called to preach, we are called to pass on the rudiments and tenets of the Faith when the occasions arise. However, as so many saints remind us through the year – and we cannot be reminded of this too often – everyone's mission to others begins at home with the self. Our demeanour must speak of Christ and reveal Christ: often it reveals nothing but a rather selfish individual.

In our prayers: thanks for the life, example and intercession of Saint Francis Xavier; for Christians of the East and Far East; for those who evangelize by means of the written word; for those who do not yet know Christ.

Saint Francis, pray for us, and for all missions, missionary organizations and all works dedicated to the spreading of the gospel.

December 4   Saint John Damascene *(Doctor of the Church)*

John was born in 657 and brought up in the court of the Khalif of Damascus. Christianity was tolerated and John received a proper classical and Christian education. A new Khalif began to discriminate against Christians, causing John to leave and join the monastery of Saint Sabas (December 5), outside Jerusalem. He spent his time writing in his cell. He was ordained priest, and preached and taught in Jerusalem. John left us a large body of work, including three important essays against Iconoclasm. He died in 749 and was declared Doctor of the Church in 1890.

Rise, Sion, rise! And looking forth,
Behold thy children round thee!
From east and west, from south and north,
Thy scattered sons have found thee;
And in thy bosom Christ adore
For ever, and for evermore.
(Hymn by Saint John Damascene, translated by J.M. Neale)

John responded with enthusiasm to his call to the written word. The written word is the most permanent and far-reaching tool of the evangelist and teacher. With it the faithful can learn more about the Faith and instruct the faithless. John's work still has that value to this very day. He was particularly passionate against the Iconoclasts. The sight of a religious painting, sculpture or icon can be of immense spiritual value to the Christian. Art can stimulate meditation and carry the pilgrim into a deeper exploration of the Christian Mysteries. Today, these things are so important, as we consider the use made, say, in advertising of the images of idols in society – the idols of money, of sexual gratification, of glamour, sport and celebrity. The Christian images are the very antitheses.

In our prayers: thanks for the life, example and intercession of Saint John Damascene; for religious booksellers and publishers; for icon painters and sculptors.

Saint John, pray for us, and for all tract writers of orthodox material.

December 5   Saint Crispina *(Martyr)*
(Also today, Saint Sabas [*Abbot*].)

Crispina was a young married woman of position in North Africa, who was beheaded in 304, during Diocletian's persecution of Christians, for refusing to sacrifice to the Roman gods.

Our God is in the heavens; he does whatever he pleases. Their idols are silver and gold, the work of men's hands. They have mouths, but do not speak; eyes, but do not see. They have ears, but do not hear, noses, but do not smell. They have hands but do not feel; feet, but do not walk; and they do not make a sound in their throat. Those who make them are like them; so are all who trust in them. The Lord has been mindful of us; he will bless us . . . he will bless those who fear the Lord, both small and great. (Psalm 115.3–8,12,13)

To refuse to bow down to the idols worshipped in secular society may set the Catholic apart but, nevertheless, we have to live in modern society unless we are called to the cloister. We have to live with the idols of pleasure and leisure all around us – and they often, it seems, are the most popular topics of general conversation. We are called to be aloof from anything that threatens to stand in the way of our worship of God.

In our prayers: thanks for the life, example and intercession of Saint Crispina; for the strength to resist the temptations of idols.

Saint Crispina, pray for us, and for all who remain faithful.

December 6   Saint Nicholas of Myra *(Bishop)*

Nicholas was a fourth-century bishop of Myra, in Asia Minor, who, during his episcopate, was imprisoned for his faith, under Diocletian. He was a thoroughly holy man. Though many extraordinary stories have attached themselves to this saint, it is likely that he inherited sufficient wealth to enable him to carry out charitable acts throughout his ministry – usually involving the rescue from poverty (and thus from the certainty of early death) of humble families with children.

But when the disciples saw it, they were indignant, saying, 'Why this waste? For this ointment might have been sold for a large sum, and given to the poor.' But Jesus, aware of this, said to them, 'Why do you trouble this woman? For she has done a beautiful thing to me. For you always have the poor with you . . .' (Matthew 26.8–11a)

Let us, therefore, not be shy about Santa Claus! Let us not hesitate to promote the Santa Claus of Christmas and to identify Father Christmas with Santa Claus. Let us not be embarrassed about assuring children of Nicholas's benevolent and holy life on earth and his eternal life in the company of the saints and martyrs in the heavenly realms. Let us not be cautious that Nicholas will pray for us and for others, along with all the saints. He may not pluck demands for toys from our chimneys and return that way with a generous haul, but through Nicholas we are able to arrive at the Incarnation and Nativity of Our Lord, and give others the joy of these Truths.

In our prayers: thanks for the life, example and intercession of Saint Nicholas of Myra; for confidence in our use of the life of Saint Nicholas in our endeavours to spread the gospel of Christ at Christmas; for all the children of the poor.

Saint Nicholas, pray for us, and for all places dedicated in your name, for Russia, Sicily, Greece and Germany.

❧

December 7 Saint Ambrose *(Bishop and Doctor of the Church)*

Ambrose was born in 340 in Gaul. He was made Bishop of Milan in 374. Immediately, he shared his wealth among the poor of his diocese. He preached and taught with great authority against the prevalent heresies of the day. He reformed the Liturgy in his diocese and corrected the deterioration in the standard of the singing schools where the chant was taught.

Thee let the secret heart acclaim,
Thee let our tuneful voices name,
Round thee our chaste affections cling,
Thee sober reason own as King. (Saint Ambrose, trans. C.B.)

Reform and repair in our lives is a necessity of our daily routine. Reform, we remind ourselves, is not innovation but a return to purity by removing the accretions of life acquired during the normal course of living. In society, falling standards usually herald an official change in standards, often supported by legislation, so that the fallen standards become the new. Our happy duty is to the standard that never changes – the standard of Christ whose divine melody never corrupts and is never corrupted.

In our prayers: thanks for the life, example and intercession of Saint Ambrose; for the maintenance of Christian standards in society.

O Trinity of blessed light,
O Unity of princely might,
The fiery sun now goes his way;
Shed thou within our hearts thy ray.
To thee our morning song of praise,
To thee our evening hymn we raise;
Thy glory suppliant we adore
For ever and for evermore. (Saint Ambrose, trans. J.M. Neale)
Saint Ambrose, pray for us, for all choristers and organists, and for all places dedicated in your name.

༄

December 8 The Immaculate Conception of Our Lady

By the grace of Almighty God, Our Lady was conceived in the womb of Anne (July 26) free from any blemish of Original sin. In conveying God's message, Gabriel (September 29) addressed Mary as being already 'full of grace' and, therefore, already in a state pure enough for God's purpose.

O Glorious Maid, exalted far
Beyond the light of burning star,
From him who made thee thou hast won
Grace to be Mother of his Son.
That which was lost in hapless Eve
Thy holy Scion did retrieve;
The tear-worn sons of Adam's race

311

Through thee have seen thy heavenly place.
Thou wast the gate of heaven's high Lord,
The door through which the light hath poured,
Christians rejoice, for through a Maid
To all mankind is life conveyed.
(O Gloriosa Femina, anon, ninth century, trans. P.D.)

Mary's state at conception was a baptized state. She would be fit to say 'yes' to God and fit to become the Mother of God. Baptism frees us from the control of Original sin and its infection by allowing us to recognize it for what it is. We continue to sin because we remain subject to our natural passions and inclinations. God calls us to keep a balance and control over ourselves so that we do not become slaves to those passions and inclinations. Absolution constantly returns us to that state of grace.

In our prayers: thanks for the life, example and intercession of Our Lady; for the teaching contained in the dogma of the Immaculate Conception; for a desire to set our sights on Christ at all times.

Holy Mary, pray for us, and for the United States of America and all its people.

December 9 Saint Peter Fourier *(Founder)*

Peter was born in Lorraine in 1565. He entered the Order of Augustinian Canons at Chaumousey. He was ordained in 1589, and in 1597 was given the parish of Mattaincourt. There he tirelessly performed charitable acts without discriminating against those who were not Catholic. He established a free school under a new foundation. Peter reformed the Canons Regular of Lorraine, which became the Congregation of Our Saviour. Peter was a holy man, often much frustrated in some of his endeavours. He died in 1640 and was canonized in 1897.

Whom have I in heaven but thee? And there is nothing upon earth that I desire besides thee. My flesh and my heart may fail, but God is the strength of my heart and my portion for ever. (Psalm 73[72].25,26)

Certainly the alienation of those who are not Catholic or even Christian is hardly the appropriate by-product of a charitable act. If the light of

Christ shines from us we can control the destination of that light only by switching it off, and we know how to do that well enough.

In our prayers: thanks for the life, example and intercession of Saint Peter Fourier; that we resolve to show Christ to everyone who crosses our paths and comes into our lives.

Saint Peter, pray for us, and for all religious foundations dedicated to the education of children.

December 10 Saint John Roberts *(Martyr)*

John was a Welshman who became a Catholic in France, trained in the English College in Valladolid, and then became a Benedictine monk. He joined the English Mission and entered the country four times and was three times banished. John was renowned for his work with the plague victims of London. Finally, he was arrested while still in Eucharistic vestments. He was tried for treason and hanged at Tyburn in 1610. He was canonized in 1970.

And Jesus came and said to them, 'Go therefore and make disciples of all the nations, baptizing them in the name of the Father and of the Son and of the Holy Spirit, teaching them to observe all that I have commanded you; and lo, I am with you always, to the close of the age.' (Matthew 28.19,20; quoted by Saint John Roberts at his trial)

Some are given great ordeals and trials to overcome or to be vanquished by. Here John worked compassionately among the infections and contagions of plague-ridden London – needless to say, an extraordinarily dangerous mission. He also served isolated and abandoned Catholics hungry for the sacraments – an equally dangerous mission. Generally speaking, our vocations do not involve perilous duties or even particularly difficult ones; John's signpost puts our slight duties into perspective!

In our prayers: thanks for the life, example and intercession of Saint John; for victims of plague and those who care for them; for all who are persecuted.

Saint John, pray for us, and for all who work in hazardous conditions.

December 11   Saint Damasus I *(Pope)*

Damasus became pope in 366, amid considerable controversy and accusations. For many years he fought to clear his name. However, he was unstinting in the entertainment he provided in his quarters, and gained a reputation for the luxury of his living. In contrast, Damasus carried out vast improvements in the catacombs so that the holy martyrs' relics could be more appropriately housed, that people could visit these relics along clean walkways, and breath fresh air from the shafts he built. And the foundations for the government of the Church were put in place during this period. Damasus financially supported Saint Jerome's (September 30) translation of the Holy Bible. Damasus died in 384.

Let not those rejoice over me who are wrongfully my foes, and let not those wink the eye who hate me without cause. For they do not speak peace, but against those who are quiet in the land they conceive words of deceit. They open wide their mouths against me; they say, 'Aha, aha! our eyes have seen it!' Thou hast seen, O Lord; be not silent! O Lord be not far from me! Let those who desire my vindication shout for joy and be glad, and say evermore, 'Great is the Lord, who delights in the welfare of his servant!' Then my tongue shall tell of thy righteousness and of thy praise all the day long. (Psalm 35[34].19–21,22,27,28)

The story of this saint is unusual, to say the least. Was Damasus's reputation largely born of the whisperers' tales? It is not uncommon, these days particularly, for a person to acquire a bad reputation on account of one misleading newspaper headline. Whisperers and murmurers provide the same service. Damasus's irrefutable contribution to the future of Christ's Church is quite apparent to us; the honouring of the saints and their relics is an important ingredient in our lives. Indeed, our private daily prayer is so fruitfully guided by the saints, who have presented us with their very different signposts for our own benefit and that of others.

In our prayers: thanks for the life, example and intercession of Saint Damasus; for the opportunity to worship in the light and knowledge of the saints in one great communion; for those who are misunderstood and whose characters are blighted by untruth and exaggeration.

Saint Damasus, pray for us, and for all who work in the government of the Church.

🕮

December 12 Our Lady of Guadalupe; Saint Jane Frances de Chantal *(Foundress)*

The American Indian peasant Juan Diego received the privilege of visions of Our Lady on a mountain outside Mexico City in 1531. A magnificent basilica now stands there. In 1910, Our Lady of Guadalupe was declared 'Virgin Patroness of Latin America', and, in 1945, 'The Queen of Mexico and Empress of the Americas'.

Jane was born in 1572 in Burgundy. She was widowed with three children but, after a time, under the inspiration of Saint Francis de Sales (January 24) and influence of his teaching and, later, with the spiritual direction of Saint Vincent de Paul (September 27), she founded the Congregation of the Visitation of the Virgin, dedicated to the visiting and care of the poor, sick, needy and destitute. By the time she died in 1642, there were over 60 convents of the Visitation established throughout France. Jane was canonized in 1767.

As he walked by the Sea of Galilee, he saw two brothers, Simon, who is called Peter, and Andrew his brother, casting a net into the sea; for they were fishermen. And he said to them, 'Follow me, and I will make you fishers of men.' Immediately they left their nets and followed him. (Matthew 3.18–20)

'I am your mother of great mercies, and I am the mother of all nations of the world.' (Spoken by Our Lady to the American Indian peasant, Juan Diego)

Jane was plucked from widowhood and given the sizeable task of founding a Congregation in Our Lady's name whose purpose was to minister to all the needy. In so doing, Jane 'raised the profile' – as modern publicists would say – of those in dire need of help. The Congregation was enormously successful and the work done quite extraordinary. Our Lady continues to intercede for us all and for the poor of Latin America, together with those who were the focus of Jane and her followers.

In our prayers: thanks for the lives, examples and intercession of Our Lady and of Saint Jane Frances de Chantal; for the poor of Latin America and of France.

Holy Mary, Lady of Guadalupe, pray for us and for the people of Latin America.
Saint Jane, pray for us, and for the poor and needy of France.

December 13   Saint Odilia *(Abbess)*

Odilia was born blind in Alsace and sent away by her father on account of her sex and her defect. She was educated in a convent and baptized at 12 by the Bishop of Regensburg. She recovered her sight after he had anointed her eyes with holy oil. Odilia forgave her father for his less than fatherly treatment, and he endowed a monastery for her in his castle at Obernai. Odilia and her nuns cared for the sick in their hospice and fed the hungry of the area. She died in 720.

As he passed by, he saw a man blind from his birth. And his disciples asked him, 'Rabbi, who sinned, this man or his parents, that he was born blind?' Jesus answered, 'It was not that this man sinned or his parents, but that the works of God might be made manifest in him.' (John 9.1–3)

It is remarkable to read of the faith and dedication of Odilia. Her eyes were opened to the glories of the Creator's handiwork for the first time, and she saw immediately how man's action so often sullied the Creator's craft. There she saw her lingering bitterness and forgave her father; she saw those who were less fortunate than she had been, and immediately dedicated her life to them. To what extent are we blind to our faults and to the distress of others?

In our prayers: thanks for the life, example and intercession of Saint Odilia; for sight enough to see our faults and for sight enough to see the needy; for the generosity to forgive; for those who are blind; for those who are hungry.

Saint Odilia, pray for us, and for all who strive to emulate your example.

December 14   Saint John of the Cross *(Doctor of the Church)*

John was born in 1542 in Old Castile. He was for a time a nurse in a clinic for the treatment of venereal diseases. He became a Carmelite after studying with the Jesuits, and a priest in 1567. John was closely acquainted with Saint Teresa of Avila (October 15). He too was a mystic, and his written output was considerable – both prose and poetry. During some grave difficulties between the two Carmelite foundations, he was imprisoned and cruelly treated. John died in 1591, was canonized in 1726 and declared Doctor of the Church in 1926.

In his 'Spiritual Canticle', John of the Cross pleads that man might understand that before reaching the grove of the many riches of God's wisdom, he must first desire and enter the grove of the suffering of the Passion of Christ.

Our careful consideration and immersion in the Passion of Christ will open our minds to the Mystery that is his Passion, Death and Resurrection. Only by doing so can we begin to understand God's plan for the reconciliation of mankind. The exercise will sharpen our will to spread the true joy and happiness of a life in Christ. And John was anxious that each one of us should, to the extent of his ability, enter more deeply into Christ's life as recorded in the Gospels by allowing the mind free rein.

In our prayers: thanks for the life, example and intercession of Saint John of the Cross; for those who are shunned and misunderstood; for the patience to study Scripture more deeply.

Saint John, pray for us, and for all mystic writers of prose and poetry.

December 15   Saint Mary de Rosa *(Foundress)*

Mary was born in Brescia in 1813. She served her apprenticeship in coping with the sick and dying, the deaf and the dumb, in her early years. She founded the Congregation of the Handmaids of Charity for the Care of the Sick. The Sisters gained further experience in treating the wounded and dying in the battlefield. The constitution of the Congregation was agreed and approved by Pope Pius IX. Mary died in 1855 and was canonized in 1954.

'. . . which of these then, do you think, proved neighbour to the man who fell among robbers?' He said, 'The one who showed mercy on him.' And Jesus said, 'Go and do likewise.' (Luke 10.36,37)

No sick person would fall outside Mary's embrace. Sickness was the leveller. No matter the disease or injury, the ministry of the Congregation would see it as their God-given duty to tend the condition. Like the Samaritan, Mary and her Congregation did not first question themselves about the type or nationality of the sick person or about the cause of his injuries. Where had the man been to contract this disease? Were these injuries sustained in a duel? Their mission was to the sick, without any qualifications.

In our prayers: thanks for the life, example and intercession of Saint Mary de Rosa; for all missionaries dedicated to care of the sick throughout the world.

Saint Mary, pray for us, and for all religious Orders and Congregations who tend the sick and dying.

⸎

December 16   Saint Adelaide of Burgundy

Adelaide, for the first 60 years of her life – she was born in 931 – was at the centre of the turbulent politics of the time. For 20 years she was the Empress of Rome. Adelaide was known for her peace-loving nature, and for her ability to be charitable to her enemies and forgive them. She founded and restored many religious houses and sent missionaries to the Slavs. She died in 999 and was canonized in 1097.

'You have heard that it was said, "You shall love your neighbour and hate your enemy." But I say to you, love your enemies and pray for those who persecute you, so that you may be sons of your Father who is in heaven; for he makes his sun rise on the evil and on the good, and sends rain on the just and on the unjust. For if you love those who love you, what reward have you?' (Matthew 5.43–46a)

Peacemaking can mean negotiating an uneasy compromise. It can mean, ultimately, that the parties to the agreement live amicably at arm's length. Between two individuals, it can mean perfunctory nods and an uneasy silence or an occasional awkward conversation. However, bloodshed is averted, at least. Loving enemies is a different matter altogether; the very idea is, for some, a step too far. How do we suddenly love the loathed? We begin in prayer and we consider our relationship with the enemy; we air it before God. We test our innocence in the relationship; we acknowledge our shortcomings; we own that we are fellow creatures of the one Creator.

In our prayers: thanks for the life, example and intercession of Saint Adelaide; for all peacemakers; for the patience to build bridges between ourselves and those we dislike.

Saint Adelaide, pray for us, and for Rome and for all Slavs.

December 17   Saint John of Matha *(Founder)*

John was born in Provence. He became a priest and felt his vocation to lie in the recovery of the Christian slaves and prisoners taken by the Saracens in the Second Crusade (1147–49). He founded the Order of the Most Holy Trinity, the mission of which was to penetrate the inhospitable regions of southern Spain, Morocco, Tunis and the Middle East, negotiating the release of Christians. Many hundreds, perhaps thousands, achieved their freedom in this way. John died in 1213.

The Spirit of the Lord God is upon me, because the Lord has anointed me to bring good tidings to the afflicted; he has sent me to bind up the broken-hearted, to proclaim liberty to the captives, and the opening of the prison to those who are bound. (Isaiah 61.1)

What a wonderful vocation! Courageous and brave and golden-tongued, and under the banner of the Holy Trinity, the Order gave relief, succour and freedom to the captured and joy to the wives and mothers and fathers. John harboured no hatred of the enemy; he was willing and able to discuss the release of his fellows in a sensible and friendly manner. Did the Saracen negotiators see in John's earnestness Christ's love of humanity and of the prisoners in particular? Did they wonder and marvel behind their furrowed brow?

In our prayers: thanks for the life, example and intercession of Saint John of Matha; for all prisoners of war and battle; for those who are pawns in international politics.

Saint John, pray for us, and for all kidnap victims and their families.

December 18 Saint Peter Duong, Saint Peter Truat and Saint Paul My *(Martyrs)*

The two Peters were catechists of the Society of Foreign Mission of Paris, Paul, a faithful worker and volunteer attached to the Society. The three died in horrible circumstances in the mission field in Vietnam in the late 1930s. They were canonized in 1988.

'. . . when the season of fruit drew near, he sent his servants to the tenants, to get his fruit; and the tenants took his servants and beat one, killed another, and stoned another. Again, he sent other servants, more than the first, and they did the same to them . . .' (Matthew 21.34–36)

These martyrs had been received into the joy of the Lord and were fired with enthusiasm to spread the Good News to their fellows. They were met with an open and receptive audience among their countrymen. A violent campaign against foreign missionaries and their converts erupted after a time, which resulted in the deaths of these saints. They had been shown Christ and had welcomed him within to share and to reveal. There was no complaint at an early death; there was no possibility of denying the Christ, who was now an inextricable part of them. Might we compromise in the circumstances?

In our prayers: thanks for the lives, examples and intercession of Saint Peter Duong, Saint Peter Truat and Saint Paul My; for those who face an unjust death with equanimity and faith; for those who kill readily.

Saints Peter and Saint Paul, pray for us, and for the Christians in Vietnam.

December 19   Saint Anastasius I *(Pope)*

Anastasius was a friend of Saint Jerome (September 30) and supported his efforts to stamp out the errors and dangers of unorthodox theology. He was a holy and devout man renowned for his purity of living. He died in 401.

For thou art great and doest wondrous things, thou alone art God. Teach me thy way, O Lord, that I may walk in thy truth; unite my heart to fear thy name. I give thanks to thee, O Lord my God, with my whole heart, and I will glorify thy name for ever. (Psalm 86[85].10–12)

Throughout the ages there have been elements anxious to soften difficult concepts and liberalize demanding morals, but happily, the purity of the Faith is, nevertheless, maintained. Attacks upon the Church usually result in a strengthening of resolve. In our own day there are those who wish to push the Church away from orthodoxy in its moral teaching because society nowadays likes to promote, among other things, the 'marriage' of single sex couples; to provide contraceptives to schoolchildren; to make available abortion on demand.

In our prayers: thanks for the life, example and intercession of Saint Anastasius I; for all orthodox teachers of the Faith; for society generally.

Saint Anastasius, pray for us, for the Holy Father and the Roman Curia.

December 20   Saint Philogonius of Antioch *(Bishop and Martyr)*

Philogonius was a lawyer of note. In 319, he was made Bishop of Antioch and under his direction his diocese blossomed, as Saint John Chrysostom himself (September 13) once noted. The peace-loving and gentle Philogonius was imprisoned during the persecutions of Maximinus, and died there naturally (or was put to death) in 324.

For this reason I, Paul, a prisoner of Christ Jesus on behalf of you Gentiles – assuming that you have heard of the stewardship of God's grace that was given to me for you, how the mystery was made known to me by revelation, as I have written elsewhere briefly. When you read this you can perceive my insight into the mystery of Christ . . . that is, how the Gentiles are fellow heirs, members of the same body, and partakers of the promise in Christ Jesus through the Gospel. (Ephesians 3.1–6)

As John Chrysostom pointed out at Philogonius's funeral, Philogonius was familiar with the etiquette of the courtroom, and with the appropriate and customary behaviour of the courtroom. At his elevation to the See of Antioch, he made himself so familiar with the behaviour required for the court of heaven that, on his death, his translation must have been seamless. We are called to aspire to the ways of heaven here on earth. It is difficult because it means living in a rather different way and we often fall short of the ideal. Are we ever mistaken for a courtier of heaven?

In our prayers: thanks for the life, example and intercession of Saint Philogonius of Antioch; for care and attention to the way we live; for trust in the love of our Saviour.

Saint Philogonius, pray for us, and for all bishops.

December 21   Saint Peter Canisius *(Doctor of the Church)*

Peter, born in 1521, entered the Society of Jesus and was given the mission to reintroduce Catholic teaching in the Ingolstadt University in Germany and in other colleges and schools. Saint Ignatius (July 31) then gave him a second mission in Vienna. Peter began to write a series of catechisms for various age groups. He continued to write and publish until his death in 1597, after a long illness. John was canonized and declared Doctor of the Church in 1925.

And the Gospel must first be preached to all nations. (Mark 13.10)
Bless the Lord, you priests of the Lord, sing praise to him and highly exalt him for ever. Bless the Lord, you servants of the Lord, sing praise to him and highly exalt him for ever. ('The Song of the Three Young Men', Daniel 3.62,63)

A facility with the written word was clearly a gift most necessary for Peter's calling. He quickly realized that the written word assisted the convert to retain the teaching he had received from the lips of the priest. He realized that there was need of such help for all ages and abilities, even for those who had long professed the Catholic Faith. We know well that the most effective way of propagating the Faith is by example, but the firming and deepening of understanding is often best conveyed by the written word. Our own reading is important – not least of Holy Scripture itself.

In our prayers: thanks for the life, example and intercession of Saint Peter Canisius; for those who write about the Faith for the instruction of others; for those who seek after knowledge of the Faith.

Saint Peter, pray for us, and for all societies and publishers dedicated to the promulgation of the Catholic Faith.

December 22 Saint Frances Xavier Cabrini *(Foundress)*

Frances was born in 1850 near Pavia, and founded the Missionary Sisters of the Sacred Heart. In 1889, the Sisters left for New York. Frances' mission was to the Italian immigrants, and particularly the poor, the orphaned, the imprisoned, the destitute, and the lonely of her race. She lived a holy and self-giving life and died in 1917. Frances was canonized in 1946.

Therefore be imitators of God, as beloved children. And walk in love, as Christ loved us and gave himself up for us, a fragrant offering and sacrifice to God. (Ephesians 6.1,2)
Preach the word, be urgent in season and out of season, convince, rebuke, and exhort, be unfailing in patience and in teaching. (2 Timothy 4.1)

The mission to the lonely and to those who feel out of place is a worthy enterprise. It was of enormous importance in New York in the nineteenth century, as it is today in this country among the new arrivals from, say, Poland and many other countries. There is a duty on the shoulders of the faithful to welcome brothers and sisters in the Faith who find themselves on these shores. The universality of the Church must be practised as well as preached. (The use of Latin serves the Church well in this respect.)

In our prayers: thanks for the life, example and intercession of Saint Frances Xavier Cabrini; for all who offer comfort to the dispossessed and the immigrant; for those who are alien in other lands.

Saint Frances, pray for us, and for New York and the Italians of that city.

December 23 Saint Margaret d'Youville *(Foundress)*
(Also today, Saint John of Kanti.)

Margaret was a French Canadian and was born in 1701. As a widow, she gathered around her a band of helpers and together they fed and cared for the sick, the blind and the elderly. She founded the private Order that, by 1747, became the Sisters of Charity of the General Hospital. She cared not only for the elderly infirm but also for English and French soldiers injured in battle against each other. No one was refused. Margaret died in 1771 and was canonized in 1990.

Now Simon's mother-in-law lay sick with fever, and immediately they told him of her. And he came and took her by the hand and lifted her up, and the fever left her; and she served them. That evening, at sundown, they brought to him all who were sick or possessed with demons. And the whole city was gathered together about the door. And he healed many who were sick with various diseases, and cast out many demons . . . (Mark 1.30–34a)

The thorough goodness and undiscriminating love of Margaret is the epitome of the Christian Way. The Sisters of Charity were there to serve anyone in any sort of need. They were acting the gospel truly and perfectly. Not for them the reaction of the priest and the Levite; they were dedicated to a wide definition of 'neighbour'. If I know (or know of) the needy, then they are in close proximity to me; and if in close proximity, then they are my neighbours.

In our prayers: thanks for the life, example and intercession of Saint Margaret d'Youville; for the cultivation of selfless generosity; for eyes that see.

Saint Margaret, the Mother of Universal Charity, pray for us, and for Canada.

December 24   Saint Sharbel Makhlouf

Sharbel was born of a Christian family in 1828. He educated himself while still a shepherd; he then entered the monastery dedicated to Our Lady of Maifouk. Sharbel was ordained in 1859 and spent his last 23 years in a life of asceticism in Saint Peter and Paul's hermitage. In his day and after his death, it was a popular place of pilgrimage. Sharbel died in 1898 and was canonized in 1970.

And in that region there were shepherds out in the field, keeping watch over their flock by night. And an angel of the Lord appeared to them, and the glory of the Lord shone around them . . . (Luke 2.8,9)

The shepherds who guarded the lambs bred specially for sacrifice in the temple were the first Jews to pay homage to the promised Saviour. Sharbel too was a shepherd. As the sheep gathered around him on the hillside in the late afternoon, he saw his mission clearly. He journeyed to the stable of his Lord by translating to a hermitage and there lived a life of example to others in prayer and meditation, giving quiet counsel to those who sought it. Sharbel always prayed in the language of Our Lord.

In our prayers: thanks for the life, example and intercession of Saint Sharbel Makhlouf; for the enthusiasm to respond to the call to the stable to worship the Lord; for those who are alone this Christmas who would rather not be alone.

Maranatha! – our Lord has come; our Lord is here!
Saint Sharbel, pray for us, and for shepherds throughout the world.

December 25   The Nativity of Our Lord;
Saint Albert Chmielkowski *(Founder)*

Albert was born in 1845 in Poland. For safety, his parents sent him to Paris where he became a painter of note. He returned to Poland, became a Jesuit and then founded the Brothers of the Third Order of Saint Francis, Servants of the Poor, dedicated to the care of tramps and outcasts. Albert died in 1916 and was canonized in 1989.

And the angel said to them, 'Be not afraid; for behold I bring you good news of great joy which will come to all the people; for to you is born this day in the city of David a Saviour, who is Christ the Lord. And this will be a sign for you: you will find a babe wrapped in swaddling cloths and lying in a manger.' And they went with haste, and found Mary and Joseph, and the babe lying in a manger. And when they saw it they made known the saying, which had been told them concerning the child; and all who heard it wondered at what the shepherds told them. (Luke 2.10–12,16–18)

Albert saw in the plight of the outcast, Christ himself, thrown out of the vineyard and killed by those who would steal it. Our Lord's loving face gazed from the pathetic, hunted features of those he tended, and they saw in Albert the same face, the face from the cross as Mary looked up at him, the face from the mountainside as he preached and taught with amusing banter and absurd hyperbole to capture the attention of the crowd, the face from the manger, innocent and perfect, that stared up at Mary his mother close by.

In our prayers: thanks for the life, example and intercession of Saint Albert Chmielkowski; thanks for the gift of the Holy Incarnation; for all those of no fixed abode; for religious Orders specializing in comfort for the neglected.

O Wonderful, mysterious generation!
O most astonishing Nativity!
O glorious child! O Deity incarnate!
So had the prophets, by thy spirit moved,
Declared thou should'st be born, thou Son of God!
So, at thy dawning, angels sing thee praises,
And to the earth glad tidings bring of peace.
(Feast of the Nativity, Sarum Missal)
Saint Albert, pray for us, for Poland and for the artists who gather in Paris.

December 26 Saint Stephen *(Martyr)*

The proto-martyr Stephen, a deacon, is shown to us with some vividity in Acts 7.2–53. He must have been a captivating preacher and an orator of assurance and authority. His wonderful thumbnail sketch of the history of the Hebrews and the prophets can hardly be bettered. But his message about the Messiah was too much for many, and he was taken away and stoned to death in about 35.

'. . . You always resist the Holy Spirit. As your fathers did, so do you. Which of the prophets did not your fathers persecute? And they killed those who announced beforehand the coming of the Righteous One, whom you have now betrayed and murdered, you who received the law as delivered by angels and did not keep it.' And as they were stoning Stephen, he prayed, 'Lord Jesus, receive my spirit.' And he knelt down and cried with a loud voice, 'Lord do not hold this sin against them.' (Acts 7.51b–53,59)

Stephen was asking his blind and deaf persecutors why they did not see what they had done throughout history, why they did not know what they had done when they crucified him about whom the Prophets were unanimous. As the mob stoned Stephen did these questions linger in the air and mingle with his cries of forgiveness? In today's world the Church's words are still drowned by the clamour of evil, but we do not despair because we know that the last to be hired will receive the same reward. Our calling, one way or another, is to the middle of that clamour.

In our prayers: thanks for the life, example and intercession of Saint Stephen; for all who are persecuted.

Saint Stephen, pray for us, and for all places dedicated in your name.

December 27   Saint John *(Apostle and Evangelist)*

John was the brother of James I; they were the sons of Zebedee and, probably, cousins of Jesus. John is commonly identified with 'the beloved disciple' of the Gospel of John, his name omitted from the text through modesty. Even if John did not complete the final version of the Gospel as we now know it, it is likely that his reminiscences and personal accounts are at its core. John probably lived into very old age in Ephesus and died in about 100.

And going on a little farther, he saw James the son of Zebedee and John his brother, who were in their boat mending their nets. And immediately he called them; and they left their father Zebedee in the boat with the hired servants, and followed him. (Mark 1.19,20)
When Jesus saw his mother and the disciple whom he loved standing near, he said to his mother, 'Woman, behold your son!' Then he said to the disciple, 'Behold, your mother!' And from that hour the disciple took her to his own home. (John 19.26,27)

Jesus' younger cousin, John, was specially chosen because he was to become the protector of Mary and the man who would represent us all as he accepted Mary as his mother. Our calling is, of course, also to kinship with Jesus himself – to be his brother, his sister or cousin. Do we not, therefore, number with the 12, the 70, the countless successors of the successors throughout the ages in one unbroken communion of prayer to the glory of God?

In our prayers: thanks for the life, example and intercession of John; for the dedication to nurture our kinship with Christ, the Word made flesh.

Saint John, pray for us, and for all places dedicated in your name.

December 28   The Holy Innocents *(Martyrs)*

Matthew records the killing of babies and small children by Herod the Great in Bethlehem. This, of course, was not in the least out of character. Herod was notoriously paranoid about claimants to his throne – after all, he had had ten wives – and he guarded it jealously even though he possessed the throne only at Rome's pleasure. Wise men (from Babylon, perhaps?) were renowned as seers and interpreters of astronomical events, and often travelled to investigate their predictions further. Any hint of such a prediction confirming the messianic prophesies of Israel would have sent Herod into paroxysms of jealous fury. The babies and small children who died, died for Christ.

Then Herod, when he saw that he had been tricked by the wise men, was in a furious rage, and he sent and killed all the male children in Bethlehem and in all the region who were two years old or under, according to the time which he had ascertained from the wise men. (Matthew 2.16)

The world would wring its hands and tearfully place flowers at the scene of the massacre were this event newly recorded extravagantly on the front pages. The world might hold vigils until Herod were convicted. But why do we show this love for only some of the victims of man's cruelty and, save for the few, ignore the plight of 500 or so children each day (in this country alone) chemically aborted or ripped from the womb?

In our prayers: thanks for the example and prayers of the Holy Innocents; for all lost innocence, for those with unwanted and inconvenient pregnancies; for those who have aborted their children; for all organizations dedicated to the unborn child.

O Holy Innocents, pray for us, and for all unborn children.

December 29 Saint Thomas of Canterbury *(Bishop and Martyr)*

Thomas was consecrated Archbishop in 1162. He was a proud and, sometimes, bad-tempered man, who, however, knew his faults well. Not surprisingly, his public life was better known than his private life, which largely took the form of prayerful asceticism and generosity to the poor. Thomas was murdered in Canterbury Cathedral in 1170 at the age of 52. Responsibility for Thomas's murder was accepted by King Henry II, who made public penance for the offence.

O God, insolent men have risen up against me; a band of ruthless men seek my life, and they do not set thee before them. But thou, O Lord, are a God merciful and gracious, slow to anger and abounding in steadfast love and faithfulness. Turn to me and take pity on me; give thy strength to thy servant. (Psalm 86[85].14–16a)

Thomas was a statesman as well as an archbishop, as archbishops of Canterbury had to be in those days. Thomas knew that he courted the king's anger from time to time; he was adamant in his protection of the Church from the interference and greed of the crown, and it was for this faithful stance he was killed. We are all called to defend the Church by the way we live, and we may be called upon at any time to promote it in other ways. Are we constantly alert to the very voice that called Samuel?

In our prayers: thanks for the life, example and intercession of Saint Thomas of Canterbury; for the courage to defend the Church when required to do so.

Saint Thomas, pray for us, and for all places dedicated in your name.

❧

December 30 Saint Anysius *(Bishop)*

Anysius was made bishop in 383. He was noted in his day and afterwards for his great qualities as a bishop. Anysius was a friend of Saint John Chrysostom (September 13) and worked hard to have him restored to his See. Anysius died in 410.

Ascribe to the Lord, O heavenly beings, ascribe to the Lord glory and strength. Ascribe to the Lord the glory of his name; worship the Lord in holy array. The voice of the Lord is upon the waters; the God of glory thunders . . . upon many waters. The voice of the Lord is powerful; the voice of the Lord is full of majesty. The Lord sits enthroned as King for ever. May the Lord give strength to his people! May the Lord bless his people with peace. (Psalm 29[28].1–4,10b,11)

From time to time the principal vocation of a saint seems to rest with his or her support of another. This may be the case here. There were, of course, many who supported Saint John Chrysostom in his difficulties, but Anysius risked his own exile by supporting him with such dedication. Support for the greater man inevitably means that the spotlight falls upon that man. In all his humility Anysius was content for that to be the case; his only concern was for the orthodoxy and purity of the Faith. A part of our Godly living concerns our ability to place ourselves second (or much lower, perhaps) to another with greater ability.

In our prayers: thanks for the life, example and intercession of Saint Anysius; for those who need our support.

Saint Anysius, pray for us, and for those who have fallen away from the Church's teaching.

December 31 Saint Catherine Labouré (Also today, Saint Sylvester I [*Pope*].)

Catherine was born in 1806. She joined the Sisters of Charity of Saint Vincent de Paul. At the convent in the Rue de Bac in Paris, Catherine received a number of visions of Our Lady in response to which the 'miraculous medal' was struck at the instigation of the Archbishop of Paris. Catherine herself remained silent about the visions until only a few months before she died. Her life was one of silent devotion to God. She acted, through her confessor, when prompted by the visions to do so; otherwise she led a simple convent life. Catherine died in 1876 and was canonized in 1947.

When I attend chapel, I place myself before our good Lord and say 'Lord here I am, tell me what you want me to do.' If he gives me something to do, I thank him. If he gives me nothing, I thank him because I do not deserve anything more than that. And then I tell God all that is in my heart; I tell him my joy and my pain, and then I listen. If you listen, God will speak. When he speaks to you, approach in an unaffected manner. (Catherine Labouré)

Catherine's simple lesson to us is a most valuable one. 'If you listen, God will speak.' We have to be open and receptive to his voice. We must allow ourselves time to pray, to thank, to ask for forgiveness, to intercede and to listen. Catherine was granted visions of Our Blessed Lady only because she was open to what God had in store for her. The consequence of her visions was the attraction of the 'miraculous medal' to so many pilgrims and the good, told and known, untold and unknown, that has been done.

In our prayers: thanks for the life, example and intercession of Saint Catherine Labouré; for the patience to wait and listen.

Lord, here I am, tell me what you want me to do.
Saint Catherine, pray for us, and for all who are content to be humble and humble enough to be content.

Additional Prayers

The daily devotions may be used without addition or in the following way:

In nomine Patris, + et Filii, et Spiritus Sancti.

In the name of the Father + and of the Son, and of the Holy Spirit. Amen.

(The devotion supplied for the day.)

(The devotion supplied for the day.)

Christe, Fili Dei vivi, miserere nobis.

Christ, Son of the living God, have mercy on us.

Pater noster, qui es in caelis, sanctificetur nomen tuum. Adveniat regnum tuum. Fiat voluntas tua, sicut in caelo et in terra. Panem nostrum quotidianum da nobis hodie. Et dimitte nobis debita nostra, sicut et nos dimittimus debitoribus nostris. Et ne nos inducas in tentationem: sed libera nos a malo. Amen.

Our Father, who art in heaven, hallowed be thy name. Thy kingdom come. Thy will be done on earth, as it is in heaven. Give us this day our daily bread. And forgive us our trespasses, as we forgive those who trespass against us. And lead us not into temptation, but deliver us from evil. Amen.

Ave, Maria, gratia plena, Dominus tecum; benedicta tu in mulieribus, et benedictus fructus ventris tui, Jesus. Sancta Maria, Mater Dei, ora pro nobis peccatoribus, nunc et in hora mortis nostrae. Amen.

Hail Mary, full of grace, the Lord is with thee; blessed art thou among women, and blessed is the fruit of thy womb, Jesus. Holy Mary, Mother of God, pray for us sinners, now and at the hour of our death. Amen.

Beata Dei Genitrix, Virgo Maria, Sanctique omnes intercedant pro nobis ad Dominum.

May the blessed Virgin Mary, Mother of God, together with all the saints, intercede for us with the Lord.

Gloria Patri, et Filio, et Spiritui Sancto. Sicut erat in principio et nunc et semper et in saecula saeculorum. Amen. Alleluia *(vel)* Laus tibi, Domine, rex aeternae gloriae.

Glory be to the Father, and to the Son, and to the Holy Spirit. As it was in the beginning, is now, and ever shall be, world without end. Amen. Alleluia *(or)* Praise to thee, O Lord, King of everlasting glory.

❦

Our Father, who art in heaven, hallowed be thy name.

Thy kingdom come. Thy will be done on earth, as it is in heaven.

Give us this day our daily bread.

And forgive us our trespasses, as we forgive those who trespass against us.

And lead us not into temptation, but deliver us from evil. Amen.

O Heavenly Father, praise and thanks for thy goodness, kindness and mercy; for thy great benefits to me, in particular for . . . ; for the glimpses of heaven I see on earth; *[for the life (lives), example(s) and intercession of . . .]* Help me live on earth as a citizen of heaven. Encourage me to be generous, and assist me to be an instrument of thy divine generosity, and an agent of peace and loving-kindness. Give me strength to fulfil the vocations thou hast given me. Give me only what I need but look with love upon my family and friends . . . ; relieve and comfort the sick, dying and bereaved . . . ; *[Pour thy steadfast love upon the . . . ; help and comfort those who . . . ; give guidance and wisdom to . . .]* Look mercifully upon the souls of the faithful departed . . . *[and especially those who have lost their lives . . .]* Forgive those who sin in ignorance and those whom I have caused to sin. Forgive my sins of negligence and omission, and my sins of commission . . . forgive me when I fail to forgive others. Preserve me from *[temptation to the sin of . . . and]* every act of evil. Grant these things through Jesus Christ, thy Son, who lives and reigns with thee in the unity of the Holy Spirit, one God, for ever and ever. Amen.

From Advent until Candlemas

Alma Redemptoris Mater, quae pervia caeli porta manes, et stella maris, succure cadenti, surgere qui curat populo: Tu quae genuisti, natura mirante, tuum sanctum Genitorem: Virgo prius ac posterius, Gabrielis ab ore, sumens illud Ave, peccatorum miserere.

Mother of Christ! Hear thou thy people's cry, Star of the sea and portal of the sky! Sinking we strive, and call to thee for aid, Mother of him who thee from nothing made: O by that joy which Gabriel brought to thee, Thou Virgin first and last, let us thy mercy see.

From Candlemas until Maundy Thursday

Ave Regina caelorum, Ave Domina Angelorum. Salve radix, salve porta, Ex qua mundo lus est orta: Gaude Virgo gloriosa, Super omnes speciosa: Vale, O valde decora, Et pro nobis Christum exora.

Hail, O Queen of Heaven enthroned! Hail by angels mistress owned! Root of Jesse, gate of morn, Whence the world's true light was born. Glorious Virgin, joy to thee, Loveliest whom in heaven they see! Fairest thou where all are fair! Plead with Christ our sins to spare.

From Easter until Trinity Sunday

Regina Caeli laetare, Alleluia: Quia quem meruisti portare, Alleluia: Resurrexit, sicut dixit, Alleliua. Ora pro nobis Deum. Alleluia.

Joy to thee, O Queen of Heaven, Alleluia! He whom thou wast meet to bear, Alleluia! As he promised hath arisen, Alleluia! Pour for us to him thy prayer, Alleluia!

From Trinity Sunday until Advent

Salve Regina, Mater misericordiae, vita, dulcedo et spes nostra, salve. Ad te clamamus, exsules, filii Hevae. Ad te suspiramus, gementes et flentes in hac lacrimarum vale. Eia ergo, advocata nostra, illos tuos misericordes oculos ad nos converte. Et Jesum, benedictum fructum ventris tui, nobis post hoc exsilium ostende. O Clemens, O pia, O dulcis Virgo Maria.

Hail, holy Queen, Mother of mercy; hail, our life, our sweetness and our hope. To thee do we cry, poor banished children of Eve; to thee do we send up our sighs mourning and weeping in this vale of tears. Turn then, most gracious advocate, thine eyes of mercy towards us; and after this our exile, show unto us the blessed fruit of thy womb, Jesus. O clement, O loving, O sweet Virgin Mary.

Before Mass (or at any time)

Deus, cui omne cor patet,et omnis voluntas loquitur , et quem nullum latet secretum: purifica per infusionem sancti Spiritus cogitationes cordis nostri; ut te perfecte diligere, et digne laudare mereamur.
Conscientias nostras, quaesumus, Domine, visitando purifica: ut veniens Dominus noster Jesus Christus, Filius tuus, paratam sibi in nobis inveniat mansionem: Qui tecum vivit et regnat in unitate Spiritus Sancti Deus, per omnia saecula saeculorum. Amen.

O God unto whom every heart is open, every desire known and from whom no secrets are hidden; cleanse the thoughts of our hearts by the inspiration of thy Holy Spirit, that we may perfectly love thee, and worthily praise thy holy name. Cleanse our thoughts, we beseech thee, O Lord, by thy visitation, that when our Lord Jesus Christ, thy Son, shall come, he may find within us a dwelling prepared for him; who lives and reigns with thee in the unity of the Holy Spirit, God, for ever and ever. Amen.

After Mass (or at any time)

Anima Christi, sanctifica me.
Corpus Christi, salva me.
Sanguis Christi, inebria me.
Aqua lateris Christi, lava me.
Passio Christi, conforta me.
O bone Jesu, exaudi me.
Intra tua vulnera absconde me.
Ne permittas me separari a te.
Ab hoste maligno defende me.
In hora mortis meae voca me.
Et jube me venire ad te.
Ut cum Sanctis tuis laudem te
In Saecula saeculorum. Amen.

Soul of Christ, sanctify me.
Body of Christ, save me.
Blood of Christ, inebriate me.
Water from the side of Christ, wash me.
Passion of Christ, strengthen me.
O good Jesu, hear me.
Within thy wounds hide me.
Suffer me not to be separated from thee.
From the malicious enemy defend me,
And bid me come to thee,
That with thy saints I may praise thee
For ever and ever. Amen.

For the Queen and the Royal family

Quaesumus, Omnipotens Deus, ut famula tua Elizabeth regina nostra, qui tua miseratione suscepit regni gubernacula,virtutum etiam omnium percipiat incrementa; quibus decenter ornata, et vitiorum monstra devitare, et ad te, qui via, veritas, et vita es, cum principe consorte et prole regia, gratiosa valeat pervenire: per Christum Dominum nostrum. Amen.

Almighty God, we pray for thy servant Elizabeth our Queen, now by thy mercy reigning over us. Adorn her yet more with every virtue, remove all evil from her path, that with Prince Philip and all the Royal family she may come at last in grace to thee, who art the way, the truth, and the life. Through Christ our Lord. Amen.

For the dead

Deus, veniae largitor et humanae salutis amator, quaesumus clementiam tuam; ut nostrae congregationis fratres, propinquos et benefactores, qui ex hoc saeculo transierunt, beata Maria semper Virgine intercedente cum omnibus Sanctis tuis, ad perpetuae beatitudinis consortium pervenire concedas. Per Christum Dominum nostrum. Amen.

O God, who freely grants forgiveness and desires the salvation of all mankind, grant we beseech thee in thy mercy that all our brethren, families and benefactors who have passed from this life may by the intercession of the blessed Mary ever virgin and of all thy saints partake with them of everlasting bliss. Through Christ our Lord. Amen.

+ Requiescant in pace. Amen.

+ May they rest in peace. Amen.